THE ROARING REDHEAD

The Roaring Redhead

Larry MacPhail—
Baseball's Great Innovator

Don Warfield

Diamond Communications, Inc.
South Bend, Indiana

1987

THE ROARING REDHEAD
Copyright © 1987 by Diamond Communications, Inc.

Manufactured in the United States of America

Diamond Communications, Inc.
Post Office Box 88
South Bend, Indiana 46624
(219) 287-5008

Library of Congress Cataloging-in-Publication Data

Warfield, Don, 1921-
  The roaring redhead.

  1. MacPhail, Larry. 2. Baseball—United States—Promoters—
Biography. I. Title.
GV865.M316W37   1987   338.7'61796'0924   [B] 86-13437
ISBN 0-912083-18-2

To my dear friend, Milt Herrick,
who planted the seed and nurtured
the book chapter by chapter.

CHRONOLOGY:
Larry MacPhail

Born — Cass City, Michigan, February 3, 1890.

1906-10 — Beloit College, U. of Michigan
Graduated and received Law Degree from
George Washington U.

1910-15 — Law firm in Chicago

1917-19 — France, Captain in U.S. Army

1919-33 — Columbus, Ohio

1931-33 — Headed Columbus Red Birds

1933-36 — Headed Cincinnati Reds. First night game in
Majors May 24, 1935.

1937 — Banking business with father in Michigan

1938-42 — Headed Brooklyn Dodgers

1942-45 — Colonel, U.S. Army

1945-47 — President, New York Yankees

1948-57 — Horse & Cattle Breeding

1953 — Bought Bowie Racetrack

1957-75 — Down on the Farm, Glenangus

Died — October 1, 1975.

1978 — Elected to Hall of Fame

Contents

Preface

It is amazing to me that no one has ever written a biography of Larry MacPhail. He was the most innovative and exciting baseball executive of his time and certainly one of the most complex and fascinating characters in the history of sports. Brilliantly analytical, down to the smallest detail, he also had an uncontrollable temper. He was driven to and past the point of violence many times by the combination of drink and an absolute refusal to face any form of failure. No one who knew him has ever forgotten him. And his impact on the game of baseball may never be equalled. Consider the following list of firsts he accomplished:

1. First night game in the major leagues.
2. First televised game.
3. First to introduce "Old Timers' Games" to the Majors.
4. First to establish pension funds for club employees throughout all levels of baseball.
5. Headed first committee for players' pension funds—probably the finest in all of sport.
6. First to use airplane travel for baseball teams.
7. First to shake New York City by broadcasting all home and road games.
8. First to introduce yellow baseballs which, although a long way from being accepted in baseball, are coming to the fore in both tennis and golf.
9. First to regularly schedule doubleheaders.
10. First to install a stadium club.
11. First to introduce season ticket plan.
12. First to develop and introduce protective batting helmets.

Not only did he accomplish these firsts in the short period

of 13 years in baseball, 11 in the major leagues, but he also guided three teams—one in the minors and two in the majors—from virtual bankruptcy to financial stability. He built the foundation for championship teams for years in two major league cities and continued the dynasty in a third.

He is remembered best for these achievements in his meteoric career in baseball, but few people know of his great record in two world wars and his successful endeavors in horse and cattle breeding.

In this book I have tried to present a fair and accurate picture of Larry MacPhail. However, one man who knew him very well, Red Barber, said that "he is a hard man to capture in print."

Whenever possible, attempts have been made to give credit to those writers whose quotes have been used. When this has not been done, it is also possible that some students and historians of the period will recognize the many and varied sources from which the material has been gathered.

For the general baseball buff, for whom this book is intended, minute citations of sources would serve no useful purpose.

Finally, this study attempts to rectify a glaring omission in baseball lore, and the author assumes full responsibility for its point of view.

Don Warfield

Foreword

Bill Veeck had planned to write this foreword because he had such a high regard for Larry MacPhail. A number of years ago Veeck established the Leland S. MacPhail Promotional Trophy, which is awarded annually by a committee that judges which minor league team has done the best job of promotion during the previous year. It is presented by his son, Leland Stanford (Lee) MacPhail, Jr., former president of the American League and recently retired president of the Major Leagues Player Relations Committee.

In many ways Larry and Bill were kindred spirits, both mavericks who thumbed their noses at the baseball establishment. Each had headed a minor league team and three major league teams, and each had two pennant winners and a world championship.

Although Bill was unable to write the actual foreword, information and stories from the several meetings he and I had have been included in this book.

There are a number of sources from which this biography was created, starting with a diary kept by my mother-in-law (then Ida Green), when she and Larry (then Rusty) were an item at Beloit College for five months in 1906 and 1907.

His widow, now Mrs. James (Jean) Bauer of Cass City, Michigan, has been kind enough to loan me a suitcase full of newspaper clippings, magazine articles, etc., much of which has never been published, as well as many great pictures. Without this material, it would have been most difficult, if not impossible, to cover the life of Larry MacPhail.

Also contributing greatly to their father's biography were his sons, Lee and Bill, and his daughter, Mrs. Walsh (Marian) McDermott. Bill, formerly head of sports for CBS, currently works in that same capacity for Ted Turner's CNN in Atlanta, Georgia. Lee, especially, has been most supportive, reading most of the chapters from strictly a factual standpoint, and also furnishing most of the pictures.

In addition, the author has had many taped personal interviews and/or exchanged correspondence with, among others:

Walter (Red) Barber, member of the Hall of Fame, dean of all baseball announcers, who worked for many years with Larry in Cincinnati and New York;

E.J. (Buzzie) Bavasi, who recently resigned as vice-president and general manager of the California Angels, and who got his start in baseball when he was hired by MacPhail;

Albert B. (Happy) Chandler, former United States senator and governor of Kentucky, and the second commissioner of baseball, mainly as a result of MacPhail's efforts;

Spurgeon (Spud) Chandler, one of the star pitchers during Larry's three years as owner of the Yankees;

John Galbreath, owner of the Pittsburgh Pirates for so many years, highly successful businessman and longtime resident of Columbus, Ohio, dating back to MacPhail's entry into baseball as general manager of the Columbus Red Birds;

Arthur (Red) Patterson, former New York baseball writer and pugilistic opponent, later publicity director of the New York Yankees under MacPhail and executive vice-president of the California Angels;

Harold (Peewee) Reese, new member of the Hall of Fame and great shortstop of the Brooklyn Dodgers. To acquire Reese, MacPhail bought the entire Louisville ball club;

Frank (Spec) Shea, rookie pitcher and one of the stars of Larry's World Champion New York Yankees in 1947;

George Sisler, Jr., president of the Columbus Clippers and two-time winner of the Leland S. MacPhail Promotional Trophy;

Horace Stoneham, former owner of the New York and San Francisco Giants and frequent competitor of MacPhail's;

Irwin Weil, professor of Russian literature at Northwestern University, son of the former owner of the Cincinnati Reds, and nephew of Frances Levy, Larry's secretary and public defender during his days when he directed the Reds.

1

Standing at the Station

If ever man and situation were met, this was it. The Brooklyn Dodgers and Larry MacPhail were synonymous. The two were one.

In January of 1938 MacPhail had taken over a team in total disarray. Now, in 1941, four baseball seasons later, he had brought them from the consistent depths of the second division to the top of the heap, king of the hill.

He had taken the castoffs of other teams, bought a player here and there, patched the lineups and generally infused a winning attitude and spirit to bring about something that had not happened in the borough for over two decades. Now, it all came together.

Whit Wyatt had just pitched a real gem—a four-hit shutout over the Boston Braves in Beantown—and Brooklyn had won the game, 6-0. The entire team had been following the score of the game of the second-place St. Louis Cardinals inning by inning, and when Branch Rickey's team had lost, the race was all over. The Dodgers had won their first pennant in 21 years!

The clubhouse was bedlam, but nothing compared to the wild celebration ahead. The team hurriedly packed to catch the train and the special cars John McDonald had arranged for their triumphal ride to New York City. MacPhail's traveling secretary and general factotum had planned well, ordering plenty of huge steaks, beer, whisky and even champagne.

Larry had tried to reach his manager, Leo Durocher, to congratulate him but, in all the confusion, had only gotten through to McDonald.

Red Barber had been broadcasting the game off the ticker to the delirious fans of Brooklyn. He also had announced the arrival time of the train at Grand Central Station. It turned out that more than 30,000 rabid fans were waiting for them, a fact that was relayed to Durocher on the train. As they headed southwest through Providence, New London, New Haven, Bridgeport and Stamford, word of their progress was sent ahead and the fans' anticipation grew.

In the meantime, MacPhail, not wanting to miss out on the big celebration, hopped in a taxi and headed for the station at 125th Street, the last scheduled stop before Grand Central.

Accompanying him from the office were Jean Bennett Wanamaker, his private secretary and, later, second wife, and Branch Rickey, Jr., son and namesake of his one-time close friend and business associate but, later, bitter enemy.

The activity on the approaching train was starting to pick up. The ebullient third baseman, Cookie Lavagetto, had his pocket knife open and went through both cars cutting off everyone's tie just below the knot. Not to be outdone, the Dodgers' slugging first baseman, Dolf Camilli, had gotten out his straight razor and had sliced a number of belts and suspenders in two.

Durocher finally cut off the bar and shoved the players into the dining car for their steak dinner. No one was feeling any pain when Tony Martin, the nightclub singer who had been traveling with the team and who was a good friend of Leo's, got up and announced that he would sing a victory song.

"The hell you will! Sit down," yelled Lavagetto, "this is our celebration."

As the train got nearer to the 125th Street Station, Durocher heard rumblings that some of the players planned to miss the melee at Grand Central and get off at the earlier stop. John McDonald had neglected to tell Leo that MacPhail planned to board the train there and Leo, not wanting to disappoint the fans waiting for them, ordered the conductor not to stop.

The look of shock on Larry's ample, beet-red face was one of total disbelief and dismay. The train roared past him at 50 miles an hour with the wind almost knocking him over.

When the crowd finally dispersed at Grand Central and Durocher found his way back to the New Yorker Hotel, he located MacPhail and, with a big grin on his face, glowed:

"We did it, Larry! We did it!"

Without even a hello and with a big scowl on his face, Larry glared at him and stormed:

"Did you tell the conductor not to stop at 125th Street?"

"Well, yes," Leo stammered. And, before he could say another word he heard Larry scream:

"You're fired! You're through!"

Incredible! Durocher and the Dodgers had just clinched the pennant, all of Brooklyn was up in the clouds, and suddenly he's fired. He dragged himself up to bed, dog-tired and emotionally spent.

At 7:00 the next morning his phone rang. It was MacPhail.

"Guess I went a little overboard last night. I found out later why you told them not to stop at 125th Street. Let's forget it. Why don't you stop off at the office on the way to the ball park and let's figure out how to beat the Yankees." That's all there was to it.

This was all typical and vintage MacPhail—one of the most fascinating and complicated personalities to burst on the world of sport. He did not appear on the professional baseball scene until he was 40, but in the short period of 13 years, he became a Halley's comet flashing across the baseball firmament.

Leland Stanford MacPhail (ne McPhail) was born in the small midwestern town of Cass City, Michigan on February 3, 1890. He was later to change the spelling of the first syllable of his last name to "Mac" because he was proud of his Scottish heritage and thought the inclusion of the letter "a" connoted a more immediate impression of his Caledonian background.

His mother, born Catherine Ann MacMurtrie, was a close friend of Mrs. Leland Stanford, the wife of the famous railroad builder, governor and senator from California. Because of this friendship for Mrs. Stanford, Larry's mother named her son after the famous Californian.

Larry's childhood was not unusual for a boy born in the typical American family of comfortable success. His father was Curtis W. McPhail, a small town banker in Michigan. Gradually, the senior McPhail acquired several small banks throughout central Michigan until he owned or controlled more than 20.

The family had lived in Grand Rapids but, during Larry's childhood, moved to Ludington, a small city north of Grand Rapids on Lake Michigan. As early as 14, he showed his interest and prowess in music by playing the organ at the Sunday services of the Episcopal Church in Scottville, a town just east of Ludington.

His primary and secondary school education included six years at the Staunton Military Academy in Virginia, training which pointed him toward a career in the military. Upon graduation at the age of 16, he applied to the United States Naval Academy and passed the examinations for entry.

However, the young teenager changed his mind about a life in the Navy and, instead, chose a more prosaic role, that of a liberal arts student at Beloit College in southern Wisconsin.

As a freshman he joined the Beta Theta Pi Fraternity and in late October started dating Ida Green, an attractive girl from Janesville, a town about the same size as Beloit.

With other friends they would make frequent trips to Rockford, a larger city in Illinois a few miles south of the state line, to see various stage presentations at the theater there, including two never-to-be-forgotten productions entitled *Strongheart* and *Brown of Harvard*.

If those times were much simpler than our own, they were also more formal. Ida's diary reveals she called him Mr. McPhail (even originally Mr. McFail) for many weeks even though they seemed to see each other almost every day, either at the library or in the evening or both, usually in the company of mutual friends.

Their social activity also included fraternity and other dances in the Illinois town of Cherry Valley, marshmallow roasts and long walks hand-in-hand along the tree-lined streets of Beloit—typical college romance activity. Ida and Mr. McPhail (it wasn't until January that she first referred to him in her diary as L. McPhail and later that month as "Rusty") frequently went to church Sunday mornings and often to Vespers services in mid- or late-afternoon.

One evening they went to Janesville to see DeWolf Hopper in a play called *Happyland*. Hopper was not only famous in various Gilbert & Sullivan roles, but it was he who almost made a career of reciting the tragic denouement of the mighty Casey striking out for the Mudville nine in *Casey at the Bat*.

In December they went to several concerts of the Girls and Boys Glee Clubs and a Pan-Hellenic dance at which she "never had a better time." Early in January Ida and "Rusty" went again to Rockford to see Shakespeare's *Merchant of Venice*.

The romance was budding and Rusty presented Ida with boxes of candy and even a small amethyst pin. In February, the two lovebirds traveled by sleigh to a fraternity party at the Beta Theta Pi house and Ida acquired a "Beta" banner that "was a peach."

By late February it was "Mac" and Ida going to classes and studying at the library every day and, in the evenings, going to basketball games (Ripon trounced Beloit in a conference matchup), the Elks' minstrels, stage plays, lunch at a Japanese tea garden and other convivial activities.

Then, without warning, the storm clouds appeared and, as was to happen so often in his life, Mac's temper exploded. After a Beloit freshman party, the two "fought all the way home." The next day Mac walked home with Ida "to finish up the fight." The romance was over.

This was Larry's only year at Beloit but he always retained a fond interest in the affairs of the college and several times in later life attended reunions of the class of 1910.

He was the eighth man to be enshrined in the College Athletic Hall of Honor at Beloit on October 27, 1967. His plaque reads in part:

" 'Larry' MacPhail, one of the most colorful figures in American Baseball history, had one brief season of glory on the 1907 baseball team of Beloit College, playing first base on a team which met Purdue, Nebraska, Wisconsin and Notre Dame (as well as a high school, a prep school and a city team)."

As is so often the case with young people at this stage in

their lives Larry did not know what direction his life should take. However, toward the end of his freshman year he decided to become a lawyer and transferred to the University of Michigan to enter law school. His eyes gave him some trouble and, after the first semester, he dropped out of school.

Then, coming to another fork in the road to a legal career, in the fall of 1908 he entered the junior class of George Washington University in Washington, D.C. and received his law degree in June of 1910.

The ebullient young barrister sought employment in Chicago and joined Davis and Rankin, a firm of corporation lawyers. In October Larry passed the Illinois state bar examination, permitting him to practice law before the Illinois State Supreme Court.

Although records are made to be broken, one that may forever withstand the vicissitudes of time is one that this 20 year old set during the ensuing period—he lost his first 200 cases!

The great California earthquake of 1906 spawned thousands of lawsuits. Because of the immediate needs of the people of San Francisco and the surrounding areas, supplies and aid in many forms were needed. This caused many perishable products to be sidetracked along the rail routes to the West Coast, and in turn resulted in heavy losses to the shippers.

The Union Pacific Railroad was the main target of the innumerable lawsuits, and they retained Davis and Rankin to represent them. Cattlemen had sued because of the loss of poundage to their livestock and farmers had claimed excessive spoilage to their produce.

MacPhail's firm assigned Larry to handle the lawsuits and, not too unexpectedly, he lost every case in the lower courts in Chicago. The decisions were eventually reversed in the Court of Appeals when it was determined that the earthquake was an "act of God."

Larry was undaunted and when, at this tender age, the Messrs. Davis and Rankin did not see fit to make him a full partner, he resigned.

He then joined the law firm of Fowler, McDonnell and Rosenberg who added his name to theirs on the masthead and he became a full partner.

During the summer of 1907, after the breakup of the romance with Ida Green, Larry had been ready for new romantic interests and it was not long before this void was filled.

The entire eastern shore of Lake Michigan from the Indiana border north to Canada has always attracted many families from the Chicago area to its beaches and resorts. The Frank Thompson family of Oak Park, Illinois, a western suburb of Chicago, started vacationing at Hamlin Lake, just north of Ludington. Thompson was a vice-president of the American Car & Foundry Company of Chicago, a large manufacturer of railroad equipment. Their youngest daughter was a lovely young girl named Inez Frances Thompson and almost immediately the two 17 year olds became attracted to each other. The romance flourished and, by the end of the third summer, they decided to get married.

It took some time for both families to get used to the idea because of the youth of their children. But, since Larry was already a practicing lawyer, and Inez had graduated in June from Ferry Hall, a "select ladies' school" in Lake Forest, Illinois, they felt the young couple's financial future seemed bright.

On October 19, 1910, Larry and Inez were married at her family's home in Oak Park. They honeymooned for two weeks in Washington and the East and started out married life in Austin, a section of Chicago just east of Oak Park, with Larry commuting to his office in downtown Chicago.

The young couple had their first child in 1912, a daughter, Marian Ann.

During the next several years Larry developed close relationships with several corporate clients, one of the most important of whom was the Huddleston-Cooper Company, a department store in Nashville, Tennessee. They were having difficulties and needed someone to head up the store. When, in 1915, they offered the presidency to Larry, he decided to take up the challenge, and the young family moved to the southern capital city.

Ross Huddleston and Emmett Cooper were partners in the firm and they recognized MacPhail's verve, enthusiasm and business ability. In addition to the presidency, he became a full partner and chief executive of the store.

"Mac" was only 25 when he moved to Nashville. Years later, at the time of the MacPhail-Topping-Webb purchase of the Yankees, the two partners in the store were interviewed.

"I'm not surprised a bit," said Huddleston. "Mac always had a lot of business daring about him. And, I believe he had the quickest mind I've ever seen. He didn't ponder over anything. He was a restless sort of person and he always acted in a hurry. He knew what he wanted, though, and usually got it."

Cooper recalled:

"He was a born promoter. Although he was new in the clothing business, he was full of ideas and innovations. The first thing he did was to put a children's barber shop in the store.

"Then, trying to build up the children's clothing department, he followed that up by putting in a child's library. Parents could leave their children there while they did their own shopping.

"One thing I remember best about Larry was the World Series broadcast he used to put on from the second floor. A telegraph wire was installed and the play-by-play was announced out of the Church Street side of the store. A big crowd used to gather on the steps of the First Presbyterian Church."

It was at this time, also, that Larry got to know Fay Murray, owner of the Nashville Vols baseball team. Later, he was to hire their manager, Charley Dressen, for the Cincinnati Reds. His friendship with Murray also led to his son, Lee, (who was born during their stay in the Tennessee capital) working for the Vols' owner in the cattle business in South Carolina after his graduation from Swarthmore College and before his career in baseball.

In addition, Larry's legal background was of great help to him during this period and his efforts resulted in improving the financial health of the company.

However, things were happening in Europe that were to alter his future completely—the "gathering storm" that brought on the first World War.

2

The Attempt to Kidnap the Kaiser

In 1921, a reunion of the 30th Division was held in Nashville, Tennessee, and the guest of honor was General John J. Pershing, head of the Allied Expeditionary Forces in the first World War. During the ceremonies and comraderie that followed, "Black Jack" was asked what his real thoughts were about the attempted kidnapping of the Kaiser. With a twinkle in his eye he replied:

"You know, I am not a rich man, but I would have given a year's pay to have been with those boys in Holland!"

Leland Stanford MacPhail, then Captain MacPhail, halting linguist and co-conspirator of the plot, loved to tell the tale of the wild escapade. The facts of the case are a matter of record. It is only the colorful interpretations that vary.

The key protagonists in this story, his Imperial Majesty Wilhelm II of Germany and ex-Senator Luke Lea of Tennessee, were as different as chalk and cheese except in one highly important personality trait. Each man was imperious and accustomed to having his own way. In the plot hatched in the ingenious mind of one, he became the HUNTER and the other, hidden away in a remote castle in Holland, the HUNTED.

Because this event happened over 67 years ago, it is important to establish the attitudes and emotions of the time, especially in the minds and hearts of the American people.

Rather than the German people, the Kaiser was perceived to be the arch-villain against whom the wrath of the Allies was directed. The malevolent, spike-helmeted emperor was depicted in tens of thousands of war posters with captions such as "The World's Greatest Criminal" and "Down with the Kaiser."

Editorials from newspapers across the country screamed for his arrest and trial for war crimes. In England, even before the end of the war, David Lloyd George was campaigning on a platform of "Hang the Kaiser." Brand Whitlock, our distinguished ambassador to Belgium (another Tennessean who will play a prominent role in the story later on) vividly reflected the mood of the American people when he wrote the following words in reference to the Kaiser's abdication and flight to sanctuary in Holland:

> The end, the denouement, the triumph of justice in the last act, the villain sneaking off amid ruins—a cinema story couldn't have done it better. What more fitting end for this miserable William Hohenzollern after thirty years of cheap theatricalism, to run away, thus, this cheap hero of melo-drama! There is something ridiculous, grotesque, in the spectacle, those three (the Kaiser, the Crown Prince, and Hindenburg) afraid to confront the people they have duped so long. One would laugh—were it not for those millions of dead whom their megalomania has sacrificed. And one has the sentiment, a hard implacable sentiment of justice, that they must not be permitted to escape thus; they must pay, they must pay!

The Treaty of Versailles, in Article 227, called for the arraigning of the Kaiser "for a supreme offense against international morality and the sanctity of treaties" and provided for a special tribunal of five judges from the United States, England, France, Italy and Japan to conduct this trial. However, the Dutch government refused to extradite the Kaiser. Holland was neutral in World War I and allowed him to continue to comport himself as if he were still an emperor.

The *Literary Digest*, an important weekly news magazine in America at the time, conducted a survey of 381 judges as to their opinion of what should be done with the Kaiser. Of these, 354 wanted a public trial. A breakdown of their recommendations for his punishment shows that 137 opted for exile, 106 for capital punishment, 51 for imprisonment and 7 for "other penalties."

This, then, was the mood of America at that time.

The HUNTED has been identified.

The HUNTER was ex-Senator Luke Lea of Tennessee, the colonel in charge of the 114th Field Artillery Regiment of the Allied Expeditionary Forces. Both by temperament and experience Lea was ideally suited for the role he was to play as leader in the kidnapping attempt. Much like his sidekick, Mac MacPhail (he wasn't to be known as Larry until later), Lea was a big, flamboyant, impetuous man who had a way of letting nothing deter him once his mind was fixed on a goal.

At 33, Lea had been the youngest man, except for Henry Clay, to be a member of the United States Senate. Andrew Jackson had also represented Tennessee in the Senate and there was much in Lea that reminded one of Old Hickory. As a matter of fact, his paternal grandfather, Judge John Overton, had been Andrew Jackson's law partner and his second in several duels.

This, then, was the temperament and background of the man who, as the HUNTER, almost achieved undying fame as the leader of a band of eight intrepid soldiers, whose mission was not only to kidnap the Kaiser, but also to deliver him to President Woodrow Wilson who was in Paris at that very moment.

But we must not get ahead of the story. It had been on April 6, 1917, the very day Congress declared war on Germany, that Mac MacPhail, Luke Lea and several others formed the First Tennessee Field Artillery, the only all-volunteer regiment in the armed forces. Inasmuch as there was neither precedent nor machinery for the integration of volunteer units into the national service, the regiment was incorporated into the Tennessee National Guard for just a day and then nationalized. The outfit thereupon became the 114th Field Artillery, of the 55th Brigade, 33rd (Old Hickory) Division. Luke Lea was in command as lieutenant colonel until October 18, 1917, when he was promoted to colonel of the Regiment. Mac was appointed regimental adjutant and assigned to command Battery B at St. Mihiel and, later, the First Battalion in the Argonne offensive. The brigade commander, incidentally, was

Gen. George Gatley, a resourceful and intrepid soldier, but unfortunately one destined to become known not so much for his military prowess as for the fact he was the father of Ann Harding, a prominent film actress of the time.

As commander of Battery B, Mac participated in the St. Mihiel offensive and in the Meuse-Argonne drive, two of the most famous battles of World War I. Ironically, on the morning of November 11, 1918, later to be commemorated as Armistice Day (and still later Veteran's Day) they were busily engaged in an artillery duel in the Woere sector. Shortly before 11 o'clock, when the cease-fire went into effect, he sustained a slight shrapnel wound and caught a whiff of poison gas. He had gone through the war with nary a scratch, but his luck ran out only an hour or so before the guns were silenced!

In December the regiment was stationed in Luxembourg and served as part of the Army of Occupation. It was during this period that news filtered through that the Kaiser had abdicated and taken refuge at Amerongen, a small town near Utrecht in Holland. MacPhail's own words record what happened next:

"Luke Lea's bitterness knew no bounds. To Luke, as to most Americans, the Kaiser was evil incarnate and it was simply unthinkable that he should go unpunished. Repeatedly, Luke harangued me on the Kaiser's crimes. 'He thinks he's safe now, but he will not get away with it!' he would announce portentously. At other times he appeared to be brooding. It didn't even begin to occur to me that a grand design was taking shape in that fertile brain of his until a few days before Christmas. Luke had been to Paris on leave and had returned only that afternoon.

" 'Mac,' he said in a conspiratorial whisper, 'come to my quarters. I've got something to ask you.'

"Wondering what the mystery was all about, I went with him to his quarters. He was billeted in the home of the local priest and when we got into his room he shut the door with care and, turning to me, said: 'How would you like to join me in an effort to take the Kaiser from his lair and present him to President Wilson in Paris?'

"I stared at him uncomprehendingly and probably goggle-eyed. 'You're kidding!' I finally blurted out as the thrust of his question got through to me.

"But, he was in dead earnest. So determined and confident was he, in fact, that he swept me along with him. Luke had a magnetic personality and an electric presence that few could resist. With wildly beating heart, I listened to him explain how we could bring off this scheme. While in Paris he had somehow managed to acquire some fine French maps drawn to a scale of one to five thousand (our artillery maps, incidentally, were not nearly as rich in detail drawn as they were on a scale of one to ten thousand). Pointing dramatically to a spot on one of the maps he said, 'This is where the Beast of Berlin is hiding.' I peered closely at the map. It showed every house, road, and almost every tree in the neighborhood of Amerongen, Holland, where the former German emperor had obtained asylum at the chateau of Count von Bentinck. Holland was a neutral country, but Luke was confident that he could arrange to get us across the border separating Germany and Holland in the vicinity of Cleve, which was occupied by units of the Belgian army. I stood bemused as Luke again rapped out the question: 'Are you with me, Mac?'

"I wasn't sure that Luke was sane at that moment and, as I heard myself replying in the affirmative, I wasn't sure that I was sane myself. Luke's enthusiasm was so infectious and the scheme so wildly appealing, I just reacted instinctively. I also had tough pioneer ancestors! I remember thinking in a detached sort of way, 'It's crazy, absolutely crazy, but I wouldn't miss it for the world.' Later, when I had time for sober second thoughts I realized that our chances for success were extremely slim, but I shrugged it off with the comforting rationalization that the worst thing that might happen to us would be arrest and deportation by the Dutch government. If that happened, it could be the fastest way of getting home."

When Mac agreed to accompany him, Luke asked him to recruit the balance of the party. He promised to undertake the job and first went to see Capt. Thomas P. Henderson, also of their regiment. Tom was calm, judicious, and cool in emergencies—a great fellow to offset Luke's impatience and rashness. Tom didn't exactly catch fire when Mac explained what was afoot, but when it was pointed out to him that the worst that could happen to them was that they would get home a hell of a lot quicker, his reluctance crumbled. In like manner, he also selected Lt. Ellsworth Brown who was in charge of their communications section.

Three enlisted men were later chosen to complete the initial group of seven—Sgt. Dan Reilly, Sgt. Owen Johnston and Corp. Marmaduke Clokey. The two sergeants were excellent mechanics and fearless soldiers and Clokey, Colonel Lea's motorcycle orderly, was as cool a man under fire as any man could be. All were fellow Tennesseans.

On the 29th of December, 1918, Luke went up to brigade headquarters and put in for a five-day leave for the entire party. Leave was granted from January 1 to and including Sunday, January 5, 1919, "with permission to visit any place not prohibited by orders from General Headquarters, American Expeditionary Forces." It was a "Special Orders" by command of Brigadier General Spaulding, who tried to find out from Luke where he intended to go, but Lea, not wanting the general to be responsible for the trip, declined to tell him.

The general again read the order that had been prepared by Lea for his approval and exploded. "It's the damnedest order of leave I have ever read. But it violates no general or special order, so I'll sign it."

Loaded down with blanket rolls and an auxiliary supply of gasoline, they headed for Liege in the regimental car, a seven-passenger Winton. This car had earned a reputation for complete unreliability and within 30 kilometers had justified its reputation. As luck would have it, an army truck heading back to camp passed by and Clokey was put on board with instructions to return with the regimental car of the 115th Regiment commanded by Col. James A. Gleason, a close friend of Lea's who could always be counted on to help a friend in need.

About midnight Clokey not only returned with the car, an eight cylinder Cadillac, but also with another adventurous volunteer, Sgt. Egbert Haile. In the meantime, the resourceful Reilly and Johnston had repaired the Winton so that shortly after midnight the trip was resumed in both cars. They drove all night and arrived in Liege about seven the next morning, dead tired and half-frozen.

However, fully aware that they had only until the night of the fifth to fulfill their mission, after breakfast they drove on to a Belgian army gasoline depot. In his best college French, Mac asked the officer on duty to supply them with the needed fuel. He replied that he could not do it without the permission of his superiors and that would take several days. Mac then became his most persuasive. "We are engaged in extremely important business and I want to remind you that if America had not come to her rescue, Belgium would still be in German hands." This got the job done and they were able to fill both gas tanks.

From Liege they motored on to the Dutch border at Maastricht where they hoped to obtain passports that would enable them to enter Holland. However, the Belgian officer said it would take several weeks before they could be issued. But, Luke had an ace up his sleeve—he was personally acquainted with Brand Whitlock, the U.S. minister, and later ambassador to Belgium. Lea had been a senator when Whitlock's nomination had come up for confirmation and had been in the forefront in approving his appointment. They headed for Brussels and arrived there after a long, cold drive.

Whitlock received them most courteously and promised to do all he could to help them with the Dutch Legation. But first he advised them to apply for American passports which they did. He had excellent relations with his counterpart in the Dutch Legation and this turned out to be most fortunate. The Dutch minister, whose country had been pro-German during the war, was now most interested in fostering good relations with the Americans and Lea, with his publishing background, implied that he could be helpful in supplying "good press" in America for the Dutch. The minister, therefore, not only visaed the passports which arrived the next morning, but also issued them a "laissez passer" which expressly stated that the entire party could travel throughout Holland by car and in uniform.

A translation of the "Laissez passer" reads as follows:

Legation of Holland in Belgium
Valid for temporary free entrance and exit by motorcar.

The Minister-Resident of H. M. the Queen of Holland, has the honor of requesting the Custom and Excise Officers in Holland to give, when passing custom examination, all facilities permitted by the existing regulations, to the most honorable Senator Colonel Luke Lea, who is proceeding to Holland (and return by motor car, on official duty from the U. S. Government accompanied by five other members of the mission in uniform).

Brussels, Jan. 4th, 1919

The Minister-Resident

(Signed)   Van Vollenhoven

Lea had objected to the phrase "official duty" and tried to have them use "Journalistic Investigation," but they assured him that it was only a "matter of form." This piece of paper proved to be a godsend for the whole expedition.

So armed, the cavalcade headed back to Liege through a blinding snowstorm with the Cadillac forced to push the ailing Winton up some of the steeper grades. When they arrived in Liege they were told that the borders into Holland were closed for the night because of the weather. They had to spend another night in the hotel and time was starting to become a real problem.

Before dawn the next morning, now the 5th of January and the last day of their leave, they headed for the Dutch border. There they were told that no Americans were welcome in Holland and gruffly told to turn back. This is when the "laissez passer" performed its magic. When the border guards saw this official document their brusqueness and rudeness were replaced immediately by courtesy and consideration. The party then proceeded to the border town of Maastricht where the entire project almost ended in disaster.

By this time they were ravenous and entered a cafe for breakfast. Mac, of course, took over at this point to order for everybody. He studied the menu, got into deep discussion with the waiter and was delighted to find that a breakfast of ham, eggs, bread, jam and coffee cost only three francs. The franc at that time was worth a little over 15 cents so they all decided to really live it up and have three breakfasts apiece—a veritable feast for the grand sum of $1.35 each. They also treated themselves to a quart of Scotch whisky for only 10 francs.

After polishing off all the food and washing it down with several highballs apiece, they were anxious to get going and Mac called for the check. Then, reality set in! He had misunderstood the waiter and had forgotten that they were now in Holland where the golden guilder, not the franc, was the medium of exchange. By emptying everyone's pocket they were finally able to settle the bill and proceed on to Amerongen.

About dusk they ran into a snag that changed the whole course of events. They came to a branch of the Rhine and found that the bridge had washed out. There was a ferry and the ferryman agreed to take them across. But, no amount of cajoling could convince him to wait for their return and they all realized that there was no way they could bring the kidnapped Kaiser back with them without the kidnappers being captured. Nonetheless, they decided to go on in the incredible hope that Lea could persuade the Kaiser to accompany them to Paris. Today, this naivete would be unbelievable but, it seems, there was nothing in the nature of reality that would deter Lea and MacPhail in their mission.

About 30 miles south of Amerongen the party happened upon an encampment of English cavalry, a fact that astounded the Americans. They were outraged and, rightly or wrongly, assumed that, being so close to the refuge of the Kaiser, the English must be protecting the enemy in his lair. And this at the very time that the English head of state was demanding the trial and execution of the abdicated German emperor.

This chance encounter recalled a day in England about a year earlier when they, the officers of the newly arrived 114th Field Artillery, were invited to tea by his Royal Highness, the Duke of Connaught. Keeping in mind the utter contempt and loathing the Americans felt toward the Kaiser, they were nonplussed when the Duke proudly informed the American officers that "I bear the same kinship to His Majesty, the

Emperor of Germany, as I bear to his August Majesty, the King of England; I am the uncle of both."

The intrepid band of Tennesseans moved on as quickly as possible and arrived at Amerongen about eight o'clock the night of January 5, 1919. A local citizen gave them directions to the castle of Count von Bentinck on the outskirts of town. There, as Colonel Lea had anticipated, they were confronted at the gate by what he described as a typical German "square-head." When the guard saw the group of American soldiers and heard their demand that they be presented immediately to the officer of the day, he reacted with astonishment. Colonel Lea then turned his flashlight around on himself to show his Sam Browne belt and shoulder insignia. The guard reacted instinctively, clicked his heels and opened the gate.

The officers were then shown into a large comfortable library and were shortly greeted by Count von Bentinck, the son of the old count, who was dressed in a long-tail evening coat. He was a tall young man who carried himself with a military bearing, but wore no decorations. Startled at being confronted by three American officers in uniform, he nervously asked in precise English, "What is the nature of your visit?"

After Colonel Lea introduced the count to Captain Mac-Phail and Captain Henderson, he replied that he would reveal the object of their visit only to the Kaiser himself. The count was very agitated, excused himself and left the room. They could hear him talking to someone in the next room in German and recognized him saying, "Your Majesty." They also heard him on the telephone speaking in Dutch.

While they were waiting, the door opened and a German soldier, dressed as a butler, entered bearing a silver tray with three glasses of port and a canister of cigars. While they were thus relaxing the count returned and indicated that the Kaiser refused to see them unless they revealed the purpose of their visit. Again, Colonel Lea refused to discuss this with anyone but the Kaiser himself.

While the sparring continued they were joined by another man also dressed in full evening wear who turned out to be the burgomaster of Amerongen, a young man who had been educated at Harvard. He suggested they leave the halting communication in German and begin conversing in English. He also asked the purpose of their visit and was refused. The count and the burgomaster then went into a huddle and shortly left the room. They were gone some time and the three American officers had time to survey the room. There was much evidence of the Kaiser's presence—a large library table ornately carved from black walnut with stationery and writing equipment all carrying the Kaiser's crest. On the table and also scattered around the room were several bronze ash trays embossed with *W* and *I* (Wilhelm and Imperator) and the Kaiser's coat of arms. Later, one of these ash trays would be the only tangible evidence remaining from this wild escapade.

The count and the burgomaster finally returned and things were still at an impasse. Luke now presented what he thought would get them off dead center—the "laissez passer." They seemed to be greatly impressed, but, even more, confused. More whispering, more retiring to the adjoining room and more waiting by the American officers.

Gradually, but surely, it became apparent that not only would they not be allowed to meet the Kaiser, they were also being detained by their "hosts." A quick exchange of glances among the three uninvited guests and they shook hands with the count and the burgomaster and headed for their cars.

Outside they found their cars surrounded by what were apparently two companies of Dutch infantry, armed with rifles and side arms. Two large searchlights shown down from the walls surrounding the castle and beside them were two machine guns. They had not the slightest idea what to expect from the Kaiser's guard, the Dutch infantry or the curious Dutch civilians who had gathered in the courtyard.

Luke quickly assembled his small group and gave brief orders. He and Mac were to ride in the back seat of the Cadillac with Haile driving and Clokey sitting next to him. Henderson, Brown, Reilly and Johnston were to follow in the Winton. Haile was instructed that under no circumstances was he to stop the car unless ordered by Lea. The Winton was to follow the Cadillac at a distance of 50 feet. It would stop only if the Cadillac stopped. If the unreliable Winton had any trouble, Reilly, the driver, was to honk the horn three times.

The eight soldiers then entered their cars, started their

engines and moved forward. Only then did they know that the cordon of military and civilians would open up to allow their passage. The timing of their departure could not have been much closer. They found out later that, within a few minutes after they had passed the outskirts of Amerongen, the loss of the Kaiser's bronze ash tray was discovered and the police in several surrounding towns had been alerted.

They sped to the Rhine tributary and, despite a long delay waiting for the ferryman to return from the other side of the river, crossed the river and the border and were back with their regiment only 36 hours later, a fact that was strongly disputed in the subsequent investigation.

The balance of the story is somewhat anticlimactic but should be told, mainly because it might have ended much more seriously in the court-martial of all concerned.

During the next few weeks the newspapers were filled with sensational accounts of the entire escapade. Luke, Mac and the other officers began to anticipate further investigation by the inspector general. Lea then reported to his brigade commander, General Spaulding, and offered to furnish all manner of information to Col. E. M. House, President Wilson's adviser, at the American Peace Commission in Paris, regarding developments in Belgium, Holland, etc. This appears to be more a smokescreen for the attempted kidnapping than actual valuable information, but General Spaulding suggested Lea write Colonel House and request a meeting. The rambling letter follows:

> A leave just concluded . . . permitted the acquisition of certain important and accurate information. This information includes the close and intimate relations of England and Belgium, to the exclusions of other nations, the plans of Belgium to acquire part of Holland, the bad blood between Belgium and Holland, facts relative to the Dutch army and radio communications, the military status of the former Kaiser in Holland, the inefficiency of the Belgian Army of Occupation in Germany, the love and devotion of the former Kaiser and Field Marshall Hindenburg by practically all Germany, the food situation in Belgium, Holland, Luxembourg and Germany, and the wish among part at least of German and Holland merchants for an entente of

Holland, Germany, Russia and Japan that could combat any alliance of England, France, Italy and the United States.

Colonel House neither replied to nor acknowledged Lea's letter. Later, when Lea was in Paris, he tried to see Wilson's close adviser but he was too ill to receive visitors.

Because of the pressure of the Dutch investigation and the complaints of the Kaiser that the visit "made me nervous," the entire kidnapping party was summoned to General Headquarters at Chaumont. Weeks dragged on during which the Inspector General of First Army, A.E.F., Col. J.C. Johnson, questioned every facet of the trip including the use of Army vehicles, the circumstances surrounding the issuance of the "laissez passer," the fact that they entered neutral territory without specific permission and the fact that they went in uniform.

There was one amusing sequence of events in regard to the "ash tray." One of the Kaiser's complaints had been that one of his prized bronze ash trays had been stolen during the visit. Colonel Lea had been questioned extensively about it. Previously Mac had been about to tell Luke about it but Lea had refused to hear about it, feeling that what he did not know could properly be deemed only rumor. He indicated that he had heard about it but, since it was only hearsay, that he could not testify to the fact. This was accepted and the long investigation was formally over.

Later, Luke must have had a premonition because, while he and Mac were having lunch, he brought up the matter:

"Mac, I have changed my ideas on the subject. I want you to retain me as your counsel and tell me every fact about the ash tray."

This Mac did and the revelation could not have been more timely. No sooner had they finished lunch than an orderly approached their table and asked Lea to report immediately to the inspector general's office.

The questioning was resumed and the general said:

"At a conference at lunch we decided that, while your testimony in regard to the Kaiser's ash tray is hearsay and therefore, not competent against anyone, it may open up a lead which will enable us to question more intelligently those who do know the facts about the missing ash tray of the Kaiser. I will, therefore, ask you to be sworn again."

After the swearing-in Lea replied:

"Mr. Inspector General, if you had asked me that question this morning I would have necessarily been forced to answer it. At lunch I became Captain MacPhail's counsel, since you had stated you were through with me as a witness. MacPhail has told me all the facts of the incident. I cannot answer your question as it is all privileged being lawyer and client."

Mac was immediately summoned and sworn in. After the routine questions of name, rank, age, residence, etc., he was asked what he knew about the ash tray. His answer was:

"On advice of counsel I decline to answer."

The investigation was finally over. The inspector general recommended that Colonel Lea be brought to trial but General Bethel, the judge advocate, in his report to General Pershing said that it would be "undignified" for the United States government to put him on trial when the whole incident was "due to poor judgment."

General Bethel then recommended that there be no court-martial, but that Colonel Lea be reprimanded. General Pershing approved this finding and on February 17 the reprimand was sent. This appears below with the key words being "amazingly indiscreet":

GENERAL HEADQUARTERS
AMERICAN EXPEDITIONARY FORCES

France, 17 February, 1919.

FROM: The Adjutant General, A.E.F.
TO: Colonel Luke Lea, 114th Field Artillery
SUBJECT: Entry of Holland and visit to the ex-Emperor of Germany

1. The Commander-in-Chief directs me to inform you that a report of the investigation of your entry of Holland and visit to the ex-Emperor of Germany, in the early part of January, has been laid before him and has received his careful consideration, and that while he is pleased to find that your actions are free from deception, he nevertheless views them as amazingly indiscreet. You should not have

entered Holland at all without the authority of your *military* supervisors. Paragraph 7 of G.O. No. 6, G.H.Q., 1918, clearly intends that leave to visit neutral countries will only be granted in exceptional cases and by authority of these Headquarters. This, however, is not the serious part of the affair. As an officer of the American Army you had no right whatsoever to present yourself at the chateau of the ex-Emperor of Germany without the authority of the President of the United States first obtained. Furthermore, it should have been apparent to you that the meaning and purpose of your visit might well have been misunderstood, as indeed it was in some quarters, and might have entailed the most disastrous consequences, both political and military.

(Signed) M.J. O'Brien
Adjutant General

3

The Columbus Days

This chapter introduces one of the most fascinating, enigmatic and unpredictable threads that ran throughout Larry's entire life in baseball—his relationship with Branch Rickey. The two men were diametrically opposite in so many ways, yet it can be said that these two giants had a greater impact on the game of baseball than any others of their time.

In March of 1919 Capt. Leland Stanford MacPhail returned from France after World War I with the 114th Field Artillery of the 30th Division. He had been recommended for promotion to major but had refused because it would have meant that he would not have been able to return with his battery. He was mustered out in April and took up residence in Columbus, Ohio.

In Columbus, Inez and Larry celebrated the birth of their third child, and second son, Bill. Their daughter Marian had been born in her mother's hometown of Oak Park, Illinois, in 1912, and Lee, Jr. in Nashville in 1917.

The 11 year period between the war and his involvement with the Columbus baseball club was one in which he sharpened his business and entrepreneurial skills in various activities.

He first organized the Standard Corporation, a glass manufacturing company, with his partner, Walter Jones. Four years later, in 1923, he sold his interest in this concern and entered the automobile business, taking over the Ohio Motors Agency, first selling the old Willys-St. Claire and later the Willys-Overland line. By his own admission, he "flooded" the Columbus market with Overlands, and sold out before its popularity collapsed.

His final business venture before his activity with the baseball club was his involvement in the construction of the Medical Science Building on North High Street. This proved to be a financial disaster and he lost everything. Of course, he was not alone since this was the beginning of the Great Depression.

During this period he became one of the most popular football officials in the Midwest, working almost all the games for Xavier College in Cincinnati, as well as many games for Ohio State, Illinois, Wisconsin, Michigan State and Minnesota plus games for Notre Dame, Tennessee, Vanderbilt, Marquette, Georgia Tech, North Carolina and Kentucky. He worked several games with Frank Lane who also went on to a colorful baseball career.

Also, during the late 20s he became active in the organization of the Central Ohio District Golf Association and the larger Ohio Golf Association. Russ Needham, writing for one of the Columbus papers, told a golf story about MacPhail which gives a further insight into his personality:

"My first close contact with MacPhail came at Canton in 1929. I had gone up there to the Brookside Country Club to cover the state amateur golf tournament for *The Citizen* and had taken John Florio, then just a promising youngster, with me."

They went out to the course as soon as they arrived in town and Florio was promptly ordered off the grounds because his club wasn't a member of the Ohio Golf Association. It turned out that Florio's club had been late in paying its dues and, although this was irritating, a phone call remedied this situation and Florio returned to the course.

Needham resumes, "But that was only an incident. Later that day the club tournament committee had treated Scotty Reston (more familiar today as James Reston, the great journalist for the *New York Times*) and Eddie Hamant, a pair of Dayton youngsters, practically the same way. They had qualified at Dayton to represent their public links, but upon their arrival at Canton were told publinks players were not to be permitted to play.

"For some reason Reston brought their troubles to me. So, that night, when we reached the hotel downtown, I laid the whole story before Larry MacPhail, who was chairman of the Central Ohio District golf committee.

"MacPhail, in characteristic fashion, promptly hit the ceiling. He first got hold of Bill Deuschle, a Columbus boy who was the defending champion. Then, he went to most of the other central Ohio players . . .

"Later he went to the state association tournament committee with the ultimatum that Reston and Hamant would play or the Central Ohio group, including the defending champion, would publicly withdraw from the tournament.

"It is unnecessary to say they all played. Florio won the tournament. Reston has since won the state publinks championship and been runnerup in the state amateur and Hamant since has become a former state intercollegiate champion.

"But, that was just an added satisfaction. The way Mac-Phail went to bat for those kids made a hit with me . . ."

Incidentally, Larry's own fine golf game led him to become a semi-finalist in the Ohio Amateur Tournament in 1928.

About this time Larry became interested in the possibility of buying the Columbus Senators, then owned by Sidney Weil who also owned the Cincinnati Reds. He formed and headed a group of business and professional men in Columbus and approached Weil with the proposition of buying the club. Weil was in bad financial shape and agreed to give Larry and his syndicate an option to purchase the club for $100,000.

MacPhail realized that his group would need to affiliate with another major league club in order to insure a supply of ballplayers. So he started to canvass the field.

His first stop was Cleveland where he had a meeting with Billy Evans, who had been a friend and former associate in officiating football games. He found that Evans was obligated to New Orleans and would not be able to supply players for Columbus.

Larry then proceeded to Chicago to talk to Comiskey, but the owner of the White Sox was out of town. While in Chicago, though, he ran into Walter Jones, his former associate in the glass business, who was a friend and former classmate of Branch Rickey at Ohio Wesleyan. He suggested that Larry see him and put in a long distance phone call to him in St.

Louis. After introducing MacPhail to Rickey, he put Larry on the phone.

"When can I see you?," he asked Rickey.

"How about 3 o'clock?" Branch answered, thinking of that hour on the following day.

"Fine," responded Larry. He rushed to the airport, grabbed a plane for St. Louis and was in Rickey's office 10 minutes and 24 hours before he was expected.

A few hours later MacPhail had sold the Columbus club to the St. Louis Cardinal organization and had become its president. Larry had his choice of a commission of $10,000 (10 percent of the purchase price) or a two-year contract as president of the club and he chose the latter. The name of the club was immediately changed to the Red Birds since all minor league affiliates of the Cardinals had names similar to the parent club.

One of his paramount demands in the deal was that the Cardinals would take no ballplayer from his club during the season without Larry's sanction. His insistence on this provision later contributed to his being fired.

Now he really had his work cut out for him. Columbus had been a second division club for 15 consecutive seasons and had not won a pennant since 1907. In 1930 they finished sixth.

He took over the new Red Birds early in 1931, just before the season started. It was too late to build a team around seasoned players and he had to be content with youngsters, untried and inexperienced. He completely reorganized the club with the help of the Cardinals. During the season approximately 75 players were on the payroll. This may have been the first time it was said: "He has three teams: one playing, one coming and one going."

These rookies made many mistakes and lost many ball games, but they never stopped hustling. On the last day of the season the Columbus Red Birds managed to slip into fourth place. MacPhail had underestimated his ball club and the first-division finish was a very pleasant surprise, not only to him, but to all the fans who had been used to an eighth-place finish.

Even more incredible than this artistic improvement was

the immediate change in the financial situation. In the previous decade, under three different ownerships, the club had lost $500,000. In his first year Larry increased the attendance by 50 percent and actually made money, the only club in the league to do so in that Depression year.

The stadium the Red Birds played in, Neil Park, was one of the oldest in the American Association, having been built in 1900, two years before the formation of that new league. However, in typical MacPhail fashion, he plunged in to work with what he had. His frantic activity now was to set a pattern for his future approach to other ancient ball parks in Cincinnati, Brooklyn and New York City.

Huge figures of red birds were painted on the fence where the town brewer had formerly advertised his malt syrup for home brew. The flagpole in deep center field had been colored a brilliant red, and signs on the foul lines told the distance to each of the fences so there would be no argument when Pat Crawford, their home run slugger, hit one out of the park. He piped canned music through the electrical announcing system both before and after the games.

All park attendants, including the female ticket sellers, were dressed in red military fedoras and red neckties when on duty. So insistent was Larry, that one old Irish groundskeeper who refused to wear the red hat was fired. After every game the vendors in the stands, with their flaming red hats and ties, lined up along the foul lines to keep the customers off the field.

He also established a new ticket policy for the kids and ladies. Boys under 16 were admitted free five days a week, and ladies, by purchasing a season ticket for the now-incredible price of $3.00, could see all home games for five cents each. Several hundred women took advantage of the bargain prices.

But all this was really a make-do approach during his first full year. All during the 1931 season MacPhail had been looking for a new location for their ball park and finally convinced Sam Breadon, owner of the parent Cardinals, and Branch Rickey that this was a necessary move. They purchased Sunshine Park on West Mound Street as the site of the new stadium, and this was to be Larry's pride and joy.

MacPhail practically lived at the ball park for the three

months prior to the Friday, June 3, 1932 opening of the new Red Bird Stadium. The $400,000 park was ready almost a full month earlier than originally planned. To accomplish this contractors had worked two and three shifts night and day for the two previous months. The day before the opening, one crew was finishing installing home plate and the pitcher's mound. Another was completing the numbering of the seats. A third crew was rushing work on the new office building and the dressing rooms and a fourth was cleaning up after the first three crews.

The new furniture for the office had been scheduled to be delivered the day before, but had not yet arrived. Larry was furious and called the store to complain vehemently. The woman on the other end of the line heard language she had never heard before and the insistent demand that the delivery be made immediately. Before she could respond she heard the loud click of the phone slammed down in her ear.

She called MacPhail back as soon as he had hung up, told him off roundly, and, in turn, slammed down the phone. Larry was fuming, hopped in a cab, and hurried down to the furniture store. As he was to do a number of times in his life, he ended up by hiring the person who had had the guts to respond in kind to his explosions. The clerk at the furniture store came to work for him.

The new stadium provided seating accommodations for 17,000 fans, 14,000 in the grandstand and another 3,000 in the bleachers. There was no advance in ticket prices over those charged at Neil Park. Bleacher seats went for 50 cents, unreserved grandstand seats for 75 cents, reserved grandstand seats for $1.00 and box seats for $1.50.

Larry had planned the Opening Day festivities just as meticulously as he had the construction of the stadium. At a Wednesday afternoon meeting of the recreation committee of the Columbus Chamber of Commerce he had vetoed any speeches. He felt the fans would be out there to see a ball game.

He had the 120-piece Knothole Gang band there in uniform for the first time, dressed in blue sailor trousers, white middies and red berets. Then, the Camp Chase Drum and Bugle Corps, resplendent in gold trousers, tin hats and blue coats, led a march to the new flag pole where they played the "Star-Spangled Banner" while a color guard from Fort Hayes fired a 17-gun salute and raised the flag for the first time.

Larry had invited and had received acceptances from a very distinguished group of dignitaries. Chief among them were: Kenesaw Mountain Landis, the first and most powerful commissioner of baseball; John Heydler, president of the National League; Governor George White, who threw out the first ball from his box near the Columbus dugout; Branch Rickey; Mayor Henry Worley, who had declared a half-day holiday for the occasion; the 30 mayors of other nearby central Ohio cities; L.W. St. John, athletic director of Ohio State University; and Thomas Hickey, president of the American Association.

The game was broadcast on radio station WAIU, the first time a baseball game in Columbus had ever been aired.

Judge Landis was mightily impressed with the whole performance and especially with the Knothole Gang band which had marched over to the box where he and Larry were seated.

He turned to Larry and said, "Young man, I want you to come to Chicago as my guest and spend a couple of days explaining how you've handled this Knothole Gang idea here. I believe you have one of the finest things in baseball in these kids of yours."

When asked about his reaction to the new stadium he added, "It's immense. There is nothing like it in the minor leagues of the country, and you have a park here that would make many of the major league clubs envious. Columbus certainly has full reason to be proud of such a wonderful layout."

In the game itself, the Red Birds did themselves proud. They clobbered the Louisville Colonels, 11-2, gaining a full game on three of the four teams ahead of them in the standings.

Two weeks later the installation of lights was completed and on June 17, the first night game was played at the stadium against St. Paul, with the Red Birds edging the Saints, 5-4, in 11 innings. Paul Dean, Pete Fowler and Kenny Ash, (who had won the 11-2 game against the Colonels on June 3) pitched for Columbus, with Ash driving in the winning run with a single before 21,000 happy and excited fans.

They kept improving all season, made a real run at the pennant and finished the season in second place. The '32 club had a paid attendance of 310,000, setting a new Columbus record despite the Depression. Not only were the Red Birds the only American Association team to finish in the black, but they also outdrew the parent St. Louis Cardinals' gate of 279,000.

At the start of the 1933 season MacPhail had what he thought was a pennant winning team. But, the Cardinals needed an infielder. MacPhail had a good one in the person of Burgess Whitehead. He was willing to let the Cards take him, and did, but only after Uncle Branch agreed to send him, in exchange, Gordon Slade, Jim Lindsey, Charlie Wilson, Ralph Judd and Art (Whataman) Shires.

MacPhail's insistence on putting the welfare of Columbus ahead of that of the parent Cardinals certainly contributed to the growing rift between him and Rickey, and their relationship, from this point on, rapidly deteriorated. Shortly thereafter Rickey fired MacPhail without ever giving precise reasons for the dismissal. By the time he left, however, the Red Bird team he had put together was already nine games in front of the pack and were never headed. They won their first pennant since 1907 going away.

The Burgess Whitehead incident was just one of the bones of contention between these two adversaries. Rickey was livid at the lavish office MacPhail had provided for himself in the Red Bird Stadium, feeling that it was more luxurious than those of most big league executives. Of course, Larry was never one to do things halfway. Branch put a bee in Sam Breadon's ear and goaded him into calling MacPhail on the carpet.

When Larry entered the Cardinals owner's office he was asked if he saw any paneling on the walls or Oriental rugs on the floor. He laughed, having no doubt about the source of the information that had prompted the question.

"Mr. Breadon," he replied, "if you could get solid walnut paneling for your office at no cost and Oriental rugs for the cost of a kitchen floor, wouldn't you do it?"

Sam pondered this question and allowed as how he would, but would MacPhail explain what he meant?

Larry would and did.

"The contractor did a remarkable job and finished enough ahead of schedule that he earned a bonus of $50,000. He told me that he greatly appreciated the help I had given him to enable him to complete the work so quickly and that he wanted to do something for me to show his gratitude. So, he acquired some walnut sections and proceeded to panel my office at a cost to him of about $5,000.

"In regard to the floor coverings, I read in the newspaper about a fire in one of the local furniture stores and that they were having a sale on some merchandise that had been slightly damaged, including some Oriental rugs. So, I bought them for next to nothing." The reluctant inquisition was over.

Another incident that may have irritated the puritanical and abstemious Rickey occurred during a trip Larry took with the team to see them play a big series with one of the contenders.

After a relaxing evening, MacPhail decided to have a nightcap with the night manager of the hotel. They were alone in the bar, except for the bartender who continued to provide them brandies on request. As the cognac warmed their stomachs, it also tended to heat up the conversation which got hotter and hotter. One thing led to another and Larry swore he would never have the Red Birds stay at that hotel again.

The more he thought about it the madder he got. Suddenly, he jumped to his feet unsteadily and demanded the manager return to the front desk with him and give him a list of all the room numbers of the rooms his players were occupying.

He then went to each room, pounded on the door and told each man to get up, get dressed, pack his clothes and move to the hotel across the street. All this in the wee small hours of the morning before the opening afternoon game.

Of course, a story like this made the round of the league like gossip over the back fence.

In late May of 1933 the rumors were flying. Rickey apparently had requested MacPhail's resignation and Larry had refused. They were at an impasse and matters continued to deteriorate.

Larry had been scheduled to address the Lions Club and the opportunity could not have been more timely. The room was packed in anticipation and you could hear a pin drop when Larry got to his feet.

On the way downtown today, a number of my friends stopped me and stated that they had been informed that I had tendered my resignation as president of the Columbus Baseball Club.

My answer, like Mark Twain's when shown the newspaper reports of his demise, is, "Those reports are slightly exaggerated."

I have learned today, from what seem to be reliable sources, however, that yesterday morning, at 11 o'clock, Mr. George Hedges, one of the directors of the club, invited several people to his offices, and told them I was going to resign, and announced the name of a good friend of mine, who would be given the opportunity to succeed me, immediately.

Your president has been kind enough to introduce me as the president of the Red Birds, but it seems that everybody in Columbus, except myself (and, honestly, I have a real interest in the matter) has been informed either that I have resigned, or that I am going to resign, and that someone else has already been agreed upon as my successor as president of the Columbus Red Birds.

Statements and announcements of this kind come as a surprise. I have issued no announcements, nor have I made previous statements to anyone in this connection. The manner in which this matter has been handled, however, and the hundreds of telephone calls and inquiries that have been coming to me since last Saturday seem to make it necessary for me to make some kind of a frank statement as to what the situation really is.

First, I have not resigned as president of the Columbus Baseball Club, and, up to this moment, my resignation has not been requested by the directors of the club.

There was considerable doubt in my own mind, last fall, whether I would renew my contract with the Columbus Baseball Club for 1933. I advised both Mr. Breadon and Mr. Rickey of the St. Louis Cardinals to this effect last fall.

At the time I was elected chairman of the executive committee of the American Association I told the president and directors of the Association that it was doubtful if I would renew my contract for 1933. At that time, I had other offers in baseball for my services this season.

However, on January 8, 1933, a contract for the season was tendered to me in writing, and both on that date and thereafter, verbally and in writing, the St. Louis club urged me to accept the contract and Mr. Rickey wrote me a personal letter asking that I accept that contract as a personal favor to him.

I state these facts only to make it clear that, after an association of two years, and based on my record for two years as president of the Columbus Baseball Club, the St. Louis Cardinals were insistent that I continue in that capacity for the season of 1933.

Therefore, I think it will be quite clear that if there are any differences of policy or opinion between the St. Louis Cardinals and myself, they have come about very recently; in fact, within the last 20 days.

I think that I have been sincere and honest in my opinions and in the recommendations I have made. Frankly, I doubt that it is either necessary or advisable to discuss these matters publicly at this time.

If Mr. Breadon and Mr. Rickey feel that my opinions are not compatible with the best interests of the Cardinals in Columbus, I am willing, under certain conditions, to resign.

I have no apology to offer for baseball in Columbus the last two years.

The Columbus club had lost approximately $30,000 a year on the average for a great many years. The teams had finished consistently in the second division. The park was obsolete. The average attendance was around 125,000 a year or less in good times.

When I became interested in the purchase of the club, I had three ambitions. First, to give Columbus good baseball and first division teams. Second, to provide a new and modern baseball park. Third, to win a pennant for Columbus in the American Association.

It was through my efforts, and in an endeavor to accomplish these aims, that the St. Louis Cardinals came into Columbus.

As a result of this association we drew nearly 200,000 people in 1931—over 300,000 in 1932—and established an all-time minor league record in spite of the Depression, for a team that did not win a pennant. We finished fourth in 1931, second in 1932, and we are going to win an American Association pennant in 1933.

Mr. Sam Breadon, president of the St. Louis Cardinals,

is a fine sportsman. He has evidenced his faith in baseball and in Columbus by an investment of over half a million dollars in building the finest minor league park in baseball in Columbus.

Branch Rickey is the outstanding personality in baseball today. His efforts, unceasing and tireless, even at the sacrifice of his own health, have saved minor league baseball in a number of leagues.

Whatever success we have enjoyed in Columbus has been due in the greatest degree to Branch Rickey's ability and to his sincere effort to provide for Columbus not only a fine stadium but a winning baseball club.

You will pardon, I am sure, the necessity of taking up this much time in a discussion of something that has nothing to do with the team on the field or with Ray Blades or that sterling athlete, Charles Arthur Shires.

I want to say just a few words about the Red Birds. I haven't been overly optimistic in baseball seasons nor prone to utter enthusiastic predictions. But, I have good reason for being confident that, with a fair share of the breaks, the Red Birds of 1933 will win the pennant in the American Association.

Two of the reasons are here with me today—Ray Blades, the manager of the club, and Art Shires, its captain and first baseman. These fellows typify the spirit and morale of your entry in the American Association pennant race.

Blades will make a great manager because he is intelligent—because he knows baseball—because his judgment is good—because he has and plays no favorites, and because he works harder, hustles harder, and loves to win harder than anybody on the squad.

Shires typifies the spirit and morale of the club and will make a fine field captain. The picture the newspapers paint of Art is not really accurate. Art is good "copy."

Moreover, he is intelligent, and he has had good sense enough to capitalize on the publicity that he has received. He has made mistakes—sure, who hasn't, between the ages of 17 and 25?

But, you are going to like Art. You are going to like him because he is a fine athlete—because he is a team player— because he likes to win, and because he will give as much of himself out there on the field to win for the team as any player in baseball today, without exception.

I am proud, as president of the Red Birds, to present to

you your manager and your field captain—Ray Blades and
Art Shires.

While this meeting was going on, Branch Rickey, unable
to bring about MacPhail's resignation, and apparently unwill-
ing to fire the popular Red Bird president and thereby incur
the wrath of the Columbus fans, was seeking legal advice that
would bring about his termination.

He found it in a provision of Ohio law requiring that a president of an incorporated company in the state must also be
a stockholder of record. A meeting of the board of directors
of the ball club was called and the following statement was
issued:

> At a special meeting of the shareholders of the Colum-
> bus Baseball Club, Incorporated, 9998 shares out of 10,000
> shares issued and outstanding, being present in person or
> by proxy, H.R. Tingley was unanimously elected to the
> board of directors of said company.
>
> Mr. Tingley succeeds Mr. L.S. MacPhail, whose quali-
> fying share has been transferred to Mr. Tingley, thus
> necessitating the election of a director to take the place
> of Mr. MacPhail.

Under the laws of the state of Ohio, a director of an incorporated company as well as the person holding the office of
the president of that company must also be a stockholder.
Since MacPhail was no longer a stockholder, having held only
one share which had now been transferred, he was therefore
ineligible to serve as president of the company.

When MacPhail was elected president of the Red Birds he
had been issued one share of stock which he was required to
sign, in blank, thus enabling the board of directors, at their
discretion, and at any time they chose, to transfer the share
and thus terminate him without notice or his approval.

Officials of the ball club refused to discuss the situation
further. Branch Rickey was quoted as saying, "there is nothing
else that can or need be said at the present time."

For the next few days the sports pages of the three Columbus papers, as well as occasionally those of other cities in the
American Association, were filled with nothing else but a

discussion and an analysis of the change at the top in the Red Bird organization.

With Rickey's refusal to amplify the formal announcement, his position may have suffered in comparison, but most of the sentiment favored MacPhail. The fans were so happy about the dramatic change in the fortunes of their team in such a short period of time, and after such a dismal record for so many years, that they, naturally, rallied around the man they credited for bringing about this change.

Lew Byrer, in his daily column, "Sportive Spotlight" in the *Columbus Citizen*, tried to dissect the developments. He first listed all the rumored reasons for the firing—that Larry was not an organization man, placing the good of the Columbus club ahead of that of the parent organization, that he was impulsive and inclined to carry out his decisions without regard to how they affected others, that he was an expensive operator, and other criticisms—and then proceeded to knock down each of them. Having done that, he went on to give his opinion:

> Uncle Branch has believed what he's read in the papers about being a baseball genius. He rejoices in that role.
>
> In St. Louis, Rochester, Houston and other Cardinal baseball sites he is so recognized and acclaimed. When he arrives in one of those cities there are headlines in the newspapers and Uncle Branch makes brilliant speeches before the Rotary, Kiwanis and other luncheon clubs.
>
> But, Uncle Branch is a native of Portsmouth, Ohio. He went to college at Ohio Wesleyan. Many of his boyhood and college friends live in central Ohio.
>
> And in central Ohio Uncle Branch has been unfortunate enough—from his viewpoint—to select a resident executive who was colorful and made news.
>
> I believe Columbus sports scribes, unwittingly, did Larry a real harm in building their stories of the club around him instead of Uncle Branch. And I believe that very fact had more to do with the ouster than any other one thing.

Frank M. Colley, in his column, "Wise and Otherwise" in the *Columbus Dispatch*, chose not to take sides in the controversy. He was highly complimentary of MacPhail and predicted the following:

We don't think for a minute that Larry MacPhail is through with baseball. In fact, we believe that he will go much higher in the game than the mere presidency of a club in the American Association. The time will come, we believe, when he will be ranked among the leaders in the game.

Robert E. Hooey, in his daily sports column, "That's No Hooey" in the *Ohio State Journal*, approached the story in a similar fashion to Lew Byrer—that the Columbus press corps had given too much publicity and credit to MacPhail in the previous two years and that Rickey was jealous of this. He concluded his story with these paragraphs:

> It is true that MacPhail is not an organization man. And, he never will be. He cannot take orders. He cares to do things himself. It is probably better in the long run for the Cardinal system that MacPhail be ousted. The flareup was bound to come between Rickey and him.
> But the Columbus public will long remember the unusual method Rickey and his board of directors took in disposing of MacPhail.
> It is to be remembered that Rickey failed to meet two conditions of MacPhail's when the latter was asked to resign. One concerns finances, which is more personal than public business. But, the chief one—a statement from Rickey as to the reasons why he wanted MacPhail to resign—was never given.

Shortly after MacPhail's departure, the Columbus club was accused of paying several players more than the $400 per month salary limit stipulated by the league rules. Whether this development actually cast any shadow of suspicion on Larry or not, he was determined that the entire matter be investigated and that he, personally, be cleared of any wrongdoing.

Columbus was convicted and fined by the American Association of violating this rule. They appealed the conviction to Judge Bramham, president of the National Association of Professional Baseball Leagues. This appeal was denied. MacPhail was not mentioned in the matter at all, but Larry was determined that no stigma be attached to his name.

He called Judge Landis, the commissioner of all of organized baseball, and asked for a complete investigation of the matter. The judge called in the players involved and held a hearing to determine who was involved. The hearing proved that MacPhail had nothing to do with the illegal signings and Judge Landis issued a statement to that effect.

4

On to Cincinnati

Larry was not to be out of baseball very long. He went on a hunting and fishing trip to the upper peninsula of Michigan to relax, and, during this time, received feelers from the Milwaukee Brewers and was discussed in many sports articles in cities throughout the American Association.

Meanwhile, things were going from bad to worse for Sidney Weil in Cincinnati. The $100,000 he had raised three years earlier from the sale of the Columbus farm club had not helped for long. Weil was well liked and highly respected in the National League, but seemed to be dogged by misfortune throughout his four years at the helm of the Reds. Each year the team seemed to get worse and soon it appeared that they had a lease on last place. They finished the 1933 season in the cellar again with a record of 58 wins and 94 losses.

Weil was so discouraged that, after the season, he decided to retire. For the last three years the Central Trust Company had held his stock and, when he turned the club back to them, he resigned not only as president, but also as a director of the club, issuing the following statement:

> I deeply regret that I was not able to fulfill the sincere ambition and desire which actuated me in becoming interested in the Cincinnati Baseball Club, namely to give Cincinnati a winning team. During the four years of my stewardship I exerted every effort and resource at my command toward this end but without avail. My handicap of lack of funds was no secret to you.
>
> I hope the new members of the Board of Directors will have the necessary financial backing that I have lacked and I wish them every success.

I cannot close my baseball career without a word of thanks and gratitude for the loyalty and friendship shown me by the fans during these four years of stress.

Mr. Charles W. Dupuis, president of the bank, who had been controlling every financial move of Weil during the last three years, also resigned and appointed two other officers of the bank to replace him on the Board of Directors, Mr. Thomas M. Conroy and Mr. David C. Jones.

The previous year, Larry and a group of his friends had attempted to buy the Reds, but felt that it would be foolish to buy any major league club without the backing of at least $1,000,000.

This previous contact, plus the reputation earned from his phenomenal success at Columbus, made Larry the ideal candidate in the new board's search for an experienced and dynamic baseball man to change the fortunes of the Cincinnati baseball club.

On November 7 MacPhail was elected to the new five-man board, along with Conroy and Jones. The other two members were attorney Maurice L. Galvin and Joseph Meagher, who represented the estate of Louis Widrig, a heavy stockholder of the club during the regime of August Herrmann. Meagher had served as secretary and treasurer of the club since the death of Mr. Widrig and continued in that capacity. Tom Conroy was elected vice-president and put in temporary charge of the club's business. But almost immediately thereafter Larry was also elected vice-president and general manager with virtually complete control of the operation.

MacPhail still needed to be approved by the rest of the league and in a two-day meeting of the National League on December 12-13 one of the main topics of discussion was Larry's qualifications for membership in the league.

Attending the meeting were the following owners: Mr. Conroy of the Reds; Mr. Wrigley of the Chicago Cubs; Mr. Fuchs of the Boston Braves; Mr. Breadon and Mr. Rickey of the St. Louis Cardinals; Mr. Bondy and Mr. Stoneham of the New York Giants; Mr. Benswanger of the Pittsburgh Pirates; Mr. Gilleaudeau of the Brooklyn Dodgers; Mr. Nugent of the

Philadelphia Phillies; and Mr. John Heydler, president of the National League.

The following quotations are an excerpt from the minutes of this meeting and are included in detail to illuminate another facet of the intriguing relationship between Rickey and MacPhail:

> *Mr. Conroy:* You have a copy of the letter that Judge Bramham (William G. Bramham, President-Treasurer of the National Association of Professional Baseball Leagues) wrote us. We went into the thing very thoroughly; and, on top of that, Judge Landis was in Galveston with Mr. Mac-Phail at that time. Mr. MacPhail wanted to have a hearing, demanded a hearing, and he went down there to Galveston to demand a hearing, and was with Judge Landis during that time.
>
> *Mr. Wrigley:* You understand, I am not making any criticism of any individual. What I am thinking of is, whoever goes in there, it naturally will be to the advantage of everyone to have somebody in there who everybody will get behind, the fans, the newspapers and everybody else, and say, "Here is a new ball club for Cincinnati, with a fine fellow in there running it." It makes a fine feeling, a fine spirit. That is the only thing I have in mind.
>
> *Mr. Conroy:* I understand.
>
> *Mr. Wrigley:* I do not know Mr. MacPhail at all.
>
> *Mr. Conroy:* I understand exactly what you had in mind. I am sorry in one way, and glad in another way, that this matter was brought up, because it will clear up a lot of the atmosphere, and, as somebody said, "Do away with a lot of the rumors."
>
> *Mr. Wrigley:* Oh, yes; there have been lots of rumors in connection with it.
>
> *Mr. Conroy:* Yes, and nobody was more interested in tracing the source of those rumors, than we were; and we went into it very thoroughly. I would dislike very much to see anything brought up simply on the proposition of rumors, that would put any stigma upon a man's character, or anything in connection with him, that was not a fact.
>
> *Mr. Wrigley:* Oh, no.
>
> *Mr. Conroy:* Because, as I say, we have gone into the matter very thoroughly, and it is not fair to let something hang over a man who is all right in every way, shape and form.

As a matter of fact, as I said before, we are sold on him, and we have a very high regard for him.

Mr. Fuchs: Mr. President, I would merely like to say this, whatever my own part in this thing has been, I have had in mind justice to Mr. MacPhail, first, because of the fact that this proposition did go around, and it was talked about and is being talked about. Therefore, instead of giving this man a Scotch verdict, let us be satisfied fully, in justice to him, as well as to the league. Now I do not know of any man who could clear up the entire situation better, who has a better sense of fairness, or who is more jealous of the good name of the league, than Mr. Branch Rickey. I wonder whether it would be embarrassing to him to state the situation as he knows it, because he has been associated with this gentleman as an officer of the Columbus Club. I believe a statement from him might be very helpful.

President Heydler: Mr. Rickey.

Mr. Rickey: I do not know whether it will be embarrassing or not, but it is a perfectly frank inquiry, and a perfectly honest approach on the part of a mind like yours, or any other mind here. I have no doubt about that. I shall not go into detail on the controversy that occurred in Columbus; but, if there is any lingering inquiry in the mind of anyone present after I finish, not simply as a matter of curiosity, but as having a bearing on this thing, I will answer questions as to that also. I am perfectly able to answer anything in connection with that particular phase of your deliberations here.

That controversy which happened in Columbus resulted in the retirement of Mr. MacPhail from the presidency of the Columbus Club. Now, as I use that word 'controversy,' it has reference to an entirely different state of affairs than the so-called "player affidavits" matter. The retirement of Mr. MacPhail was decided upon prior to any knowledge that I had that certain agreements had not been sent in. But, there was absolutely no connection between those two things. There is to be no stigma placed on the moral standing of Mr. MacPhail; there was no attack upon his character per se in any way because of the controversy with Mr. MacPhail, just referred to, and I say so with no qualification one way or the other. Those matters were entirely divorced.

I would not have any member of the National League feel that his retirement from Columbus had even the remotest connection with the thing that happened immediately thereafter. At the time that this thing had become discussed, about his retirement, that part of it was not in the picture at all; we did not know about it at that time.

Now, that is a statement of the facts, and is subject to proof by documentary evidence all the way through; everything is written, every bit of it. Now, that is the case.

Mr. Fuchs: Well, then, I take it that, in your opinion, Mr. MacPhail is qualified to come into this National League in any capacity?

Mr. Rickey: Well, that is purely a matter of opinion now. I would rather talk factually about him, in answer to that question, and then let you gentlemen draw your own conclusions. My opinion is that Mr. MacPhail is a man who will benefit the league in Cincinnati, tremendously. Now, whether that answers your question or not, I do not know, but I am ready to make that statement very forcibly—apart from minor criticisms, to which we are all subject, that come from impulsive natures at times, that may have occurred since he has been identified with the league, things such as Mr. Conroy and I were speaking about the other evening. I am referring to little things; it might be that he would be too trusting, for example, to put a concrete case before you. Larry MacPhail would be very trusting, let us say, to a friend of his, a newspaper man, John Jones, and he has him out to dinner tonight, and he casually observes a certain thing, makes a certain observation about something he proposes to do, let us say. He tells him that in confidence, as a statement in confidence, to be respected as such. From the standpoint of your own practical experience in baseball, that would have been a subject matter that MacPhail, perhaps, should not have told that man, but he did it, trustingly, and then the first thing he knows, something comes out somewhere. Well, now, I have known other baseball men, in their early days, to make the same mistake, if you can call it a mistake.

Mr. Bondy: Mr. President, do you not think that you would get a quicker answer to the question if you took a roll call, and a vote? Then you will know exactly how the men stand on this question, and that would answer it.

Mr. Fuchs: I want to ask permission first to have Mr. Rickey give us completely his version of it.

Mr. Breadon: I suggest that the President call for a vote, to ascertain if Mr. MacPhail will be satisfactory to be a member of this league.

Mr. Bondy: I will second that motion, if it is a motion.

Mr. Breadon: I so move.

President Heydler: Including St. Louis?

Mr. Breadon: Certainly, I do not care.

Mr. Conroy: Ask St. Louis to vote first.

President Heydler: What was that suggestion?

Mr. Bondy: Start with St. Louis.

President Heydler: You want a roll call on the question of whether Mr. MacPhail will be acceptable to the National League.

Mr. Breadon: Yes.

Mr. Rickey: I was just going to add, there might be things like that, that you would object to, but that do not occur with more experience, in my opinion. In other words, those are minor things, that all of us have done maybe in earlier years. But, he is a fast learner, he has a lot of aptitude, a lot of enthusiasm, a lot of industry. He will deal with you in a straightforward fashion, right across the table; and his enthusiasm, controlled and directed in the right direction, will help to make the Cincinnati club a winner, and make more money for the league; there is no question about that.

Now, when it comes to questions which somebody might think they would like to ask, about why that controversy arose, we think that is a matter which does not concern the league. It is not a matter that you would be concerned with even if you knew the facts.

Mr. Fuchs: You say it is nothing that reflected on his character?

Mr. Rickey: No.

Mr. Fuchs: All right; that is the point of issue.

President Heydler: Call the roll.

Asst. Secretary Giffels: New York?

Mr. Stoneham: Aye.

Asst. Secretary Giffels: Boston?

Mr. Fuchs: Yes.

Asst. Secretary Giffels: Pittsburgh?

Mr. Benswanger: Yes.

Asst. Secretary Giffels: Brooklyn?

Mr. Gilleaudeau: Yes.

Asst. Secretary Giffels: Philadelphia?

Mr. Nugent: Yes.

Asst. Secretary Giffels: Chicago?

Mr. Wrigley: Yes.

Asst. Secretary Giffels: Cincinnati?

Mr. Conroy: Not voting. I have expressed myself.

President Heydler: I think we should hear from Cincinnati.

Mr. Conroy: Then, I vote yes.

President Heydler: That is a fine endorsement by the league of Mr. MacPhail. I do not see how anyone could ever question that hereafter, at any time.

One interesting comment was made later by Judge Bramham about that meeting. Larry had occasion to send this excerpt of the minutes of that meeting to him on September 18, 1935. On September 20 Judge Bramham sent Larry the following reply on the letterhead of the Office of the President, The National Association of Professional Baseball Leagues:

Mr. L. S. MacPhail, Vice-President,
Cincinnati Baseball Club,
812 Traction Bldg.,
Cincinnati, Ohio.

Dear Mr. MacPhail:

I am returning to you herewith the enclosure in your letter of September 18th, which I have read with the greatest interest. The gentleman was certainly walking on eggs in his talk and testimony, but there was finally enough smoke to embarrass him greatly if he should ever take a back track.

There are two kinds of folks in this world—one, the fellow who lives and speaks right out in the open; the other, a genuine representative of the character "Dr. Jekyll and Mr. Hyde." I prefer those who come within the first classification.

With kind regards, I am

W. G. Bramham, President

Also, in the morning edition of the *Cincinnati Enquirer* on the same Tuesday, November 7 on which the new board of the Cincinnati Reds was formed, Jack Ryder wrote an article which appeared on the front page. In it he said the following:

Last year (meaning the season just ended) the Columbus team finished as champions, but President MacPhail
was deposed from office in mid-season because he was
honest enough to expose to the minor league officials the
duplicity of the Cardinals in sending him players whose
salaries violated the American Association agreement on
the limit of the amount to be paid to each player.

MacPhail assumed the position of "goat" without a mur-
mur . . . and refused to comment on the matter.

On the 6th of November, the day before MacPhail was
elected to the board, he was interviewed about his plans for
the Reds were he to be put in charge. Larry said:

I am a believer in young blood for a ball club. If I am
president every effort will be bent in that direction. Furthermore, I wish it made emphatic that Cincinnatians will
have the controlling interest in the club and that it virtually
will be home ownership, a situation that cannot help appealing to the fans of Cincinnati. Previously, several friends
and myself tried to buy the club, but the negotiations fell
through. I want Cincinnati to have a winning team and I
do not believe that the present aggregation measures up
to the specifications.

It is going to be a big task to rebuild the Reds, but I
believe it can be done. Of course, it would be foolish to say
that we could step out and obtain a winning team the first
year. It can be done eventually with sufficient working
capital and I imagine that can be arranged.

There is an interesting sidelight to the club that MacPhail
inherited. The Reds of 1933 had started the season with an
infield made up of Sunny Jim Bottomley, the veteran Cardinal
first baseman obtained from Branch Rickey for Owen Carroll
and 11 minor leaguers, at first; Joe Morrissey at second; Leo
Durocher at short; and Andy High at third. After the first 16
games, Weil announced another major transaction with the
wily Rickey, actually one that helped both clubs. Durocher,
who had been the Reds' great fielding shortstop for three years,
was traded to the Cardinals along with two pitchers, Dutch
Henry and Jack Ogden, for Paul (Oom-Paul) Derringer, third

baseman Earl (Sparky) Adams and pitcher Allyn Stout. It
turned out to be a good trade for both teams.

In his typical fashion, MacPhail started right in hyping the
team in the winter months. He had the Cincinnati fans agog.
He was always too shrewd to promise more than he could
deliver, but by Christmas I am sure he had the fans dream-
ing with "visions of pennants dancing in their heads" in the
not-too-distant future. Lou Smith, in the *Cincinnati Enquirer*,
said that "in the 1934 pennant race, Larry MacPhail is 12,000
words ahead of the field."

His first move was to analyze the club's roster. He immediately asked waivers on every member of the team so that
he could determine how much interest there was on the part
of the other clubs in making trades with the Reds.

Even before the minor league meeting was held in Gal-
veston on the 17th of November Larry had completed two
trades. First, he shook the fans of Cincinnati by trading the
great control pitcher, Red Lucas, to the Pirates for their second baseman, Tony Piet, and outfielder Adam Comorosky.
Then he sent second baseman George Grantham to the Giants
for pitcher Glenn Spencer.

His next move was the outright purchase of Gordon Slade
from the Cardinals. Slade had been one of the five players
MacPhail had insisted on receiving in compensation for
Burgess Whitehead when the Cardinals had called Whitehead
up from Columbus.

Then, Larry contacted Chick Hafey and flew to the West
Coast to talk with him face to face. There had been rumors
that the great outfielder had become disenchanted with the
Reds and wanted out. MacPhail was able to convey his own
enthusiasm to Hafey who was happy to stay with the team
under the new regime.

Donie Bush had been the manager of the Reds when Mac-
Phail took over, but although Bush was a good friend of his
and he respected him, Larry preferred to have a playing
manager. This was accomplished in another trade. He sent
Glenn Spencer to the Cardinals in exchange for pitcher
Sylvester Johnson and catcher Bob O'Farrell, whom he later
installed as manager. He had originally wanted Jimmy Wilson

in that position, but was unable to get him. O'Farrell had been the Cardinals' manager in 1927.

Three weeks earlier, MacPhail had acquired infielder Mark Koenig from the Phillies for shortstop Otto Bluege and infielder Irvine Jeffries.

The excitement he was creating spilled over into other National League cities. Even urbane and blasé New York reacted to his visit there in early January. The *Evening Post* carried the following article:

> There are two baseball stories in New York today. One concerns Babe Ruth. The other, Larry MacPhail, a figure less glamorous than Ruth, but one whom you'll hear from shortly. For a baseball owner, MacPhail is a revelation. He talks. He doesn't evade. He takes you into his confidence. He thinks baseball needs promotion, and he's ready to promote.
>
> And if you think all that doesn't constitute a peculiar article in the baseball world, just add up the number of denials that preceded the appointment of Jimmy Wilson as manager of the Phillies. Add them up and spell baloney.
>
> MacPhail is progressive and baseball needs that virtue as much as it needs Babe Ruth's color. If it is at all possible to lift the Cincinnati club out of the cellar into the dividend-paying class, the Reds new vice-president will do it. He can't miss making his presence felt in baseball.
>
> Thus far that's the story of Larry's visit to New York. He's here ostensibly to trade, but pending the completion of prospective deals, he'll talk freely on baseball, affairs of the Cincinnati club included, however ridiculous it would seem to put the two in one class.
>
> "First, I'll make a couple of denials," MacPhail said, "and you can put them on the record. We're not considering Burt Shotton for the post of manager of the Reds. Chick Hafey is not on the trading block and we won't trade Jim Bottomley for Don Hurst.
>
> "Yes, I think Hafey is worth more than Chuck Klein. I never did place that $150,000 price tag on Chick. I merely gave my opinion—and I still think so—that Hafey's record for batting and fielding is better than Klein's. The figures for the last seven years bear me out."

The Braves apparently do not think MacPhail's estimate of Hafey's worth is exaggerated. They offered him $75,000 and three players for the star center fielder. Generous as this offer was, MacPhail refused it, preferring to retain Hafey as the nucleus of his club.

"You can't buy much with that money, at least no one who can approach Hafey in ability. Now I have a pretty good outfield with Hafey, Comorosky and Johnny Moore. I think the acquisition of Comorosky and Tony Piet helped the club no end, even if we did give up Red Lucas.

"Jim Bottomley, Piet, Mark Koenig and Sparky Adams make a more than competent infield. I figure that we've got one of the strongest clubs that ever finished last in the league. With a little improvement we'll make trouble for the others and pick up a few places ourselves."

Larry now had some real momentum going, but there was only so much he could do without adequate financial backing. He was the talk of the town and felt that now was the time to strike in appealing to the civic pride of one or more of the wealthy Cincinnatians. One of the men he arranged to see was Powel Crosley, Jr., millionaire manufacturer of radios and refrigerators, and president of the Crosley Radio Corporation.

This was not the first time Crosley had been approached to lend his financial support to help bail out the local team, but he had never been approached by anyone having the persuasive powers of a Larry MacPhail.

The first meeting lasted for five hours and Crosley, who was mainly interested in keeping the club in Cincinnati, offered to back MacPhail in heading the corporation as president of the club. Larry, however, declined and, in a subsequent conference, convinced Crosley that he should take the presidency himself and take an active part in the running of the club.

He agreed and, in announcing his decision to head the organization, told the press "I was never interested until Mr. MacPhail came into the picture. He has built an efficient organization, and I am confident we will make a success of the venture."

There are two versions of the clinching arguments Larry

used to convince Crosley. One was the promise that he could rename the park Crosley Field. This may have been part of it, but it seems somewhat more likely that MacPhail persuaded him of the promotional value of the team to his radio station, WLW, even if the team did not make money.

On February 4, 1934, the day after MacPhail's 43rd birthday, Crosley purchased controlling interest in the club. He bought $175,000 worth of preferred stock and took an option on 80 percent of the common stock. Later, he exercised part of this option and bought 51 percent of the common. MacPhail had what he wanted when Crosley informed him that he would provide the money for MacPhail to buy ballplayers. Crosley was then wise enough to leave the operation of the club in the hands of experienced baseball men.

Mr. Crosley already owned two radio stations—the aforementioned powerful WLW and the lesser station WSAI. He had hired a young Florida announcer who had won an audition at WLW in 1933, a man whose career became intertwined with MacPhail's for many years thereafter, Mr. Walter L. (Red) Barber. MacPhail believed in radio, not just as a novelty, but as a means to promote the game to all segments of the populace. He especially wanted to broadcast the out-of-town games back to Cincinnati to keep up the interest in the Reds all season long.

For several years prior to 1934 the Reds' games had been broadcast on a minor station, WFBE, with a colorful local sportscaster, Harry Hartman, doing the games. In 1934, not only did Hartman continue, but Barber started his broadcasts on Crosley's less-powerful WSAI and, for that year only, an announcer by the name of "Oatmeal" Brown did the games on station WKRC. For the year 1934 all three stations would be on the air, each paying $2,000 for the privilege and retaining the rights to raise their own advertising revenues.

They scheduled 85 games, 72 of which would be out-of-town games. Barber planned on airing not only all 85 games, but also repeating a resume of each game in the evening followed by occasional interviews with National League players.

MacPhail was especially interested in getting the women of the Cincinnati area involved in the success of the team and felt that the more games they could hear on radio, the more likely they would be to join their husbands at the ball park.

Now, he was ready to move. He knew he needed to develop a farm system as soon as possible and that he was almost starting from scratch. First he hired Frank Lane, a former associate in officiating football and basketball games, as his assistant. In Frantic Frank, as he became known later, Larry recognized his own qualities of dedication and imagination that would more than make up for his lack of experience in baseball. The two made a great team.

Almost immediately they started acquiring farm clubs at all levels of organized baseball, either through outright purchase or by setting up working arrangements. The first six included Toronto of the International League; Wilmington, North Carolina of the Piedmont League; Beckley, West Virginia, of the Middle Atlantic; Bartlesville, Oklahoma, of the Western Association; Mt. Airy, North Carolina, of the Bi-State; and Jeanette, Pennsylvania, of the Penn State Association. Today, it is hard to imagine many towns of the size of the last five supporting baseball, but in those days of less mobility and little extra money to spend, there was great local pride in the hometown teams.

Early in the season Larry amazed the fans by making still more trades. He picked up two veteran pitchers who, he thought, might not only win a few games, but also add to the gate attractions—Dazzy Vance and Fred (Sheriff) Blake.

It was to become a trademark of MacPhail that, wherever he went in baseball, he wanted to spruce up the parks, make them colorful and attractive and make them places of excitement for fans of all ages. Cincinnati was no exception. He repainted the park, put fancy uniforms on the ushers, and hired cute girls to sell cigarettes to the fans.

Another of MacPhail's many firsts also occurred this summer—the first transporting of a team by air. He was always looking for ways to hype the team, so he chartered two American Airlines planes to fly the Reds from Cincinnati to Chicago. A few of the players refused and proceeded to the Windy City by train, but most of them caught the spirit and piled in the Ford Tri-Motors. WLW even put a shortwave transmitter on board and Red Barber broadcast back to the station in Cincinnati. He and the engineer got off in Indianapolis with the equipment and drove on back to the Reds hometown, their fans having heard the historic broadcast live.

Unfortunately, the 1934 edition of the Cincinnati Reds proved to be no improvement over the 1933 edition, and the cellar again loomed as their likely final resting place. By May 7 the team was in bad shape, having lost eight straight. Larry, never one to sit back and wait, made more moves. He sent outfielder Johnny Moore and Pitcher Sylvester Johnson to Philadelphia for another outfielder, Wesley Schulmerich, and pitcher Ted Kleinhans. Then he made two purchases from the minors—Tony Freitas, a diminutive southpaw pitcher from St. Paul, and Harlin Pool, an outfielder from Sacramento.

Even with the changes, the infield was usually composed of Jim Bottomley at first, Tony Piet at second, Gordon Slade at shortstop and Mark Koenig at third. In the outfield, Schulmerich replaced Moore in right, but Hafey was still his regular center fielder with Comorosky in left.

In the pitching department, the regular four-man rotation consisted of Paul Derringer, Si Johnson (no relation of the recently traded Sylvester), Benny Frey, and the rookie, Tony Freitas. Dazzy Vance proved to be over the hill, having started and lost two games. The catching was well handled by Ernie Lombardi, who was also their best slugger. But, the team was floundering, and seemed to have no direction. They were winning about one game out of three and showing no improvement. Also, Larry was becoming more and more disenchanted with O'Farrell's leadership ability and started looking for a new manager.

He searched in many areas of the country and finally found his man, Charley Dressen, who was managing the Nashville, Tennessee club in the Southern Association. Lee Allen, in his book on the Reds, tells an interesting story about Dressen and the start of his long-lasting association with MacPhail:

> Dressen had been only an average player for the Reds in the seven years he had played, starting in 1925, but he always had been recognized as a smart performer. He paid a great deal of attention to small details and was enamored

of what he called "inside baseball." He had landed the managerial job at Nashville through a bit of daring.

After his release by the Reds, Dressen found himself at the end of his career without a job and without money in the midst of the nation's worst Depression. He was contemplating joining the police force at Decatur, Illinois, when he learned that Nashville was considering a change in managers. Borrowing money for the journey to the Tennessee city, he applied to Fay Murray, owner of the Nashville club, for the job.

Murray made it clear that he was interested primarily in winning and how did smart young Mr. Dressen propose to win? Charley said that he would take over the team then and there, and if he didn't win more games than he lost during the remainder of the 1932 campaign, Murray wouldn't have to pay him a cent in salary. That rather strange proposal was accepted. Dressen took the job and had a record of thirty-eight victories and as many defeats when the last day of the season came around. Nashville won the final encounter, 12 to 8, thereby earning Chuck's salary, and although Murray later told Dressen that he would have paid him off anyway, he would not have gone along with him as a manager unless he had shown a winning record.

Then, in 1933, the Giants, crippled by an injury to Johnny Vergez, their third baseman, needed infield insurance for the World Series against Washington. Dressen, still active as a player at Nashville, was selected. He sat on the bench in the autumn classic, but achieved a bit of immortality in the eleventh inning of the fourth game, at Washington. The Giants had the lead, 2 to 1, but the Senators had three men on base and only one out. At this stage, Cliff Bolton, a reserve catcher whom Dressen knew from Southern Association play, was sent in to bat for Monte Weaver, the Washington pitcher. The Giant infield went into a huddle, speculating whether to play in and cut off the run at the plate or drop back for the double play. Dressen, acting under impulse, for he hadn't been consulted, rushed from the bench out on the field and told manager Bill Terry, "Set the infield back. I know Bolton. He's slow, and if the infield is back you can get two."

"O.K.," Terry agreed. "Play for two, boys."

Bolton hit into the double play, Ryan to Critz to Terry. It ended the game, the Giants winning, 2 to 1.

That was an example of Dressen's attention to detail, but it was rather spectacular, and Larry MacPhail, sitting in the grandstand that afternoon, made a mental note that Chuck Dressen might be worth consideration as a manager.

MacPhail considered two people as candidates to become the new manager in addition to Dressen—Wade Killefer in Indianapolis and Oscar Vitt at Los Angeles. After quick plane trips to those two towns he went on to Atlanta where Dressen's Nashville team was playing. He made the decision to hire Dressen, but could not close the deal while he was there.

An hour after he escaped a harrowing landing at the Cincinnati airport he received a long-distance phone call. Nashville's first-string catcher had just broken his leg and they were desperate for a replacement. This was all Larry needed. Sure he would help them out. Not only would he send them his third-string catcher, Jack Crouch, but would also sweeten the deal by adding a pitcher, Walter Hilcher, and $5,000. All he wanted in return was Dressen. Murray was over a barrel and, reluctantly, agreed to the trade. MacPhail had his new manager.

On July 29, Dressen became manager of the Cincinnati Reds. On the same day MacPhail bought a rookie infielder, Alex Kampouris, from Sacramento and he was installed at second base.

The season was too far along to improve much on the field, but the remaining weeks gave Dressen time to evaluate the players MacPhail kept bringing up from the farm system. Among these were two who looked very promising—Frank McCormick, a young first baseman, and a rookie southpaw pitcher named Lee Grissom.

Even though they finished the season in the cellar for the fourth consecutive year with a record of 52 wins and 99 defeats, it did appear that there was light at the end of the tunnel—a rather prophetic thought for a momentous event of the next season, 1935.

5

The Lights Go On

In late 1934 and early 1935 the country was still in the depths of the Depression. Even with all the hoopla that Larry created to bring out the fans, the total attendance in 1934 was only 206,000. Financially, the Reds were in dire straits. Cincinnati was the smallest town in the majors and, therefore, had far less potential drawing power than the other cities. MacPhail pondered the situation and came up with what he thought was the solution—limited night baseball. It had saved many of the minor league teams from total collapse and would be a real shot of adrenalin for the Reds. However, he could not possibly anticipate the tremendous resistance with which this proposal would be met by the other owners in the league.

The history of the development of "baseball under the lights" is interesting, but difficult to trace. Although several areas take credit for the first night game, the two that seem to have the greatest right to lay claim to the event were in New England and the Great Plains States in the early 1880s. Two amateur teams played a game at Nantasket Beach, Massachusetts in 1880.

The other game took place in Fort Wayne, Indiana on June 2, 1883, with a group from the M. E. College hosting a professional team from Quincy, Illinois. It was a seven-inning game won by Quincy, 19-11. The Jenney Electric Light Company furnished 17 lights, each with 4000 candlelight power to light up the field. An excerpt from a glowing article in the *Fort Wayne Daily Gazette* the next day follows:

Last night was the occurrence of the long looked-for event that was to make Fort Wayne historic and cause her name to be mentioned wherever civilization extends.

Baseball is the American national game but it was reserved for the city of Fort Wayne to be the first in the world to play it at night and by the rays of artificial sun. The degree of illumination was such that the game was well played, although an alarming number of strikes were called by Umpire Morrissey.

The crowd was very large and, although the turnstiles registered 1,675 admissions, there were at least 2,000 present.

The first night game in organized baseball was played in the Western Association on April 18, 1930 between teams from Independence, Kansas and Muskogee, Oklahoma. Night baseball in the minor leagues caught the public's fancy immediately and became the savior of the game, but the owners of most parks had to wait for the manufacturers of floodlights to catch up with the demand.

Si Burick, sports editor of the *Dayton Daily News* for so many years, recalled a nostalgic meeting he had with Larry at the first night game at Shea Stadium on May 6, 1964. Burick was also with MacPhail that historic night when it all began in Cincinnati in 1935, and recalled Larry's reminiscences:

"I was with Columbus when the Indianapolis owner, Norman Perry, put a lighting plant into his park after consulting with me, and later, after Norman's good results, I had them put into our park in Columbus."

Putting lights in Crosley Field was a great idea, but it had a flaw. The National League had a rule against night ball. More than that, it required unanimous league approval to put in lights.

"I prepared a 40-page brief on lighting," Larry said, "and had it ready for delivery at our annual winter meeting in December. But, first I had to visit the commissioner (Judge Kenesaw Mountain Landis) who was trying to make a free agent of one of our players. The conference took a long time and I got fidgety.

"Finally, Landis shouted, 'MacPhail, what's your hurry?' I told him I was due at a National League meeting in 20 minutes to present my brief on night ball. He dismissed me with this statement:

" 'Young man, you can write this down. Not in my life-time or yours will you ever see a baseball game played at night in the majors.' "

Going into the meeting with the old man's words still ringing in his ears, MacPhail was stopped by the late Charles Stoneham, owner of the New York Giants.

"I'll never vote for night baseball," Stoneham warned.

"Do me a favor," MacPhail pleaded, "and listen to my argument before you make up your mind. I make you this promise. If we are permitted to play night games next season, and if you are then dissatisfied, I'll never use the lights again, no matter how much we invest in them."

Stoneham agreed to listen.

"I talked for three solid hours from my brief," Larry laughed. "When they called for a vote, Charlie abstained. There were seven yes votes, including my own. I asked for seven night games—one with each club—and got them."

The Cincinnati ball club purchased what was then the finest lighting system in baseball for Crosley Field.

"The cost," MacPhail recalled, "was $150,000, and we borrowed every nickel of it."

And Landis, who had predicted there would be no night ball in his or MacPhail's life span, attended a game under the lights in Cincinnati in mid-season.

Larry had researched recent developments in outdoor light-ing and finally awarded the contract to General Electric who had led the field in innovations. They installed 632 strategi-cally placed lights throughout the park, completely overcom-ing the fear of shadows that would affect the quality of play.

The details of the first night game in the majors were described by Red Barber in an article in the magazine *Modern Maturity*. He was the regular broadcaster for the Cincinnati Reds, and, certainly, one of the greats in the sports broad-casting field.

The game had been scheduled for the night of May 23, but it was cold and rainy, so was rescheduled for the next night. In typical MacPhail fashion, he had a drum and bugle corps, high school bands and plenty of fireworks to celebrate the occasion.

Over 20,000 fans poured into Crosley Field for the big event, over ten times the number that would have attended an afternoon contest with the lowly Philadelphia Phillies. With darkness overtaking the setting sun and the expectant crowd suddenly quiet in anticipation, President Franklin Delano Roosevelt, in the White House 500 miles away, touched the telegraph key and the entire park was bathed in brilliant light. The huge crowd gasped and cheered.

The game itself was an artistic success for the appreciative hometown fans. Dressen had saved the ace of his staff, Paul Derringer, for the game and Jimmy Wilson started Joe Bowman. The Reds won, 2-1, with the Phillies getting only six hits and the Reds just four.

The fans took to night ball with relish. With the Depression on, most of the people who could attend afternoon games during the week were retired or unemployed and they couldn't always afford the price of the ticket. Here was a solution. Now, the fans could relax at the ball park in the evening after a hard day's work.

However, it wasn't that simple. The diehards among the owners wouldn't give up without a fight. What blasphemy! Didn't MacPhail realize there were traditions to uphold? Probably the most intransigent of the detractors was Clark Griffith, owner of the Washington club. He called baseball at night "bush league stuff" and "just a step above dog racing." One of his most famous quotations was:

"There is no chance of night baseball ever becoming popular in the bigger cities. High class baseball cannot be played under artificial light. Furthermore, the benefits from attending the game are largely due to fresh air and sunshine. Night air and electric lights are poor substitutes."

However, it was Griffith, the Old Fox, who later did a complete about-face and went overboard in being among the first to insist on unlimited night ball.

Ed Barrow of the Yankees said, "Night baseball is just a fad. It will never last once the novelty wears off."

Frank Navin, owner of the Detroit Tigers, agreed: "Night games will be the ruination of baseball. It changes the players from athletes to actors."

Bill Terry, then playing manager of the New York Giants,

had these words of caution: "It'll increase the dangers of the bean ball."

Even Ford Frick, then president of the National League, when asked how he felt about it shortly after the first game, answered: "It would be suicidal to play as many as 10 games a season at night."

Returning briefly to Si Burick's article written at the time he and MacPhail were reminiscing at the opening of Shea Stadium in 1964, we see how the efficiency of lighting systems had improved in 29 years. The 632 lights in 1935 gave off about 1 million watts, and the opening night at Shea had 1600 lights giving off about 2 million watts.

That night at Shea, Franklin Delano Roosevelt Jr., then assistant secretary of commerce, pressed a button at home plate to illuminate the "old-fashioned" part of the new lighting system, the same type of lights as in Crosley Field in 1935. Then, MacPhail pressed a second button and the amount of light more than doubled with the mercury vapor lights, brand new at that time. Incidentally, the Reds again played in that game and again won, this time 12-4 before 32,421 fans.

The first seven night games for the Reds attracted 123,991 paid admissions and contributed greatly to the fact that the Reds' attendance more than doubled over the previous year. In 1935 they drew 448,000 fans compared to 206,000 in '34.

Incidentally, at the beginning of 1934, MacPhail had introduced a profit sharing plan for the ballplayers that was based on increased attendance. He had set a goal of 275,000 for the season. If the Reds reached this figure, each player would receive a bonus of 5 percent of his salary. In the event the attendance reached 325,000 the bonus would be increased to 10 percent and if they drew the unlikely figure of 350,000 the percentage would be raised to 15. Since the total attendance was only 206,000, no bonuses were paid and there is no record that this plan was continued into 1935 with the advent of the night games.

As dramatic as was the "first night game in the majors," MacPhail still knew that he had to improve the team on the field. In the off-season he returned to the trade wars and studied the records of all the youngsters in his farm system. No fewer than five of his new men became regulars—in the infield, Billy Myers at short and Lew Riggs at third, plus Ival Goodman in the outfield. In the pitching department, he brought up two rookies from Toronto—a southpaw named Al Hollingsworth and a right-hander from Cincinnati, Gene Schott. He had traded Mark Koenig to the Giants for Myers, and had bought Riggs and Goodman outright from Rickey's Cardinals. In addition, he purchased Sammy Byrd from the Yankees. Byrd had achieved some recognition in New York as Babe Ruth's late-inning replacement.

Dressen's starting lineup for the 1935 season consisted of old reliable Ernie Lombardi catching, Bottomley, Kampouris, Myers and Riggs across the infield, and Byrd, Hafey and Goodman in the outfield. The pitching corps was still anchored by Derringer and, also, still included Si Johnson, Frey and Freitas. Schott and Hollingsworth were valuable additions, plus a huge relief pitcher from Maine, named Don Brennan.

The new optimism appeared justified as the team split their first 32 games. Hafey had a bad habit of leaving the team unexpectedly and without notice, but the addition of a couple of other seasoned outfielders—Babe Herman and Kiki Cuyler—filled that gap pretty well.

In the first five night games, the Reds were 3 and 2, beating the Phillies, Dodgers and Braves, and losing to the Pirates and Cubs. But, the big attraction was the sixth night game on July 31. It was against the World Champions of 1934—the now-famous Gashouse Gang of the St. Louis Cardinals with the brothers Dean (Dizzy and Daffy), Leo Durocher, Pepper Martin, and Joe (Ducky) Medwick.

The night games had proved so popular that MacPhail had arranged with the railroad companies to run special excursion trains into Cincinnati from cities and towns all over the Ohio valley. The entire region for miles around had adopted the Reds. The combination of their improved hometown team and the arrival of the world champions caused so much excitement that the advance sale of reserved seats to out-of-town fans exceeded all expectations.

The local fans buying general admission tickets came to the park early to get good seats for the big game. Soon all those seats were taken and the milling crowd, their spirits buoyed by the products of those fine German breweries of Cincinnati, eyed the roped-off vacant area of the reserved seats. The trains, bringing in the fans from West Virginia, Kentucky and Indiana who were entitled to those seats, were late. The young ushers were overmatched, and soon the local fans took over. Then, the trains started arriving and all hell broke loose in the stands. It was bedlam.

The game was very exciting, with Paul Dean pitching against Tony Freitas, but it was nothing compared to the battle in the stands. Soon, the crowd overflowed on the playing field. MacPhail was nowhere to be found and the fans without seats stormed the office demanding their money back. Larry's secretary, the very capable and resourceful Frances Levy, barricaded the office and handed out the refunds through the mail slot in the door.

Even in the pandemonium, somehow the game finally ended, with the Reds winning, 4-3, on a game-winning single in the last of the 10th by reserve infielder Billy Sullivan. MacPhail blamed the police for not bringing out a riot squad and the chief of police blamed MacPhail for selling more tickets than he had seats, a disagreement with the authorities which was not that unusual for MacPhail. However, the fact that there could be a sellout at Crosley Field was, in itself, an amazing change in the affairs of the Reds.

More needs to be said about Frances Levy whose quick thinking saved Larry from trouble more than once. Though in his three years with the Reds he came to rely more and more on Frances Levy, their relationship did not start out smoothly.

Miss Levy was Sidney Weil's maiden sister-in-law whom he had hired when he took over the Reds in 1929. She was well-versed in the protocol, customs and rules followed in the big leagues and, when she stayed on to work for the roaring redhead, assumed that these procedures would continue to be followed. She did not yet know MacPhail.

Fran Levy's background was extremely modest and she was used to doing as she was told in a job. However, most of the things she had been asked to do or letters she had been asked to write were predictable and routine. Her strength and fortitude had not often been tested by her brother-in-law. Things would be different working with MacPhail.

Their first run-in occurred almost the first day when Larry had wanted something done that was not standard procedure.

Miss Levy reacted:

"But, Mr. MacPhail, you can't do that!"

"What do you mean I can't do that?," Larry screamed.

"Well, the league rules say that—," Miss Levy responded.

"I don't give a damn what the league rules say. That's the way I did it in Columbus," MacPhail interrupted.

"Yes, that may be true. But, this is the major leagues, Mr. MacPhail," his secretary countered.

Larry exploded. "You're fired!"

Miss Levy was aghast. "Honest, Mr. MacPhail, I didn't mean it that way," she said.

Again he yelled, "You're fired!"

Then, she left the room and 10 minutes later the phone rang and he apologized and said:

"I'm sorry. I checked and it has to be done your way. Please come back in."

This sort of thing was to happen quite frequently and very quickly Miss Levy developed a real affection for her unpredictable boss. As a matter of fact, she often defended him publicly and, very often, saved him from himself. He would end up saying:

"Miss Levy, you're absolutely right."

Larry learned to rely on her and their friendship lasted through the years.

The team moved up two places in the league in 1935, finishing sixth. It was not a dramatic change, but enough to create a feeling of anticipation.

The 1936 season showed continued improvement, but still nothing worldshaking. The personnel changed somewhat with a rookie, George McQuinn, taking over for the aging Jim Bottomley at first base.

Interestingly, the previous year MacPhail had acquired first baseman Johnny Mize from the Cardinals on a tryout basis, if he could pass the physical exam. He had a knee problem which would require surgery. Rickey, who received a percentage of the sale price of any player he sold, was asking $55,000 for Mize and MacPhail insisted on having an orthopedic specialist check him out. The doctor thought there would be considerable risk involved in the operation and, on this advice, MacPhail decided to pass. He stayed with the Cardinals, had the operation, and, of course, starred for many years to come.

During the season McQuinn, whom they had acquired from the Yankees, proved to be unable to hit National League pitching, and MacPhail brought up another rookie from the farm system, Les Scarsella, who filled the position adequately. The rest of the team remained pretty much intact and the players, with another year of experience, were able to move up one more notch, finishing in fifth place with a record of 74 wins and 80 losses.

Then, without any warning, and for reasons that no one has ever adequately explained, MacPhail suddenly tendered his resignation as vice president and general manager, declaring he "may go fishing for a while."

He emphasized that there was no friction involved and both he and Crosley declared their relationship had been "most pleasant."

Larry had made the newspaper headlines on several occasions during the year as a result of altercations with the police, usually after drinking bouts. In one that had received considerable publicity, he had had a fist fight with Sgt. John Oman in an elevator in the Netherland Plaza Hotel in downtown Cincinnati. Crosley was a very conservative man who did not cotton to any kind of notoriety and when, the day after the fight with Oman, he confronted MacPhail with the story, Larry said, "Boy, isn't that great publicity?"

MacPhail's resignation was effective November 1, but he added that he had no intention of quitting baseball permanently and that he would probably be connected with the National League at some time in the future. He said he had a number of decisions to make for the Cincinnati club in the interim before his departure.

"This," he said, "ought to prove that our relationship is friendly because I will be doing things that the club would not wish me to do if it were unfriendly toward me and which

I would not do if I felt unfriendly toward the club. I feel, however, that my future is away from Cincinnati, although I shall always cherish the friends that I have made here."

Larry's statement to the press follows:

> I am not going to be with the Reds in 1937. I have resigned effective November 1.
>
> I have thoroughly enjoyed my three-year association with the officers and directors. We all take a great deal of pride in the progress that the club has made. We all feel that the Reds are established as an aggressive competitor in the National League. The club is in competent hands, in strong financial position, and its future is assured.
>
> If I have been able to accomplish anything in Cincinnati it is because I have had at all times not only a free hand, but the utmost in support from Mr. Crosley. There has not been a single instance in this entire time when Mr. Crosley has not cheerfully supported every single move that I have attempted to make in the interest of the Cincinnati Baseball Club. It will not be easy for me to discontinue associations that have been extremely pleasant.
>
> The club is composed of a manager, two coaches, a trainer and forty players. I am more or less responsible for the fact that all but three are on the club roster, and naturally I will be greatly interested in the continued success of the club. Cincinnati is the best baseball town in the United States. The Reds' fans have given me their loyal support.
>
> I am quite confident that no other baseball association that I may have in the future can possibly be as pleasant as my personal associations with Mr. Crosley and the other directors of the club. I wish the club all the luck in the world in its effort to win a pennant for Cincinnati next year.

In accepting MacPhail's resignation, Powel Crosley, Jr. issued and signed the following statement:

> With the announcement of Larry MacPhail that his connection with the Cincinnati Baseball Club will end November 1, I desire to express on behalf of the Cincinnati Baseball Club and its directors our appreciation for what he has done for baseball in Cincinnati.
>
> He deserves credit for the improvement in the ball club, for the improvements that have been made in the ball park,

and the introduction of night baseball to the big leagues. My personal association with Mr. MacPhail has always been most pleasant. We of the Cincinnati Baseball Club Company, and I think I speak for the fans of Cincinnati, wish him every success for the future.

When asked about MacPhail's replacement, Thomas Conroy, treasurer of the Cincinnati club, said that a successor had been under consideration for some time and that an announcement would be made shortly. He added that MacPhail had been helpful in discussing the merits of a number of the men who had been considered for his position.

In the three years since Larry arrived in Cincinnati to lead the Reds out of the cellar, most of his press had been great. There was one article, however, written by Joe Aston, sports editor of the *Cincinnati Post*, shortly before MacPhail's resignation that touched on fan dissatisfaction, possibly dating back to that chaotic night game when he had oversold the park.

Aston wrote that, rather than giving total support because of the rising fortunes of their team, the serious-minded and sensitive fans were criticizing MacPhail for failing to protect their rights, especially in seating arrangements and the treatment of players. In regard to the latter subject, he wrote the following:

> The Derringer suspension, for instance, caused quite a bit of unnecessary agitation, because it was accompanied with an unsatisfactory explanation. Speaking personally to Mr. MacPhail just before Paul's reinstatement Thursday, however, I heard what seemed to be a perfectly logical summary of the whole case. Said Mr. MacPhail:
>
> "At the start of spring training it was apparent that Paul did not have his mind on baseball. His pitching since the start of the regular season has proved that his mental attitude was not the same as it was last year when he won 22 games for us.
>
> "We did not publicly announce the reasons for his changed attitude, because we felt that such publicity would be embarrassing to Paul. We tried everything we knew of to help him get down to business. As the last resort we suspended him, hoping that this would cause him to snap out of his slump.

"Next to Dizzy Dean, I believe Paul is the best pitcher in the league and next to Dizzy, I believe he is getting paid more than any other pitcher. We have a right to expect him to deliver to the best of his ability."

On this explanation Aston commented:

No doubt it would have taken some careful thought to put this across to the average fan in a soothing way at the time Paul was suspended. Maybe the fans still would not have been satisfied, but there must have been some better way than merely issuing the harsh statement that Derringer had been suspended for failing to slide at the plate.

There was one other incident that caused some sparks between Crosley and MacPhail, one that was recounted by Red Barber in his book, *Rhubarb in the Catbird Seat.* It concerned James (Scotty) Reston, one of the young golfers whom Mac-Phail had helped out during the Ohio state tournament when Larry had lived in Columbus.

When he became general manager of the Reds, Larry brought young Reston down there with him. Scotty had told MacPhail that he would not play golf in Cincinnati because it would take too much time away from his job.

About the only time he did play was in a one-day tournament which he promptly won, although he had not played for some time. In the locker room after the tournament, with many people coming in and out and idly chatting about sports in general, the subject of the Reds came up.

Now, shortly after Crosley had bought controlling interest in the team, he elected to change the name of the ball park from Redlands Field to Crosley Field. In addition, he saw fit to have placed atop the scoreboard a large Crosley Shelvador refrigerator.

As he still does in his columns for the *New York Times*, Reston spoke his piece, this time about those changes at the home of the Reds. In no uncertain terms, he said that Mr. Crosley had no right to change the name of the ball park, and also showed no consideration for the past glories of the birthplace of it all by blaspheming the memories with sight of the huge refrigerator.

Naturally, word got back to Crosley who was furious. He pressured Larry to fire Reston immediately. MacPhail told him, "If he goes, I go with him!"

In timely fashion, the situation was resolved when Scotty was offered the opportunity to join the Associated Press, and he then started his brilliant journalistic career.

In retrospect, it is really difficult to imagine two men engaged in the same activity in the same town whose personalities and temperaments were more different from each other.

Powel Crosley was the quiet, conservative, successful businessman who shunned the spotlight and was constantly aware of his public image and driven by the desire to protect that image at all costs.

On the other hand, Larry MacPhail was the swashbuckling marauder, dressed to the nines in expensive, but garishly loud suits and sport coats of huge plaids and checks who thought his day was not complete unless he had done something worthy of mention in the press.

Dating back to his days in Columbus, he would storm through the lobby of the Deshler Hotel or the Neil House splitting the air with his gravelly rasping voice, a roar to cause anyone within earshot to turn and gawk in wonderment.

This same trademark of elegant but colorfully wild dress was a part of the imprimatur of his personality. This same bravado followed him in the lobbies and corridors of the Gibson and Netherland Plaza Hotels in the Queen City.

It was probably inevitable that these two men would eventually part company.

Thus, this chapter in the explosive career of Leland Stanford MacPhail came to an end and he returned to Michigan again to help his father and brother in the small town banking business.

6

Larry's Love Affair with Brooklyn

In later years, when questioned about his reasons for leaving Cincinnati, Larry said, "If I stay around here much longer, I'll have a nervous breakdown."

Regardless of the reason or reasons for his leaving baseball at that time, the frenzied pace at which he conducted his activity in the world of organized sport was replaced by the less hectic, but also less remunerative and less engaging realm of small town investments.

In the meantime, things were happening in Brooklyn that would greatly affect the future for MacPhail and provide an opportunity to bring his talents to full flower. As background material, what follows is a brief history of the Brooklyn National League franchise before MacPhail entered the scene.

The club originally joined the National League in 1890, the year Larry was born, and was founded and owned by a triumvirate headed by Charles Byrne, whose main interest was real estate. His partners were a couple of gambling casino owners named Joseph J. Doyle and Ferdinand Abell.

At the age of 24, Charles H. Ebbets, who was to become the dominant figure in Dodger history for so many years, started working for the club, more as a flunky around the office than anything else. Gradually, when the opportunity arose, he bought a few shares of stock and, when Byrne died in 1897, was able to get himself elected president although he owned barely 10 percent of the outstanding stock.

Shortly thereafter, he and Harry Von der Horst, a brewer

who owned the Baltimore Orioles, joined in an arrangement which would certainly be illegal today, but which was, to say the least, very imaginative. Von der Horst acquired 30 percent of the Dodgers in return for switching the Orioles' manager, Ned Hanlon, and some of their players to the Brooklyn team. Among them were some of the great stars of their day—Wee Willie Keeler, Iron Man McGinnity, Hughie Jennings, Fielder Jones, Joe Kelley and Wild Bill Donovan—and they brought pennants to Brooklyn in 1899 and 1900.

The glory was short-lived, though. The Dodgers fell on bad times, partly because of the raids by the upstart American League, and Baltimore was to be gone from the major league scene for 55 years.

Von der Horst tired of the situation and wanted out of his part ownership of the Dodgers. For $30,000 he sold his 30 percent back to Ebbets, who welcomed the opportunity because he took great pride in his team. He felt that whatever his ownership lacked in professionalism was more than compensated for by his devout chauvinism for team and borough.

In tough times he and his wife were perfectly willing to cut down the overhead, he by selling tickets at the park, and she by washing the players' uniforms when necessary. During the first 20 years the team had several names including, in 1900, The Bridegrooms, since many of the players had gotten married in the off-season. Later, they were called the Superbas and, still later, the Trolley Dodgers in tribute to the nimble citizens of the borough and their reaction to the cavalier attitude of the devil-may-care streetcar conductors.

By 1908, Ebbets became convinced he needed a new park. So, bit by bit he began to acquire land on the slope of Crown Heights on the edge of Flatbush. By 1913 he had the four and a half acres he felt he needed for the new park, but was up against it for the money to build it. He therefore sold a 50 percent interest in the club for $100,000 to two brothers—Edward J. and Stephen W. McKeever, who were Brooklyn contractors of Irish descent.

The park was ready by early 1913 and on April 9 they dedicated the new Ebbets Fields with the season opener against the Phillies. One report of this momentous occasion follows:

A cold, raw wind kept the attendance down to about 12,000, but did not affect the players, who put up a remarkable battle. Both Tom Seaton (for Philadelphia) and Nap Rucker (for Brooklyn) pitched brilliant ball, the former just shading the noted southpaw in a 1 to 0 shutout. The opening ceremonies were impressive, the two teams parading across the field headed by a band and Borough President Alfred E. Steers throwing out the first ball. Benny Meyer, the heavy-hitting recruit from Toronto, lost the game for Rucker in the first inning. With one out, Otto Knabe doubled to right. Meyer muffed Hans Lobert's foul in the sun field, but Casey Stengel overcame this error by making a sensational catch of a long fly from the same batter. Then, Meyer muffed Sherwood Magee's fly, letting Knabe in with the only run of the contest.

In passing, it is interesting to note that both MacPhail and Stengel were born in 1890 and died within a few days of each other in the fall of 1975 at the age of 85.

Ebbets hired Wilbert Robinson as field manager. "Uncle Robbie," as he became affectionately known to the Flatbush fans, had been a catcher with the Baltimore Orioles and had later tried his hand at saloonkeeping, both of which made him well-qualified for his new position.

Robinson remained manager of the team until he resigned in 1931, having won pennants in 1916 and 1920. After a five-year period during which two other managers had run the team, the owners hired Burleigh Grimes for the job in 1936, feeling that the ex-spitball pitcher, with a penchant for being thrown out of ball games in record numbers, would fit in beautifully with the appreciative fans of Brooklyn.

After the older McKeever died, Stephen represented their families' interests with Ebbets and the two men got along well enough. Unfortunately, in the 23 years since Ebbets had sold half the ball club to the McKeevers, their families had grown further apart and it became more and more difficult to make decisions, no matter how inconsequential. The frequent stalemates and resultant inaction translated into red ink on the books. The period from 1935-37 saw an additional half million dollars in losses, bringing the total indebtedness to

$1,200,000. The other $700,000 was made up of a mortgage on Ebbets Field of $500,000 and another $200,000 loan from the bank that covered past purchases of equipment and ballplayers from other clubs.

These were still Depression days and the bank, the Brooklyn Trust Company, which had been advancing money for the operation of the club, refused to go any further unless the controversy between the rival factions were resolved. The situation was desperate. Finally, the heirs of the two families did agree to let the bank seek out a man to solve their problems.

There was a five-man board of directors consisting of Steve McKeever, now getting along in years, Joe Gilleaudeau, Jim Mulvey, William A. Hughes, and George Barnewall, the banker who was representing the Brooklyn Trust Company. Jim Mulvey, Steve McKeever's son-in-law, had gotten to know Ford Frick, president of the National League, quite well over the recent years and contacted him for advice. Frick was almost as interested as the others in improving the situation at Brooklyn and helping them regain some of their past glories. He immediately suggested Larry MacPhail.

This name was met with great enthusiasm by the entire board, but also with skepticism about their ability to interest Larry in the job. However, the timing could not have been better for all concerned.

"Ford, we don't know MacPhail. Do you think you could contact him on our behalf?" Mulvey asked.

"I'd be happy to call him and see if he will come to Brooklyn to meet with you," answered Frick.

By this time MacPhail was climbing the walls in rural Michigan and was ready for another challenge.

His sixth sense also told him how desperate the situation was in Brooklyn. His negotiations were masterful. He literally turned down their offer three times, until the bank told him that he could write his own ticket. Larry was much more interested in the latitude he would have with the job than he was in his salary. In fact, on the latter, he was perfectly willing to have the stockholders vote at the end of the year whatever amount they figured he had earned. He knew what he could do if given the opportunity.

What he did insist on was absolute authority over all phases of the operation of the ball club—total control. He also was to be named vice-president and general manager and be given a reasonable amount of money by the bank to start the rebuilding job. This was to include refurbishing of the park, buying a ballplayer or two for immediate needs, and the wherewithal to increase and improve the farm system.

The bank agreed to all terms and the official announcement was made at the club's offices on January 19, 1938.

In the afternoon of the same day he held court at a gala affair for the press at the Victoria Hotel in New York and had never been in better form. When he wished to, Larry could charm a boa constrictor and he exuded confidence and goodwill to the entire press corps, burying the hatchet with a few sportswriters with whom he had had some disagreements when they had met in Cincinnati, and spreading happy thoughts for the future to all concerned. He did surprise many of them with his thoughts on the prospects of night games in the near future at Ebbets Field.

"As for night baseball, that's about number 10 on our list of problems," he said. "First, we've got to build a ball club. People won't come to see us play day or night if we're lousy. I'd say offhand that some other National League club will play night baseball before Brooklyn."

Now, Larry went to work. First, he secured from the bank a fund of $200,000 to start refurbishing the park. Nothing had been done for years and the place was a shambles—the stands, the dugouts, the clubhouses, the infield, everything. Paint was always the first thing Larry applied to any ball park he took over, but there was no sense in putting paint on broken seats and crumbling concrete. First things first.

The field itself left much to be desired. Among the ballplayers, both on the Dodgers and the other teams of the league, Ebbets Field had developed the reputation as one of the worst on which to play. The infield was uneven and full of stones and the outfield full of ruts. MacPhail personally walked every square foot of the playing surface and had a crew start resurfacing it. Then, the broken seats were replaced, the dugouts and clubhouses refurbished and the entire park freshened up with a bright-colored paint job, all under Larry's close scrutiny.

Also, on the drawing board were a new press box and press club, the latter a precursor of his first stadium club to be established later on. In addition there would be a lounge and bar that would serve drinks before, during and after the games.

Next, there was the subject of the ushers. This was a group as unique and fiercely independent as New York cab drivers. They thought of themselves as strongarmed policemen and, therefore, brought out the same combativeness in the Dodgers' fans. Larry always tried to create an atmosphere of fun, one that would encourage entire family participation. He had seen what Andy Frain had done with Comiskey Park and Wrigley Field in Chicago, as well as the Kentucky Derby and other sports complexes in the Middle West. Therefore, he hired Frain to bring out some of his courteous, uniformed ushers from Chicago to train local recruits to conduct themselves in the same fashion.

While this job was going on, Larry studied not only the Dodgers' roster and the individual players, but the entire farm system to see with what he had to work. His next step had to be improving the product on the field. About a month after he took over, MacPhail was ready to make his first move.

He called a meeting of the directors and told them he was going to the bank and ask for $50,000 to buy a first baseman, Dolf Camilli, from the Phillies. They were nonplussed. They pointed out that, not only did they have a first baseman, Buddy Hassett, but that if he were going to spend that kind of money, surely he would get more than one ballplayer.

Larry ignored these remarks and added, "I don't know if I can get him from Gerry Nugent for $50,000—it might take $75,000—but I'll try damned hard."

The meeting was over. MacPhail got up, left the office and marched directly to the Brooklyn Trust Company and into the office of the president, George V. McLaughlin.

"George, I need another $50,000," Larry blurted out.

"What for?" demanded McLaughlin.

Larry told him his plans and the former police commissioner sensed that here was the man who could get the job done, the one who could bail the bank out of their baseball troubles. MacPhail got the money and headed for Philadelphia. By nightfall he had Camilli for the Dodgers, and at his price.

MacPhail also needed help in the internal organization. Dating back to his days in Columbus, even before his involvement with the Red Birds, he had headed a group that had been interested in buying the Cincinnati Reds. While looking into this possibility, he was shown the books and the operation of the Reds by Sidney Weil's young secretary, John McDonald.

Although the financial condition of the club scared him off, he was impressed with the ability and forthrightness of the young man who had revealed these facts. Later, when MacPhail took charge of the Reds, McDonald became invaluable to him in more ways than just the operation of the club. McDonald, himself, described his relationship with MacPhail in an article he and Charles Dexter wrote in the *Saturday Evening Post:*

> I found myself intimately associated thenceforth with the only living loudspeaker in human form. I was MacPhail's buffer between the front office and the police, press, and public. Though my title was traveling secretary, I found myself actively engaged in operating a baseball club, doing such odd jobs as arbitrating rows, refereeing fights, scouting and signing players, hanging signs outside the park, and day by day sitting in the front row at the greatest sports show in the world.

McDonald jumped at the opportunity to continue this relationship when MacPhail asked him to come to Brooklyn with him.

The 1937 Dodgers had finished in sixth place. Almost any change would be upward—or, so it seemed. Larry had retained Burleigh Grimes as manager and spring training opened in Clearwater as usual. The club didn't seem to have any spark and the exhibition games did not indicate much improvement. One day the sportswriters caught Burleigh in a particularly low mood and questioned him about where the team might land in the National League pennant race in '38 with the present personnel.

Grimes was never one to pull his punches anyway and, after outlining the inability of his pitching staff and describ-

ing his Methuselah outfield of Kiki Cuyler and Heinie
Manush plus Buddy Hassett, the refugee from first base who
had been pushed to the outfield by the addition of Camilli,
opined that they would finish eighth. When it was pointed
out that the Phillies were still in the league, he optimistically
allowed as how they might play over their heads and finish
seventh.

When MacPhail read this in the paper, you could hear him
scream all the way from Brooklyn. He got Grimes on the
phone and told him to meet him in Greensboro, North Carolina, where two of the Dodgers' farm clubs were training.
Burleigh claimed that he had been misquoted. But when Larry
got back to Brooklyn, he told the press that if the Dodgers
were in seventh place by May 15 there would be hell to pay.

The team got off to a rough start, losing five of their first
seven games. The fans showed a commensurate restraint in
attendance and MacPhail started to reconsider his priorities
as regards night baseball. He contacted the General Electric
Company again and soon had committed to the expenditure
of $72,000 for new lighting equipment. The Giants and
Yankees were unhappy about it, complaining that New York
City was not Cincinnati and that the sophisticated people of
a city the size of New York would never go for baseball at
night.

The Giants, especially, were livid, charging MacPhail with
a breach of contract. They maintained that there had been
a three-way agreement among the Yankees, Dodgers and Giants that night baseball would be banned in the New York
metropolitan area.

That was all Larry needed to show the "peepul" of Brooklyn
and all New York how selfish and greedy the owners of the
Giants were. In an open letter to the press he came out
fighting:

> Giant officials, notably Treasurer Leo Bondy, are voic-
> ing open resentment of Larry MacPhail's action in pulling
> the Dodgers out of a three-cornered pact with the Giants
> and Yankees opposing night baseball.
> The directors of the Brooklyn Club advise me there was
> no contract, pact or understanding of any kind, nature or

description with the Giants or Yankees regarding night baseball.

If Mr. Bondy can tell us where we can get a couple of pitchers, we would appreciate his assistance. Otherwise, we suggest he confine his efforts to running the Giants.

The only "pact" my directors know anything about is an understanding engineered by Mr. Bondy several years ago that has resulted in depriving New York fans of all broadcasts of baseball games.

With his usual speed and attention to detail, Larry was ready to play the first night game by June 15, and against his old team, the Reds. The game was a sellout, with fans arriving long before dark. It was preceded by typical MacPhail fanfare—a huge fireworks display, brass bands, etc. and even a footrace in which the Olympic star, Jesse Owens, gave an exhibition.

The game itself was even more dramatic. Bill McKechnie, the Cincinnati manager, was going to start Johnny Vander Meer in the big event. In his previous start in Boston four days earlier, Johnny had pitched a no-hit, no-run game and fans wanted to see him try for another.

With the MacPhail luck working full time, Vander Meer did the impossible. He pitched another no-hit game to become the only pitcher to hurl two consecutive no-hitters in the majors. The ninth inning was especially exciting. After he had retired Hassett for the first out, Vander Meer walked the next three batters, loading the bases. Then, Ernie Koy, who normally hit Johnny well, was thrown out on an easy grounder. This brought up Leo Durocher who, after fouling off several balls, lined out to Harry Craft in center field.

There was another amusing exchange in the press the day of the game, between Bill Terry and Larry. Terry had been asked if he would attend the night game and he had answered that he might, if only to see Jesse Owens run. Larry's response in the press again showed his attention to detail:

Five years ago the New York Giants, under the able leadership of Col. William H. Terry, made baseball history by engaging in the first night baseball game in New York in which a major league club appeared. The Giants at that time requested the Brooklyn club to allow them to play a night baseball game in Brooklyn against a semi-pro club. The Brooklyn club gave its consent. The Giants received $1,000 for playing the game. It is fitting that an individual who pioneered night baseball in New York should be honored when a major league club again plays a night baseball game in Brooklyn. We are therefore extending a cordial invitation to Colonel Terry to be present at Ebbets Field tonight as an honored guest.

With grudging admiration Terry confirmed the accuracy of the facts and corrected MacPhail only to the extent of the money the Giants received, saying it was actually $1,500 instead of $1,000.

MacPhail kept the pot boiling. Three days later he pulled another coup designed to bring the fans in. Babe Ruth was probably the greatest fan attraction of all time. He was out of baseball and never could understand why he had never been asked to manage in the majors. So, Larry thought, "Why not bring him in to Ebbets Field as a coach. He could also hit a few out of the park in batting practice and thrill the fans with his power."

The Babe demanded $25,000 to join the Dodgers, but Larry contended the season was half over and insisted he would pay the new first base coach $15,000 and not one penny more. Ruth finally took it, and it was still, in all likelihood, more money than any coach had received before for half a year's work. He proved to be a real drawing card and, what with this and other crowd-pleasing ideas, MacPhail was able to increase the attendance by more than a quarter of a million over that of 1937, with a total home attendance of 750,125.

Although interest in the Dodgers was definitely on the upswing and the financial picture was improving, the artistic product on the field still left much to be desired and they ended up the '38 season in seventh place. Toward the end of the season Grimes sensed that he was not be be manager much longer and he even encouraged Durocher to apply for the job. Larry would have none of it, pointing out at least five reasons for turning him down, including Durocher's inability to handle his own affairs, let alone manage 24 other ballplayers, plus his total lack of managerial experience.

However, this did plant the seed in Larry's mind. Durocher had already determined that his future lay in managing so he took every opportunity to be present whenever any league meetings or baseball owner get-togethers would occur. It so happened that the World Series that year was in Chicago, between the Yankees and Cubs. Leo made sure that he was there, not only for the Series, but also to be around where the action was.

Larry and his half-brother, Herman W. MacPhail (whom everyone called "Max"), were staying at the Congress Hotel. Near the end of the Series, Larry called Durocher and invited him up to the MacPhails' suite. "Max," he called to his brother in the next room, "come in here and meet the new manager of the Dodgers." That's how he broke the news to Durocher.

On October 13, 1938, Larry called a press conference at the New Yorker Hotel to announce his new appointment. Word had leaked out so that there was little surprise in the news, but great interest. They asked Larry if Leo had named his coaches yet and were informed one would be Charley Dressen, his great tactician who had previously managed the Reds for MacPhail and the past year had been the manager at Nashville.

The other was Bill Killefer, who for the last three years had been manager of Sacramento in the Coast League. Killefer was no stranger to MacPhail and he told all assembled of their previous encounters in Michigan and Wisconsin. In 1905, Larry was first baseman for the Ludington, Michigan, high school team that played for the state championship against Paw Paw, whose catcher was Bill Killefer, later to become the famed battery-mate of Grover Cleveland Alexander.

Ludington won and, for years, Killefer claimed "we was robbed" by the only crooked umpire he had ever encountered. Their paths crossed again and this time Bill had his revenge in a blinding fashion.

In 1907, Larry was playing first base for Beloit College and they were engaged in a hard-fought battle with Sacred Heart in Wisconsin, whose star was Killefer. With Sacred Heart leading, 2-1, in the last of the ninth, Larry came to bat with two out and men on second and third. The pitcher ran the count to two and two and MacPhail braced for a fastball down the middle. At this point Killefer let fly with a stream of tobacco juice right in Larry's eye. Strike three! The game was over, and before MacPhail could see clearly and catch up with him, Killefer was long gone.

With gusto, Larry said that Killefer was the dirtiest player he had ever known but was a damned good baseball man and would be a fine coach for Brooklyn.

The entire conference was decidedly upbeat. The sportswriters were enjoying the liquid refreshments and asking both MacPhail and Durocher questions about the coming season.

"Leo, what do you think of the team and why do you think it will do any better than the seventh place finish of 1938?"

After giving credit to Burleigh Grimes for the job he did in the '38 season, Leo waxed enthusiastic about the younger players having one more year of experience, the older players getting better every year, etc. MacPhail, for his part, added that he knew Durocher needed more horses and he would be stirring things up in the trade marts and the farm system. All in all, the session broke up with positive visions for the future.

Another event occurred on the same day, October 13, 1938, which at the time seemed of only passing interest, but was one that was to have a profound effect on the life of Larry MacPhail. It involved an addition to the office staff.

For weeks the Dodgers' office manager had been looking for a private secretary for Larry, and had been contacting several agencies, among them the New York office of Katherine Gibbs. This agency had, in turn, been calling up an attractive 28-year-old secretary named Jean Wanamaker, who had kept insisting that there was no purpose in her even having the job interview since under no circumstances would she consider either working in Brooklyn or working for a baseball club.

Finally, at the insistence of the Gibbs' office, she did agree to have the interview, and a time of 10 o'clock was set up on what turned out to be the same day MacPhail had set up for the press conference announcing Durocher's appointment.

Miss Wanamaker arrived shortly before the appointed time and sat in the outer office to await the interview. At 4 o'clock in the afternoon she was still sitting there, having gone out for lunch and returned. During this time she saw a parade of men going in and out and much excitement in the inner office. She was stewing and about to leave when she was informed by one of the office secretaries, "Mr. MacPhail will see you now."

Her curiosity got the best of her and she had to find out what kind of man would keep anybody waiting so long.

When Larry found out she had been kept waiting in the outer office for six hours he apologized, and immediately they got into a discussion which involved the amount of money she could be making if he agreed to hire her. She had asked for $40 per week which, at the time, was "an awful lot of money."

Larry picked up a blank card, the kind they use to record the wages for personnel, and held it in his hand. He countered her request by pointing out:

"But, you don't know anything about baseball."

Jean responded, "No, not a thing, but $40 is what I have been making and that's what I intend to make."

Larry reacted, "Well, it's probably a good thing that you don't know anything about baseball, but, how about starting at $32, and, then, you know, in a month or two, we can see how things work out, and then you could get raised to $35."

Jean said, "Mr. MacPhail, let's end the interview right here," and got up to go.

Larry grinned and took out his pen.

"Wait a minute," and wrote $40 on the blank card. He added, "Well, we'll try it out on a month's trial basis."

Jean agreed, saying, "That's all right with me because I'm not sure I'm going to work in Brooklyn for a whole month, either."

Before the '39 season started there was to be another change in the setup in Brooklyn that was to have a profound effect on the New York baseball scene—radio. The five-year agreement among the three major league baseball teams in New York City, that there were to be no radio broadcasts of the games, was up at the end of the '38 season. MacPhail announced that the Dodgers were not going to renew it. The Yankees and Giants were furious.

Although the Yankees were owned by Jacob Ruppert, his

general manager was Ed Barrow, and Barrow had almost complete authority over all phases of the Yankee operation. He was unalterably opposed to giving away for free the product he had so carefully created. He was almost totally responsible not only for the development of the Yankee team, but also Yankee Stadium. Charles Stoneham, owner of the Giants, was almost as strongly against radio as Barrow.

MacPhail ignored them both. Once he had made the decision he moved quickly. Walter "Red" Barber had done a great job in Cincinnati getting the entire populace of the surrounding area excited about the Reds, and MacPhail wanted him to move to New York and do the same thing for the Dodgers. Red was anxious to come. He reported to the Dodgers spring training camp in Clearwater, Florida in February. The idea was to get to know the ballplayers in Florida and then drive up to Brooklyn and broadcast the spring training games in Brooklyn via Western Union.

MacPhail needed a 50,000 watt radio outlet and got it with station WOR. He sold the broadcast rights to three sponsors— General Mills, Socony Vacuum, and Proctor & Gamble. General Mills did most of the negotiating for all three sponsors. Their product, Wheaties, was on its way to becoming known as the "Breakfast of Champions." Socony-Vacuum felt this would be a great method of advertising their Mobil oil and gasoline products, and Proctor & Gamble saw the start of their thriving relationship with the broadcast media.

Even though they hated it, both the Giants and Yankees were now forced to broadcast their games as well. Those two teams were always scheduled opposite each other. When one was in town, the other was playing on the road. The team that was home would have its game broadcast, but never a road game. Conversely, all the Dodger games, home and road, were aired so that the loyal fans of Flatbush could follow their favorites in every game all season. During a game on a hot summer day or evening a Brooklynite could walk the streets and pick up the play-by-play broadcast through the open windows along the way.

7

Swinging into Action

MacPhail wasted no time preparing for the 1939 season. All winter long he had kept changing personnel, nothing spectacular, but trying to add here and plug a hole there. During the World Series he had drafted a pitcher, Hugh Casey, from Memphis. The Cubs gave Tony Lazzeri his outright release in December, and Larry, thinking about infield reserve and wanting to add some of that old Yankee spirit, signed him to a Dodger contract. He acquired Jimmy Outlaw from St. Louis and traded him, along with Buddy Hassett, to Boston for outfielder Gene Moore and pitcher Ira Hutchinson. Larry was in his element. When the White Sox asked for waivers on the veteran catcher, Luke Sewell, MacPhail claimed him.

Although it didn't seem like it at the time, one of the biggest moves MacPhail was to make happened right after the first of the year—the acquisition of Whitlow Wyatt from Milwaukee. He was no spring chicken, having just passed his 30th birthday. He had had some good years in the American League, mainly with the White Sox but, after a very mediocre year with Cleveland in '37, winning two and losing three, he had been released to Milwaukee. He had a banner year with the Brewers in '38, winning 23 and losing only seven. For some reason, MacPhail was the only one interested in bringing him back to the majors.

Larry made several other moves in February, none of them world-shaking except the first of many times he fired Durocher. Leo had taken several of his pitchers, catchers and coaches to Hot Springs, Arkansas, for the baths and to start getting in shape prior to spring training. They would do calisthenics in the gym in the morning and then roadwork over the hills in the afternoon. But, for a man like Leo, who appreciated the night life of the big city, Hot Springs left something to be desired.

He found out that the best eating spot in town was the Belvedere Club. So, the first Saturday night he took his coaches there for a steak dinner. After dinner they found that the big attraction was the Saturday night Bingo Game at $2.00 a card. With 50 or 60 players each pot was worth $100 to $120 and the club provided a Grand Bingo Prize of $750 at the end of the evening. Who do you suppose won the big prize? None other than Leo, who then proceeded to blow it all on champagne "for the house."

All the sportswriters who were traveling with the team knew a good story when they found it and wrote it up with a flourish. It hit the newsstands in New York the next morning and Durocher was rudely awakened in his room Sunday morning by a long-distance phone call.

"You're fired," the screaming voice yelled.

When Leo realized it was MacPhail at the other end of the line, he stammered incredulously, "What for?"

"You know damned well. Gambling! You're supposed to be a big league manager, not a big league gambler. You're fired!" ranted Larry and slammed down the phone.

Since it was the first time MacPhail had fired him, Leo didn't know how to take it and prepared to fly home. Before he could actually leave though, Larry called him back on some other matter, completely ignoring the subject of his previous phone call and it was never mentioned again.

Spring training went along well and Durocher showed his natural ability at handling men and justifying Larry's choice. Many newspapermen who had been skeptical of his selection now recognized that Leo was in charge and the team was coming together under his managerial reins.

However, later during spring training a series of events led up to the second firing of Durocher by MacPhail, this time at Camp Wheeler, Georgia. It involved the "hidden ballplayer" and describes another of the stages in the relationship between MacPhail and Rickey. To develop the story, we have to go back to March 23, 1938.

Commissioner Kenesaw Mountain Landis had been violently opposed to the entire concept of a "farm system" and his dislike focused primarily on Branch Rickey, the greatest practitioner of the idea. Over a decade before, Landis had declared that no major league club could own stock in more than one minor league club in the same league.

As Rickey kept building the size and scope of his farm system it became more and more inevitable that he and Landis would have a confrontation with the odds stacked heavily in favor of the commissioner. By early 1938, the Cardinal organization controlled teams in six minor leagues and had working arrangements with over two dozen more.

At Judge Landis' behest, Leslie O'Connor, his chief aide, had been investigating the extent of the infiltration in the minor leagues by the St. Louis team for some time and, on the March date above cut loose 74 players in the minors controlled by the Cardinals. This became known as the "Cedar Rapids Decision." Sam Breadon, owner of the Cardinals, and Rickey, the general manager, not only owned one club in the Western League, but also had an "understanding" with Rickey's good friend who owned the Cedar Rapids team in the same league.

The charges were very specific. Landis maintained that Breadon and Rickey had "tried to obtain complete control of the lower classification clubs through secret understandings" and had violated his previous edict forbidding ownership or control of more than one club in the same league. Incidentally, this decision started a rift between Rickey and Breadon, Sam figuring that Rickey had deceived him after he had been warned to sever his relationship with the Cedar Rapids owner.

The only player of the 74 whose loss really upset Rickey was a high-school boy from the sandlots of St. Louis—Harold (Pete) Reiser. The Cardinal general manager had deservedly earned the reputation as one of the greatest evaluators of baseball talent and he felt this young man could become a combination of Ty Cobb and Babe Ruth.

It seems that at this point Rickey contacted MacPhail, told him about Reiser and requested that Larry sign him and keep him out of sight in the low minors until 1940, at which time it would be legal for Larry to trade him back to Rickey. Whether this is true or not, Reiser signed with the Dodger organization for the ridiculous sum of $100.

The plan had been that Pistol Pete, the name the sportswriters had tagged Reiser with in tribute to the shots that came off his bat, would work out with the Montreal farm club, but would then be assigned to Elmira in the Eastern League for seasoning and would be out of the spotlight of either the high minors or even the Dodger club itself.

This was all well and good except for one thing. In the batter's box he was impossible to get out, and in the field, either at shortstop or the outfield he was phenomenal. His only drawback was his strong desire to go all out. He would practically climb the wall to get a fly ball and was, therefore, prone to injury. Durocher, not knowing of the plan to keep him out of sight, started playing him in center field in three exhibition games against, of all people, the St. Louis Cardinals.

All he did was get on base 11 consecutive times, including seven hits, four of them home runs. Two of the homers were from the right side and two from the left. Naturally, Durocher was ecstatic about his "find" and bragged unceasingly to the sportswriters about his ability to spot a winner. The writers didn't need much prodding since they could see how hot Reiser was and wrote glowing articles for the New York papers.

MacPhail almost had apoplexy and Rickey was steaming. Larry fired off a wire to Durocher, "DO NOT PLAY REISER AGAIN!"

First, Durocher was puzzled. Then, the more he thought about it the madder he got. "Damnit, who's running this team on the field, anyway?" he thought.

The next day they were scheduled to play the Tigers in Macon, Georgia, and Durocher penciled in the name of Reiser in center field. Leo was just changing into his baseball uniform when John McDonald, the traveling secretary who was Mac-Phail's right-hand man but was also in Durocher's corner, came in and told him, "Leo, the boss wants to see you right away and he's got fire in his eye."

The moment Durocher and McDonald entered MacPhail's suite the volcano erupted.

"You're fired! You're through! Out of the organization. Pack your bags and get out."

Then, he really started in cursing, completely out of control. He screamed at McDonald to get out his typewriter and take down the announcement of Durocher's being canned. MacPhail, under a full head of steam, was a sight to behold. He called Leo every possible derogatory name he could think of. McDonald not only could not keep up with it but, knowing his boss, deliberately made enough mistakes that Larry had to start all over again each time John needed a new sheet of paper. In fact, he got so mad he even told McDonald to include himself in the announcement of the firings because he was completely incompetent and unable even to type out the dismissal.

The suite was a twin-bedded one, with McDonald sitting on one and his typewriter on the other. MacPhail was pacing back and forth.

By this time Leo, figuring he was through anyway and mad at being called everything in the book and then some, gave Larry a shove hard enough to send him head over heels over the bed nearest the window and into a heap on the floor. The startled MacPhail popped up and, as if by magic, the storm clouds had passed. He put his arm around Leo and the entire incident was over.

Without confiding in Leo the full reason for Reiser's being optioned out, Larry convinced him that, for Pete's own good, he should be sent down for development under the watchful eye of Manager Clyde Sukeforth at Elmira.

Spring training ended without further incident and they were ready to start the season in earnest.

The Dodgers got off to a slow start, and were in seventh place after the first two weeks. Then they started winning a few games and had a short stay in second place, only to fall back again. Some of the secondary players who weren't contributing were replaced. Luke Sewell and Tony Lazzeri were both released and they picked up Lyn Lary from Cleveland for infield insurance. The starting pitching, at least the first three, was in pretty good shape with Wyatt, Casey and Luke Hamlin.

Wyatt had not only regained his form, but now was better

than ever and was fast becoming a real favorite in Flatbush. As his record became more and more impressive an incident occurred that only MacPhail could have handled the way he did.

A story appeared in one of the Milwaukee papers contending that Henry Bendinger, the Milwaukee owner, was going to contact Commissioner Landis and demand the return of Wyatt. He maintained that MacPhail had not completed the deal for Wyatt which was to include not only a sum of money, but also four ball players, none of whom had yet appeared to play for Milwaukee.

Harold Parrott, who wrote for the *Brooklyn Eagle*, picked up the story and the next edition carried banner headlines: LANDIS MAY VOID WYATT DEAL. Just as MacPhail heard the story he ran into Parrott coming out of the press box at Ebbets Field and all hell broke loose.

Larry yelled and screamed and, in front of hundreds of witnesses, called Parrott every kind of liar and blackguard he could call to mind. He told him that he was barred from Ebbets Field forever. MacPhail, in full bloom, was not just a sideshow. He was the main attraction. The nonplussed sportswriter could not get a word in edgewise.

Parrott, unaccustomed to such treatment, put in a call to Ford Frick who, after he heard the newsman's story, advised him to lay low for the rest of the day and he, Frick, would contact MacPhail and attempt to remedy the situation. After Larry had simmered down he agreed to rescind his order to bar Parrott. However, he forgot to inform the attendant and Parrott still could not get in the next day.

Parrott reported this turn of events to his editor, Edwin Wilson, who contacted George Barnewall of the Brooklyn Trust Company. The feud was getting out of hand and Barnewall, in the interest of getting together two such important entities of Brooklyn as the Dodgers and the *Eagle*, arranged a luncheon for MacPhail, Parrott, Wilson and himself with the idea that amity could be restored.

At the restaurant the next day, Larry was in great humor and proceeded to tell the other three about some great plans he had for future baseball deals, Ebbets Field improvements, etc. With the second round of cocktails Wilson thought it was time to get down to the real reason for the luncheon meeting and brought up the subject to MacPhail.

"Oh, that!" Larry effused. "Why, I'm willing to forget the whole thing."

He went right on where he had left off and nothing was ever said about it again. Whatever was left to be done in completing the transaction with Bendinger was done and Wyatt remained as the mainstay of the Brooklyn staff.

In June and early July the Dodgers had their ups and downs but Durocher, always the scrapper, was starting to instill his brand of combativeness, not only in the team but also the loyal Flatbush fans. In June it had looked as if they might finish seventh again but then they started moving up. One of the big additions to the everyday players was Dixie Walker, an acquisition which at the time seemed as unimportant as dealing for Wyatt, but one that was to be equally significant to the Dodgers' fortunes.

Walker's career up to that point had not been very auspicious. He had been the property of the Yankees for the first six years from 1930-36, bouncing back and forth from the minors to the parent club, but never performing well enough to stick with the pinstripers. In 1933 he had had a shoulder injury that again plagued him in '36. Joe McCarthy finally gave up on him and in '37 he played for the White Sox, where he hit a respectable .302.

Dixie played for the Tigers in '38 and improved that average to .308 for the seaseon. His shoulder was troubling him again, though, and in July of '39 the Tigers asked for waivers on him, and all the other American League teams complied. The Dodgers had started the '38 season with their best outfielders being Tuck Stainback, Gene Moore and Ernie Koy. MacPhail felt he had nothing to lose by picking up Walker.

As sometimes happens with a change of uniform, Dixie became an almost instant success with the Dodgers and their fans and he soon was known by the famous sobriquet "the people's choice" or, more properly on the banks of the Gowanus, the "peepul's cherce."

There was one other important addition in 1939, this in the internal staff. Branch Rickey, Jr. had been working for his father for a couple of years to learn the baseball business. As so often happens when the son of a strong and domineering father is working under his direction, he felt frustrated and stultified. Larry had recognized Branch, Jr.'s potential and asked him if he wanted to come over to his organization. With his father's consent, the young man joined Larry and felt the relief of being on his own.

Together Larry and Branch, Jr. built a bigger and stronger farm system which was under the direction of the younger man. Before the end of the year they had a string of teams, which they either owned or controlled, in leagues from Class AA to D, including Elmira in the Eastern League, Dayton in the Middle Atlantic, Pine Bluff in the Cotton States, Olean in the Pony, and Americus in the Georgia-Florida League.

In addition, they had working agreements with Montreal in the International, Nashville in the Southern, Macon in the South Atlantic, Paducah in the Kitty, Reidsville in the Bi-State, and Superior in the Northern League. With tryout camps and a good group of scouts combing the country the Dodgers had upwards of 350 young men hopeful of eventually moving up to the majors.

Another of Larry MacPhail's many firsts occurred in late August—the 26th to be exact. On that day, the first telecast of any professional sport happened at Ebbets Field. Red Barber was instrumental in arranging the details and tells about it in his book, *The Broadcasters*.

Red's good friend, Alfred H. (Doc) Morton, was at NBC and had been put in charge of wet-nursing the infant called television. There were very few sets even in existence and those that were would not be recognizable today. The top of the set was raised up on a hinge. The picture, such as it was, was shown on a mirror so that the viewer saw the reflected picture—somewhat on the order of a periscope.

Doc Morton had televised a baseball game in the late spring of '39 between Princeton and Columbia with Bill Stern at the microphone. Morton was itching to do a real live pro game. He knew that in the New York area MacPhail was the logical one to approach since Barrow of the Yankees and Stoneham of the Giants were against even radio. He did not know MacPhail personally, but did know that Red Barber knew him well. Would Red ask Larry for permission? Yes, he would and did.

Larry, of course, was all for it and, in return, asked only that a receiving set be set up in the pressroom so that the directors of the ball club and writers could watch the game. It worked to the extent that viewers could distinguish the players, but they could not follow the flight of the ball.

There was a television truck outside and two cameras were set up—one on the ground level just to the left of the foul screen on the third-base side, and the other above it in the second deck. Barber was at the camera upstairs with the Dodger fans all about him.

In his book, Red has a great paragraph about the commercials on this first professional sports telecast:

> There was no haggling with NBC and the three sponsors of the Dodgers' radio broadcasts. NBC offered each sponsor one commercial—one time between a selected half-inning—to do with as they pleased . . . three "live" commericals . . . one each by Ivory Soap, Wheaties, and Mobil Gas. There was no script, no idiot cards, no rehearsal. In the middle of the agreed inning, I held up a bar of Ivory Soap and said something about it being a great soap . . . a few innings later I put on a Mobil Gas service-station cap, held up a can of oil, and said what a great oil it was . . . and for Wheaties? This was the big production number. Right on the camera, right among the fans, I opened a box of Wheaties, shook out a bowlful, sliced a banana, added a spoon of sugar, poured on some milk—and said, "That's a Breakfast of Champions."

There was one other first connected with the telecast. The game was the first half of a doubleheader with the Reds, and, between games, Barber did "live" interviews with a number of the ballplayers—Bill McKechnie and Bucky Walters of the Reds, and Leo Durocher, Dolf Camilli, Dixie Walker and Whitlow Wyatt of the Dodgers. Although few people realized the significance of what was happening, it was quite a day.

The season moved on into September. The Reds, most of whom had been brought to Cincinnati by MacPhail or developed in the farm system he had built, had taken over first place in May and were never to relinquish it. The Cardinals had almost as firm a hold on second place, but the Dodgers were starting to capture the imagination of fans across the country.

On the final day of the season Brooklyn had a chance to finish in third place. They were scheduled to play a double-header in Ebbets Field against the Phillies. By winning both games or by winning one game and not playing the other, they would clinch third. However, a lost game dropped them to fourth.

The day dawned dark and cloudy and Larry, always up to the challenge, wanted to cover all bets. Against the weather forecaster's prediction of clearing skies he took out a $25,000 insurance policy against a rainout and paid a premium of $4,832. The stipulation in the contract was that if one-twentieth of an inch of rain were to fall during the game or within three hours before the start of the first game, payment would be made.

By one o'clock, over 17,000 excited fans were in the stands and a few minutes later it started to pour. He was now in a position to collect the $25,000 and most of the fans expected to get rain checks for next year. However, Larry thought, "Let's wait a while and see what happens." Sure enough, by two o'clock the sun came out and they were able to start the game. Although there was a constant drizzle throughout, they were able to get the game in and Brooklyn won a hard-fought thriller, 3-2.

Hugh Casey started with only one day's rest and, although he didn't finish, he rang up his 15th win for the season. Carl Doyle pitched the eighth and ninth, facing the minimum six batters.

Shortly after the completion of the first game, the heavens opened up and the field became a quagmire. The second game had to be called. The gods were really smiling on Larry now. His gamble had paid off and he now had the insurance payment, the gate receipts and third place all wrapped up in one beautiful package.

The crowd of 17,152 brought the home attendance at Ebbets Field over the million mark for a total of 1,007,762 for the season.

Larry came to the World Series in Cincinnati as the conquering hero, a fact that did not go unnoticed by his successor at the helm of the Reds, Warren Giles. The two men could not have been more diametrically opposed to each other in both personality and showmanship.

Although it was Giles who was at the head of the team that played in the Series, most knowledgeable baseball people gave almost total credit to MacPhail for putting the team together. That made Giles just the beneficiary of the work done by his predecessor. It did not set at all well with the comparatively quiet and unassuming man who followed the always flamboyant MacPhail.

Larry was already doing the impossible in Brooklyn and it was just a matter of time until his Dodgers would be king of the hill. But, in the meantime, here he was in Cincinnati to accept the hosannahs of the baseball afficionados for bringing his former team to the big payoff window.

When MacPhail came to the Series his mind and heart were completely dedicated to baseball. He was totally immersed, as was his nature, in his activity of the moment, enough so that his marriage was already starting to suffer.

Larry was not a womanizer, as such. But, there was an incident during the Series in Cincinnati. At a cocktail party before the first game Larry was thoroughly enjoying the liquid refreshments when he was approached by a very attractive young lady who asked him if he could help her get a ticket to the opening game. He told her he could get her one and would do so:

She then asked how she could pay for it and he said:

"Don't worry, we'll find a way."

8

The Dodgers Move Up in '40

There was tremendous enthusiasm at Clearwater the next spring. After all, the Dodgers had moved up four notches, from seventh to third in just one year. Over the winter MacPhail had picked up a baby-faced youngster from Louisville who was destined to become one of the all-time greats in Dodger history—Harold (Peewee) Reese.

Louisville was controlled by the Boston Red Sox and they could have had Reese for the asking. However, Joe Cronin, who was the sixth shortstop to be admitted to the Hall of Fame, was the playing manager of the Red Sox and, for whatever reason, decided that Boston did not need another short-stop and so advised Tom Yawkey, owner of the Sox.

When MacPhail heard about this he sent his head scout, Ted McGrew, to Louisville to watch the youngster play. McGrew couldn't believe what he saw and told Larry to do all possible to get him. MacPhail went to the Brooklyn Trust Company and persuaded them to buy the whole franchise just to get Reese.

Durocher had two separate contracts with MacPhail, one as a player and the other as manager. It was always a major bone of contention between the two as to the amount of play-ing time Leo would get at shortstop. MacPhail felt that as long as he was paying Durocher two separate salaries he should get full value for his money.

For his part, Leo always felt he could manage better from the bench and was happy to pencil in Reese's name in the

94

lineup. It was a constant source of irritation to Larry and the cause for at least one of the many firings Durocher experienced. However, Reese started the season at short.

The promise of spring became a reality as the season got under way. The Dodgers opened with nine consecutive wins, a feat which, at that time, tied a record set by the 1918 New York Giants. The ninth game was the best of all—a no-hitter by Tex Carleton, a pitcher who had been a mainstay with the Cardinals, and later the Cubs, but who was in the twilight of his career and had just a mediocre season in 1939 in the minors with Milwaukee. One of the Dodger scouts had suggested to MacPhail that Tex might have one more good year in the majors. Another acquisition in early May was Jimmy Wasdell, claimed on waivers from Washington.

The team continued on its trip through the West, finishing with a 12-2 win over the Cubs and a two-game lead on the pack. MacPhail, always up to the drama of the occasion, decided to fly the victorious ball club home at night. The effect was electric! Thirty thousand fans greeted the two planes at Floyd Bennett Field and about the same number showed up at Ebbets Field the next day to see their heroes play their archrivals, the Giants. Even though the Giants did not cooperate and took a one-sided contest, it was only a pause in the Dodgers' race with the Reds.

However, the outfield was a problem. Joe Vosmik, a refugee from Cleveland and Boston in the American League, was getting along in years. He had some great years at the bat but was slowing up noticeably in the field. In fact, he wore a corset to ease his aching back, an addition which did not improve his ability to reach down for a bouncing ball.

Roy Cullenbine was their cleanup hitter, but in name only. He seemed willing to hope for walks, but that was not what he was paid to do. When his batting average fell to .180 MacPhail shipped him to the Browns for Joe Gallagher who reversed the role Cullenbine had been playing. He swung at everything, but with no greater success.

Larry was always tinkering with the outfield. The previous year he had paid $25,000 for Mel Almada, a fine fielder whose ability to hit major league pitching was questionable. A few hours after consummating this deal he was riding along in his car in the country with his two sons, Lee and Bill. He proudly told them of his new acquisition. When the boys heard the news and the amount of money their dad had paid for him they doubled up in laughter:

"Mel Almada! You paid $25,000 for Mel Almada!" Bill chortled in disbelief.

Larry was furious and silenced the pair of faithless sons. But they proved to be right and Mel was sent down to Sacramento.

The situation was getting worse. MacPhail needed a hard-hitting veteran outfielder who could field and throw the ball. He let it be known that he was ready to spend money to fill this need. He immediately thought of Joe (Ducky) Medwick of the Cardinals. He contacted Rickey and, when he was told that, although the price would be steep, Medwick was not out of the question, he hopped a plane for St. Louis.

Many things came together to make Medwick the logical target for MacPhail. From the Dodgers' standpoint, he had been Durocher's roommate when Leo was with the Cardinals and they were inseparable. His hitting production had fallen off somewhat, but he had always hit well at Ebbets Field. He could be just the veteran the Dodgers needed. From the Cardinals' viewpoint, although he had still hit over .300, it was common knowledge that many of the players on that team felt that he had been less than a team player in the pennant race the year before, and that his selfish attitude had contributed to their inability to overtake the Reds.

Also, this was now 1940 and Branch Rickey, sitting in St. Louis, was trying to figure out how to reacquire Pete Reiser without raising too many eyebrows. However, Reiser had such a tremendous year in 1939 at Elmira that MacPhail told Rickey the Dodger fans would lynch him if he got rid of the rookie. He started off 1940 back at Elmira but had already stolen 28 bases and was making a shambles of Eastern League pitching, hitting .378.

With Commissioner Landis, Rickey's nemesis, watching every move, Rickey hardly felt it wise to pursue the situation and the conversation changed to other names. Rickey's contract with Sam Breadon called for Branch to get a percentage of the money received in all trades. After much discussion, the Dodgers ended up trading four players and $125,000 to the Cardinals for Medwick and a 33-year-old pitcher, Curt Davis, who had won 22 games the year before, but had gotten off to a poor start in 1940. The four Dodgers were Ernie Koy, two young pitchers, Carl Doyle and Sam Nahem, and Berthold Haas, who had been Camilli's backup at first base. Medwick and Davis flew back to Brooklyn with MacPhail.

Dodger fans were ecstatic! Now, they were sure, they had their pennant.

This was June 12, and one week later an event happened at Ebbets Field that not only greatly affected the career of Medwick, but, more importantly, brought about a tremendous change affecting safety in the sport of baseball.

The incident, itself, happened on June 19.

Durocher always stayed at the New Yorker Hotel, so, when his close friend, Medwick, joined the team, he also took up residence at the New Yorker. As luck would have it, the schedule called for his old team, the Cardinals, to come in for a big series in Brooklyn just seven days after the trade.

About noon on the 19th, Durocher and Medwick were going down in the elevator on their way to the ball park. The elevator stopped on one of the lower floors and picked up Bob Bowman, the Cardinal pitcher who was scheduled to start against the Dodgers that day. Leo, always the needler, started in on Bowman and then Medwick got into the act. Bowman took it for a while and, then, finally blew up.

"I'll take care of you! I'll take care of both of you," he said.

Leo replied, "Why, you bum, you'll be out of there before Joe and I get to bat!"

The game started and, after the Cardinals were retired, the Dodgers came to bat. On the first pitch to him, Medwick was hit in the head by a Bowman fast ball. He fell like a rock. He lay there unconscious at the plate. The Dodgers poured out on the field with fire in their eyes and, some of them, with a bat in their hands. Leo was in the lead, screaming, "You said you'd get him!"

The Cardinal dugout emptied as his teammates rushed to defend Bowman. The umpires were almost totally helpless in trying to bring about order. The fans in the stands were so incensed they seemed ready to leave their seats and join the fray. Pandemonium had set in. MacPhail went berserk!

At this point, fact and fiction become intertwined. The next day both the *New York Times* and the *New York Herald Tribune* reported that Larry rushed from either his box or the press box onto the field and challenged the entire Cardinal bench with the fans cheering him on. A year later the *New Yorker Magazine* described the incident even more graphically:

". . . The spectators . . . cheered as they watched Mac-Phail's arrival on the scene. Waving his arms and roaring in his vibrant moose voice, he galloped down the aisles of the grandstand and across the diamond to the pitcher's box. . . . As one umpire said later, 'MacPhail came down here and tried to provoke a riot.' "

Sometimes the mind has a way of erasing what it does not want to remember. Nineteen years later, in an article by the late Gerald Holland in *Sports Illustrated*, Larry vehemently denied ever having run out on the field of play during a ball game, any time anywhere.

In the many interviews I have had with people who knew him well, Larry sometimes comes off as a wild man—bombastic, colorful, rambunctious—but always with a reputation for truthfulness. His word was his bond. Holland found the same thing when discussing him with Larry's friends. Therefore, and with a little tongue in cheek, he wrote the following:

"Giving all parties the best of it, I decided that what had happened was this: the situation on the ball field when Medwick was beaned so cried out for MacPhail that the sportswriters had been the victims of a hallucination which also had afflicted the crowds in the stands with a kind of mass hypnosis. It was that—or MacPhail had subconsciously erased the memory."

At any rate, whatever actually happened on the field that day is somewhat academic now. Medwick was rushed to the Caledonian Hospital where it was found that he had a severe concussion, but no fracture. He remained in the hospital for five or six days and then returned to the team. Interestingly enough, although Medwick had been Mr. Tough Guy and mean to boot, that beaning apparently took its toll. From that day forward, he never regained his past glory and his statistics were all downhill.

Larry did not forget the lesson to be learned from the incident. He immediately contacted Dr. George Eli Bennett, professor of orthopedic surgery at Johns Hopkins School of Medicine (and the man under whose direction the first iron lung center in the world was organized at Children's Hospital in Baltimore in the early 1940s) and the two started to develop a protective helmet for ballplayers. Dr. Bennett recalled that MacPhail got a jockey's protective cap from Alfred Gwynne Vanderbilt and the two of them took it to Dr. Walter E. Dandy, also at Johns Hopkins, who was working on a protective helmet for boxers.

On February 7, 1941 MacPhail wrote a letter to Dr. Dandy in which he informed him that he was having Spalding make up six Brooklyn caps for shipment to him immediately. He wrote Dr. Dandy that they ordinarily use head sizes from 7 to 7½, but that he was having these cap bands made about a half-inch oversized and the crowns also made larger to facilitate anything he might do in connection with the insertion of a protector piece.

He asked Dr. Dandy to see if there was anything he could do to have Du Pont get out a few samples, regardless of cost, so that the caps could be fitted and used in the training camp. He added that, after using the device in the training camp, the caps and molds could be altered or constructed so that, if the device proved satisfactory, they would be available for the opening of the season.

Ten days before Dr. Bennett's death he gave a speech in which he traced the evolution of the helmet. He was not interested in personal publicity, but simply wanted the facts straight on how the helmet was developed.

"The credit belongs almost entirely to MacPhail," said Dr. Bennett. "MacPhail liked the idea, but most important, he pushed it. He worked with many persons on it, then made its use compulsory for every player in the Dodger system."

Getting back to the incident itself, manager Billy Southworth removed Bowman from the game and later, for his own protection, the pitcher was escorted by police from the park back to his hotel. MacPhail phoned Ford Frick, demanding that Bowman be barred from baseball for life or, at least, arrested for assault. He thought of going to the district attorney also, but as Medwick's condition improved, MacPhail cooled down and the season resumed.

By the end of the first week in July the pattern had been set for the rest of the season. The Dodgers were in second place, one notch higher than in '39, but they could not dislodge the Reds from first place and, for the second year running, Cincinnati won the National League pennant behind the pitching of Paul Derringer and Bucky Walters.

The Dodgers finished 12 games back, but still played exciting ball the rest of the way and the Flatbush fans couldn't wait till next year. In mid-August Peewee Reese broke two small bones in his foot and was out for the rest of the season and Cookie Lavagetto had an emergency appendectomy on the last western road trip. Durocher had to return to the lineup and played great ball and Reiser, called up from Elmira for the last 58 games, filled in for Lavagetto at third base. But it was destined that the pennant was not to fly over Ebbets Field in 1940.

There was one other typically Brooklyn incident that happened near the end of September. After a particularly galling loss, punctuated by some questionable calls by the huge umpire, George Magerkurth, the man in blue was walking off the field when a short, husky fan blind-sided him and the two went rolling around in the dust of the infield. After fellow umpire Bill Stewart broke it up, the cops finally appeared and hauled the overly enthusiastic fan off to the hoosegow. It turned out that he was on parole so his next stay in jail was not short-lived, but his loyalty to the Dodgers was unswerving.

MacPhail was really in his element. On September 11, Larry called a press conference and gave an excellent critique not only on the season, but, also, a thorough analysis of and an insight into the operation of the club:

Press Information

When league positions are set and the close of the season approaches, it is natural there should be speculation on "plans for the next year."

Writers naturally cover the matter to the best of their

abilities, and if facts are not available, they cannot be blamed for copy based upon rumor—or pure speculation.

Articles have already appeared commenting upon: (1) Trades which will send present Dodgers on their way, (2) Players whom we will attempt to secure, (3) Reported friction between Durocher and myself over who should play shortstop, and (4) The probability of Durocher's reappointment and terms of his contract.

The press is entitled to such information as we can give out without prejudice to the club. Information herein is not press release—it is neither off nor on the record—simply facts on matters in which you may be interested.

1. First, an explanation on how we operate: Our fiscal year was changed to end September 30th instead of December 31st. This enables us to have complete reports from our auditors on our operations at Brooklyn and in the minor leagues—as well as reports from business managers, managers and scouts—available October 1st. We then hold our annual meeting, at which time I submit (1) a complete operations report; (2) a budget for the coming year; (3) recommendations as to plans and policies and as to personnel for the twelve clubs we operate or with whom we are affiliated. It is reasonable that interests owning the club shall have a voice in the determination of its plans and policies. At our October meeting they pass on my reports and recommendations and we are then set to proceed for 1941 early in October instead of in January. Directors have been generous in the past in approving all my recommendations even when there may have been doubt in their own minds as to their wisdom.

2. Our attendance will probably exceed 1939—which means two straight years of a million or better. This insures a profitable operation at Brooklyn. The minor leagues have been through one of the toughest seasons in history (largely due to weather conditions). Our operations at Montreal and Olean have been satisfactory. We will have losses at all other minor league points.

3. This year's club, with the breaks in our favor, could have won the pennant. That does not mean that we will stand pat. All the other first division clubs will be improved in 1941. We will have to strengthen to maintain or improve our position. There was only one club in baseball last year with all three outfielders hitting above .300. It is possible we might have equalled that with Medwick, Walker, and

Reiser or Wasdell playing all season. The infield compares
favorably with the best in either league. We will not hesitate
to strengthen our infield or outfield if opportunity presents,
but it is apparent our best opportunity to strengthen is by
securing another starting pitcher and additional catching.

The development of the Brooklyn club has exceeded expectations. The improvement has been faster than at Cincinnati, for instance, over a like period.

Players to whose development our farm system has contributed who have already appeared on the Brooklyn roster
include Hudson, Haas, Williams, Gilbert, Reiser and Head;
Staller and Rachunok at Montreal and Kehn at Elmira are
considered outstanding prospects. We have approximately
fifteen young pitchers on our minor league clubs who, in
the opinion of our scouts, are exceptional major league
prospects.

4. My recommendations on personnel, including the
minor league clubs, will be made at our meeting in October.
The contract of the manager will be for one year and no
announcement will be made until such time as my recommendations are approved and the contract signed. I have
a well-defined idea as to what my recommendations will
be. There were a lot of silly rumors in this connection circulated last year. I am not going to discuss the matter further in the interim or issue any denials of rumors or articles which may follow.

Durocher had no experience managing when I hired him
in 1939. He did a great job in 1939 and profited as a manager
in 1940 by experience gained the previous year. If any of
you fellows want to get out on a limb again with respect
to the appointment of the manager, it is up to you.

5. I have not told Durocher in 1939 or 1940 who to play
or where or when to play them. I get rid of players as soon
as possible who do not fit in with the manager's plans. Running a ball club on the field is strictly the manager's job
and his responsibility. I don't agree with everything he does
and neither do you—and neither do any of the 1,000,000
fans who see the Dodgers play at home. I hire a manager
because I like the kind of baseball he plays over a 154-game
season and the way he handles the players—and, if I don't
like it, I make a change. That is my job and that is what
I am paid to do. If I do not have the intestinal fortitude to
put myself out on a limb in selecting managers—or in making changes—someone else should be drawing my salary.

On the record, it looks as though my guesses have been better than the criticisms. I cannot remember any loud cheering from the sidelines when Durocher was first appointed—and I get quite a kick occasionally out of reading the comment of the press on that occasion.

6. Neither Durocher, nor any other manager I have ever had has had responsibility for making deals—or for the procurement of ballplayers from other major or minor league clubs. It has been my experience that managers are most familiar with their own players, and are not in the best position to determine the abilities of players on other clubs or in other leagues. We continually scout the National, American and minor leagues, and the acquisition of Franks, Wyatt, Casey, Camilli, Coscarart, Reese, Tamulis, Davis, Head, Reiser, Wasdell, Medwick and Walker has been the result of decisions made by our scouting staff and myself. These policies will continue.

7. Reese will not be permitted to play any more baseball under any circumstances this year. Camilli will not play again until such time as club physicians report to me that he can play without risking permanent injury (I do not expect to have repetitions of the Wyatt case if it can be avoided).

8. There will naturally be another shortstop on the Brooklyn active roster in 1941 besides Reese—but, there will be only two shortstops among the 25 active players. I haven't decided whether Durocher will be on the active player list in 1941. There are things to be considered on both sides. Durocher has been picked on the last two National League All-Star teams and our club this year had the best percentage in the National League (.641, I think) in the games Durocher played at shortstop. We may have arrived at the point, however, when it is necessary to consider Leo in 1941 as a bench manager.

9. The press reports on the consideration paid for Kampouris are exaggerated.

10. We have closed contracts for the preliminary training of the Brooklyn club at Havana, Cuba. Headquarters of the club will be at Hotel Nacional de Cuba. We will play 11 games in Havana with major league and Cuban opponents. The Florida base will be at Clearwater as usual.

11. When I was in Cuba I was asked over the telephone to comment on reports that negotiations for the sale of the Brooklyn club were in progress. I knew at that time, or

thought I knew, that there were no negotiations for the sale of the club. Sale of a baseball club and offers to certain stockholders for their stock in the club are two entirely different things. Whether or not individual stockholders choose to hold or dispose of their stock is no affair of mine.

I am not interested in becoming associated as General Manager or in any other subordinate capacity with any parties who may desire to acquire an interest in the Brooklyn Club. I am not interested personally in purchasing the club. If there should be any material change in the present setup, I will be located at some other National League point than Brooklyn.

L. S. MacPhail

September 11, 1940.

9

1941—The Year Flatbush Went Crazy

Brooklyn hadn't won a pennant for 21 years and were they ready! The momentum was there and the fans of Flatbush knew that it would carry them all the way. But, there was real work to be done. MacPhail was a dynamo. As far as he was concerned, the day after the '40 season ended was the day the '41 season began.

He knew that the Dodgers needed help both on the pitching staff and behind the plate. The two men he had in mind were Kirby Higbe of the Phillies and Arnold (Mickey) Owen of the Cardinals. The Cubs had owned Higbe originally but they had lost interest in him and shipped him to the Phils, where he had just won 14 games for the tail-enders. Larry knew that other teams also would be interested in Higbe and that he had to be very careful going after him.

He felt that if Branch Rickey knew that he intended to get Higbe his chances of getting Owen from the Cardinals would be nil, because the combination of Higbe and Owen might be enough to give the Dodgers the inside track on the pennant. So he planned the operation with the precision of a brain surgeon.

He flew to Cincinnati for the World Series and knew that he could start to make his moves there with Gerry Nugent, president of the Phils. Nugent and his board of directors were always in need of money so he was perfectly willing to talk about Higbe. MacPhail swore him to secrecy and scheduled a meeting for the next day to discuss the deal.

His next move was to contact Rickey about Owen. Rickey had, of course, deservedly earned the reputation as one of the shrewdest traders in the game. He was willing to listen but gave the impression that he was not particularly interested in disposing of his young catcher.

Owen was a rough-and-tumble battler who, although he had never quite lived up to the promise of stardom, still had been the regular catcher with the Cardinals for the last four years. However, MacPhail knew he would fit beautifully in the Brooklyn mold Larry was creating, and Rickey knew he had a catcher coming up, Walker Cooper, who would hit his way into the Cardinal lineup anyway.

The seeds had been planted. Larry had dinner and was relaxing at the Netherland Plaza with John McDonald when the latter offered the information that the Giants' bigwigs—Horace Stoneham, Leo Bondy and Eddie Brannick—were entertaining Nugent at a fancy nightclub across the river with the intention of buying Higbe. MacPhail almost had apoplexy.

The following morning he called Gerry.

"What's this I hear about you offering Higbe to the Giants. You knew we had a meeting scheduled for this morning to work out the details!"

"Hey, wait a minute, Larry, I didn't tell them anything about our meeting and I haven't sold Higbe to them. But, I certainly intend to listen to all offers before I make a deal."

MacPhail rushed down to Nugent's room and immediately went on the attack.

"All right, Gerry, what are you asking for Higbe?"

"One hundred thousand dollars," was the tentative answer.

"Sold!" said Larry.

That's all there was to it. Nugent was flabbergasted since the $100,000 was merely his opening gambit. After the formality of a telephone call clearing the deal with his board of directors, a handshake confirmed the deal.

"Now," said Larry, "you have to agree to keep this quiet for the present or I'll never get Rickey to sell me Owen."

Nugent agreed. But, they were both concerned that Judge Landis would not hear of keeping any trade quiet. All Larry needed was a few days to complete the deal with Rickey. He called Landis who agreed that the details of the transaction could be forwarded to the league headquarters with a copy to the commissioner's office in routine fashion, and MacPhail had the time he needed. No bulletin would go out from Landis' office until he had returned from the World Series.

And now for Mickey Owen. With the World Series on, almost all the owners and other major league poohbahs were in town. So, it was not surprising that rumors were flying about several teams, including the Dodgers, having made offers to the Phillies for the purchase of Higbe. When Rickey confronted MacPhail on the subject Larry exclaimed:

"Can you imagine what Nugent wants for him? A hundred thousand dollars!"

They both laughed, and got on to the haggling about Owen.

"Okay, Branch, what do you want for your catcher?" asked Larry.

Rickey, always mindful of the 10 percent of the purchase price he received from the sale of ballplayers, but also in need of insurance in the catching department in case Cooper wasn't quite ready, replied:

"Sixty thousand dollars and two ballplayers, one of whom must be a catcher."

"You've got a deal," said Larry. It ended up that he traded the veteran catcher, Gus Mancuso, and a long-forgotten rookie pitcher named John Pintar to complete the deal. He had the two men he had set out to get.

The information about the purchase of Higbe was still some time in surfacing, enough so that Horace Stoneham, in an expansive mood in Toots Shor's one night, had publicly expressed the idea that the Giants would soon acquire Higbe.

MacPhail could not pass up the opportunity to needle his cross-town rival. At a hastily called press conference he smirked:

"Regardless of what you have heard to the contrary, the New York Giants will not be acquiring Kirby Higbe since he is the property of the Brooklyn Dodgers." With this announcement he produced his copy of the agreement he had signed with Gerry Nugent and beamed in self-adulation.

In New York, Stoneham was livid at both MacPhail and Nugent but, having created the situation himself, he could only stew in his own juice. MacPhail, of course, became even a greater hero to the Flatbush faithful.

Everything was starting to fall into place. The great Paul Waner—Big Poison—was released by the Pirates and, on January 31 MacPhail signed him. He didn't have the speed and agility of his earlier years, but still had some pop in his bat.

Then, they got the good news from the doctors that Peewee Reese was as sound as ever. Reese later recalled negotiating his new contract after the excellent medical reports.

This was long before the age of agents and lawyers representing the ballplayers. His father had died in 1939. So, this shy 20-year-old youngster was overmatched in listing his credentials and it was a losing battle. He entered Larry's lavish office and, after some preliminary sparring, stated his case.

"Mr. MacPhail, I think that I have proved that I can play ball up here—hopefully, anyway. My father is not here and I don't have any help—"

At this point Larry interrupted.

"Son, let me tell you something. You're on that side of the desk, and I'm on this side of the desk. You've got a job to do and I've got a job to do."

That scared the hell out of Peewee and he signed for the same thing he had played for in 1940.

MacPhail's great plans for 1941 started with what might be the most extensive spring training season of all time. He scheduled 50 games to be played before the season even started. The first four weeks would be conducted in Havana, then they would work their way north and west, finishing up in Houston and Ft. Worth. After they returned to the mainland from Cuba, the team would be divided into A and B squads at their Florida base in Clearwater on April 1.

The players and others all assembled at the airport in Miami for the flight to Havana. It took several planes and upon arrival in Cuba they were greeted by a very enthusiastic crowd standing and cheering under a huge banner which read: "Bienvenido el Club Brooklyn."

Cabs were provided for the whole entourage. A brass band marched in front of them and led the entire procession through the narrow streets of Havana to the Prado and on to the Palace. There, aides of President Fulgencio Batista gave them their official welcome and they proceeded on to their headquarters at the Hotel Nacional.

One of the great characters of baseball lore was the inimitable Van Lingle Mungo. He was the only survivor from the wild Dodger team of 1931 which had also visited Havana and Van's memory of watering holes in the Cuban capital was extensive. Because of several altercations involving the bottle in St. Louis and Pittsburgh during the 1940 season, Van had taken the pledge and, surprisingly, had been a master of decorum in his hometown of Pageland, South Carolina over the winter. But, tempted by the nightlife of this boisterous Latin city, his great resolve crumbled.

The Cleveland Indians were scheduled to play a weekend series with the Dodgers in Havana and the new phenom of the American League, Bob Feller, was ticketed to be the starting pitcher for the Sunday game. Mungo had come to spring training in great shape and Durocher was impressed. He told Van a week ahead of time that he would be facing Feller on the Sabbath. What a matchup!

Durocher was so impressed that he gave Mungo permission to stay out late both Wednesday and Thursday. But, when he asked for Friday night as well, Leo became suspicious. He waited up for him and, sure enough, about 2:00 A.M. the prodigal pitcher came in the hotel lobby, weaving like a blimp.

The following morning Leo came down hard on him and warned him against any more of the same. Van was full of promises, but privately Durocher was unconvinced. That night Mungo was nowhere to be found and the next morning he missed the team bus for the ball park. When he finally showed up Durocher sent him back to his hotel.

Shortly before game time Durocher stepped out of the clubhouse to be confronted by a storming MacPhail.

"Durocher," he screamed, "I just saw Mungo and he's dead drunk and arguing with a taxi driver!"

Leo told Larry that he knew about it and had fined Mungo $400. MacPhail said that was not nearly enough, raised it to $1000 and assigned him to Macon, Georgia, where their AAA farm club, Montreal, was training.

The game itself was very one-sided, with the Dodgers knocking out Feller early and going on to victory.

Durocher thought he had seen the last of Mungo since he had been suspended and shipped off to Miami and on up to Macon. But, that was not to be. Mungo missed the boat and Monday morning Leo was rudely awakened by the hotel manager. He said that a man was yelling and pounding on Mungo's door, waving a huge knife and threatening to kill him. He turned out to be the male half of the flamenco dancing act performing as the headliners of the hotel floor show.

In the confusion, and with some help, they were able to get Van out through the window and hidden in the basement behind some potato sacks before half the police force of Havana descended on them, all shouting "Mungo." Somehow, one of the enterprising members of the office staff got him down to the docks the next afternoon. He hid in a utility room until a flying boat was just about to leave and then snuck aboard before the cops could nab him.

The team moved on to Clearwater to complete spring training and the rest of the exhibition games in the South and Southwest. Optimism was high. Even MacPhail who had always been very cautious in predicting how high his teams would finish, threw caution to the wind and claimed the Dodgers would win the pennant going away.

During the last several weeks Waner had been playing right field on the A Team, with Dixie Walker, "The Peepul's Cherce," riding the bench. This did not go unnoticed in Brooklyn, some of whose fans responded by sending a wire containing some 5,000 signatures demanding Walker's reinsertion in the lineup. However, MacPhail was not going to be told how to run his ball club and Waner continued in right.

Finally, the season opened and the fans were euphoric—that is until the first game and series were played. The Dodgers opened at home against the hated Giants and Ebbets Field was jammed. To the consternation of the faithful, the Dodgers not only lost the opener, but the entire three-game series. Euphoria vanished and suddenly their heroes became "dem bums."

Then, things started to turn around and their heroes started winning, taking 15 out of the next 17 games. Fortune was smiling again. However, there were a few dark clouds on the horizon. Age was beginning to tell on Waner and, finally, he was relegated to a pinch-hitting role and later cut entirely. It has been noted that, for some reason, Walker was not the favorite with MacPhail that he was with the fans, but Larry finally had to face it and Dixie was back in right field.

Then, only three-fourths of the infield was playing up to pennant-winning standards. Camilli, Reese and Lavagetto looked like all-stars, but Pete Coscarart was not performing in the same fashion.

Shortly after the season was under way MacPhail and Durocher got their heads together and tried to figure out what to do about second base.

Leo said, "Larry, if you could get me Billy Herman we would be a cinch! He has the experience and would be the spark we need in working with Peewee around second base."

Sometimes timing is everything.

For many years Billy Herman of the Chicago Cubs had been the best second-baseman in the National League—always on the All-Star team. He was a real leader and, in the opinion of many baseball experts, had all the qualifications to become an excellent manager.

At the end of the previous season Gabby Hartnett was fired as manager of the Cubs. Now, it did not necessarily follow that the expertise Phil Wrigley showed in the chewing gum business was transferable to the world of baseball. He also decided to change general managers, coming up with the surprising appointment of an ex-newspaper reporter, Jim Gallagher. Then, instead of following through with the obvious naming of Herman as the new field manager, Gallagher hired Jimmy Wilson. Herman had to be unhappy and Gallagher had to be uncomfortable.

Two weeks into the season the Cubs were in town to play the Dodgers and the general manager had made the trip with them. Gallagher and Wilson were staying at the Hotel Commodore and MacPhail arranged a meeting with them in Gallagher's room. They had dinner sent up and pretty soon the scotch was flowing freely.

The transfer of Herman to the Dodgers was agreed upon fairly early and then the haggling started in earnest. As the hours passed and the drinks went down, the details of which players and how much money Chicago was to receive for Herman got more and more confused. Gallagher was the host and kept pouring the drinks for MacPhail. What he didn't realize was that, painful as it was for Larry, he was pouring his scotches down the toilet and wash basin.

About three o'clock in the morning Wilson dropped out and went to bed, but the other two kept at it and a little after 5:00 A.M. they agreed on the trade. Larry couldn't believe his good fortune, and fearful that the morning would erase the details, had the deal scribbled out on an envelope which both he and Gallagher signed.

The Cubs got $65,000 and two players—Johnny Hudson, a third-string shortstop who had a batting average of .217 the previous year, and a young outfielder, Charley Gilbert, who never did make it.

As soon as he left the room, MacPhail located Herman, got him out of bed and the two of them called Durocher's room. Larry told Billy to get on the phone.

"Hello, Leo. This is your new second-baseman talking. I'll see you out at the ball park this afternoon if your boss will let us both get back to sleep."

That's all they needed, or so they thought. Herman really picked up the team. He was like the Herman of old and fit into the Dodger infield as if he had been born there. With the Cubs he had been hitting only .194, but in the first 20 games with the Dodgers he hit at a .386 clip. He was the ideal number 2 hitter, always seeming to be able to hit behind the runner. So that is where Durocher put him, with Reiser (now a regular in right field) third and Camilli fourth.

Brooklyn won nine games in a row but still couldn't put much distance between them and the Cardinals. St. Louis won 11 straight. However, in a big series between the two teams at Ebbets Field the Dodgers took three out of four.

Then they hit a losing streak and MacPhail almost blew a gasket. The pitching started to fall apart. Wyatt was knocked out in 12 straight games and Durocher had begun to use Higbe in the bull pen because he, too, couldn't get past the first few innings.

Every day was either jubilation or chaos, depending on whether they won or lost. MacPhail could not sit still and was constantly trying to get the right mixture of experience and youthful talent, mostly the former.

One of the best moves he made in mid-season was the acquisition of pitcher Johnny Allen who had been waived by the St. Louis Browns. Allen was meaner than a collier's whelp. He had a terrible temper and eventually wore out his welcome anywhere he went in the American League, having gone from the Yankees to Cleveland and then to the Browns.

It was said that Allen would throw at his grandmother's head if she came in to pinch hit against him. He allowed as how that wasn't true, but that he might brush her back a bit just to keep her loose.

While with the Indians he even caused a new rule to be added to the books. He had cut the sleeve of his sweatshirt to ribbons so that, when he pitched, the ball would come out of a fluttering background. But, he also had set a major league record for winning percentage while with Cleveland, 15-1. So, although he was 36, he could still pitch and Larry hoped he could help out, at least here and there.

Certainly without meaning to, the Cubs seemed to find ways to help out. On August 20 they asked for waivers on Larry French and MacPhail claimed the veteran southpaw.

Larry also recognized another opportunity to help bolster his outfield and pinch hitting corps. Augie Galan had been a fine outfielder for the Wrigleys from 1934 until he broke his knee slamming into the wall at Shibe Park in Philadelphia in late July, 1940. In spring training the Cubs became unconvinced of Galan's ability to return to regular duty and released him to their farm club in Los Angeles. Augie refused to report. He went home, but continued to keep himself in shape. So, MacPhail brought him to Brooklyn and he was another shot of adrenalin.

The season moved into August and the race between the Dodgers and Cardinals was as tight as a race could be. Back and forth. Back and forth. As each day passed, the Flatbush faithful became more and more absorbed and delirious—nothing mattered but how "dem bums" did that day. Red Barber's play-by-play was on every radio in town and pretty soon the whole country was caught up in the excitement.

Could the Dodgers pull it off after 21 years? It seemed
everyone was pulling for them.

When the Dodgers were home, every day at Ebbets Field
was opening day. Among the fans, four of the regulars formed
an inspiring musical group dubbed the Sym-Phony Band
which roamed the park with everybody cheering them on and
following them off the field snake dancing after a victory.

In the center-field bleachers an institution was born—Hilda
(The Bell) Chester. For years she had sat out there ringing her
bell in encouragement to the Dodger players all through the
game. She became a symbol of the Dodger fan. Her picture
began appearing on the sports pages. She was even offered a
regular seat behind the Dodger dugout, but scornfully dis-
dained it, preferring to stay in the bleachers with her own kind
of "peepul."

Caught up in the excitement, Dan Parker, sports editor of
the *Daily Mirror*, composed a poem which was later set to
music and became the marching anthem of the Brooklyn fans:

Murgatroyd Darcy, a broad from Canarsie
Went 'round with a fellow named Rodge.
At dancing a rumba or jitterbug numbah
You couldn't beat Rodge—'twas his dodge.
The pair danced together throughout the cold weather
But when the trees blossomed again
Miss Murgatroyd Darcy, the Belle of Canarsie
To Rodgers would sing this refrain:

Leave us go root for the Dodgers, Rodgers,
They're playing ball under lights.
Leave us cut out all the juke jernts, Rodgers,
Where we've been wastin' our nights.
Dancin' the shag or the rumba is silly
When we can be rooting for Adolf Camilli,
So leave us go root for the Dodgers, Rodgers,
Them Dodgers is my gallant knights.

The bars all over town—the Ball Field Tavern, Lefferts Bar,
Flynn's, etc.—all did a thriving business whether the Dodgers
were in town or not because they all had the tavern radios
turned to Red Barber's play-by-play.

One enterprising saloonkeeper, Tony Grimeli, thought up the ultimate promotion. Anyone who would plunk down three bucks before the game could drink all the beer he could hold, be bussed to Ebbets Field where he was given a reserved seat behind first base, be bussed back after the game, and then could resume drinking all the beer he could handle till closing time. His saloon would hold only 60 people and he had a waiting list of 241. He was asked how he could make money that way.

"Only the beer is free. When those fans get back after the game and get to arguing, they switch to whisky," he explained.

Getting back to the pennant race, the Dodgers were preparing for their final western swing. They had just concluded a three-game sweep of their cross-town rivals, the Giants, while the Reds had taken two out of three from the Cardinals. This increased their lead over St. Louis to three full games, but before they faced them the Dodgers had to play the Cubs in Chicago. The first game was rained out so they had to play a doubleheader the next day. Disaster! Not only did the Cubs win both games, but the Cards swept a twin-bill from the Phils, and the lead shrank to a single game.

The stage was now set for the crucial series.

In June of '37, the summer before Larry took over the team, the Dodgers traded Tom Baker, a rookie pitcher who never fulfilled his early promise, for the gnarled veteran, Fred Fitzsimmons of the Giants, a trade which MacPhail later heartily approved.

Fat Freddy was a knuckleball pitcher who had a great career with the Giants, having won 170 games in 12 years, but most people thought he was washed up when the Dodgers acquired him. In 1939 he had won 12 games for the Dodgers, but he needed more and more time between starts because his pitching arm had shriveled up so much. Even during a game the crooked arm would pull up on him so that he would have to bend at the knees to pick up the resin bag.

In 1940, at the age of 39, he had established a phenomenal record of 16-2, but in spring training it looked as if the end of the line had come and he joined the coaching staff to help

116 • The Roaring Redhead

out the young pitchers. When the pitching fell apart Fitz was reactivated and proceeded to win his first five games before some shoddy fielding did him in in game six.

Freddy was a great competitor and, once on the mound, his personality changed from that of a very pleasant man to a snarling bull, similar to the transformation of some drivers when they get behind the wheel in traffic. Durocher wanted him to open the series in St. Louis and had given him 11 days rest to get ready.

The Cards had their ace, Ernie White, set to face them. White had beaten MacPhail's team four straight times so this one had all the dramatic buildup of a championship game.

There had been a number of rhubarbs, not only between the two teams, but also on some questionable calls by the normally excellent umpire behind the plate, Al Barlick. At any rate, the Dodgers took the field in the last of the eighth with the score tied. The bases were loaded with two outs and "Big Jawn" Mize coming to bat. Remember the old doggerel?:

I do not like thee, Dr. Fell.
The reason why I cannot tell.
But, this I know and know full well.
I do not like thee, Dr. Fell.

Well, that's the way Freddy Fitzsimmons felt about Johnny Mize, and no one ever knew why, including Mize. His favorite nickname for him was "Tomato Face." Hugh Casey was ready in the bull pen, but Leo didn't dare take Fitz out knowing how he felt about Mize. Fitz was the snarling bull out on the mound. First, he glared at Mize and then came in to get the ball from his catcher, Mickey Owen, and told Big Jawn:

"You'd better duck 'cause this ball is going right at your head!"

True to his word, Freddy's first pitch knocked the big slugger to the ground. The next pitch was a knuckleball right down the chute. One and one.

Once again, Fitzsimmons came in to get the ball and snarled at Mize:

"Here it comes again, Tomato Face."

Mize hit the dirt again. Two and one. Durocher came out

to the mound on the double to try to calm him down and warn him about the possibility of blowing the game with a wild pitch, passed ball or hit batsman, but Fitz didn't even seem to hear him. And, Leo noticed his arm was almost out of sight up his sleeve.

The fourth pitch was in the same location as the second one and, again, Mize took it for strike two.

No one thought he would do it again. That is, nobody but Fat Freddy. Mize wouldn't give any response or reaction to Fritz's curses, but again he came in to get the ball from Owen.

"You'd better be quick this time, Tomato Face."

Unbelievably the next pitch was aimed right at his head again and Mize went sprawling. So, now, with the bases jammed, two outs and the count three and two on one of the greatest sluggers in the game Fitszimmons came in again to get the ball. This time he told Mize:

"It's coming right down the middle and you'll just stand there looking at it."

He went back to the mound, scratching and turning around. Freddy had a habit of grunting every time he threw the fast ball and, sure enough, he let forth with a loud grunt as the ball headed for the plate. Naturally, Mize was expecting the fast ball but in came a slow, slow curve. Mize had started to swing, then held up and, by the time he readjusted his swing, the ball was in Owen's glove. It had come right down the middle for strike three!

The Dodgers got a run for him in the top of the 11th and Casey came in to close it out. But Fitzsimmons had pitched 10 great innings of pressure baseball and the Dodgers went two up.

The next day Howie Pollet outpitched Curt Davis and the series was evened up.

The rubber game was a classic. Whitlow Wyatt against Mort Cooper. It was a great game and the type the purists love. The Dodgers won, 1-0, on back-to-back doubles by Billy Herman and Dixie Walker.

The next series was in Cincinnati and, although the Dodgers won the first game, the Cardinals won a doubleheader and the lead was down to a game and a half. This time it was

Allen's turn for the heroics. For the year of 1941 his acquisition was one of the greatest of MacPhail's coups.

The most noticeable difference between Allen and Fitzsimmons was their disposition off the field. Fitz was normally an affable fellow. It was only when he grabbed the ball and went to the mound that he became irascible. Johnny Allen was always that way.

Ever since MacPhail had picked him up from the Browns, Allen had pitched well and had fit right into the rotation. This day his opposing pitcher was the great Paul Derringer, the man for whom the Reds had traded Durocher to the Cardinals. The first inning set the tone of the game.

Dixie Walker seldom argued with the umpires but, for some reason, got into a disagreement with Larry Goetz before he even got into the batter's box and Goetz directed Derringer to start pitching. Walker had one strike against him before he got the bat in his hands.

At the start of the last half of the first, Allen told Billy Werber the first pitch would knock him down. It did, and the battle lines were drawn. And what a game it was!

Allen pitched his heart out. He allowed one hit in the first nine innings, but he started tiring about the eighth. Durocher kept telling him that his teammates would get him a run, but the game went on through the 10th, then the 11th, the 12th, the 13th. It was one of those steaming hot days in Cincinnati and Allen was drooping more and more. Finally, he asked his manager:

"When, Leo, when?"

The Dodgers leadoff man in the top of the 17th inning was Pete Reiser. Derringer had been pitching him inside all day and getting him out. So this time, at the last split-second, Pete moved back in the box and laid into a fastball. It went out of the park over 400 feet away—the first run of the ball game.

Now, in those days it was illegal to turn on the lights during a game. If the game were called on account of darkness the score would revert to what it had been at the end of the 16th—0-0. So, the Reds started delaying the game as long as they could. First, a pop fly fell to the ground right in front of Werber. Then, routine grounders would somehow get through the infield. The Dodgers scored four more runs before their half of the inning ended.

Durocher put Hugh Casey in to pitch the last of the 17th and, in his haste to finish the game, what did he do but walk the bases full! Leo was almost a basket case. Finally, Goetz warned McKechnie, the Cincinnati manager, that they were going to finish the game if they had to play in total darkness! Somehow they finished with a groundball to Reese who stepped on second for the force and the Dodgers had won another pressure-packed game.

After this series someone asked MacPhail if he was happy he had not taken the western trip with the team—wouldn't he have just blown a gasket?

"No", he bellowed, "all I did was kick a $300 radio to pieces!"

After two more tough series in Pittsburgh and Philadelphia they moved up to Boston with a game and a half lead again. It was a two-game series and the Braves wanted to beat the Dodgers in the worst way. In fact, they were probably too tense. In the first game, Dixie Walker hit a triple with the bases loaded in the eighth inning and that won the game.

The second game was played on September 25 which proved to be the day they had been waiting for. Wyatt pitched a real gem—a four-hit shutout—and Brooklyn won, 6-0. They had been following the score of the Cardinal game inning by inning and, when St. Louis lost, the Dodgers had won their first pennant in 21 years!

What followed was the wild victory train ride back to the Big Apple from Boston—through the cities of Connecticut to the cheering throng of 30,000 at Grand Central Station in New York City.

It also brings to mind again the never-to-be-forgotten vision of the shocked visage of the roaring redhead, mouth agape in disbelief, standing at the 125th Street Station as the train raced by and the umpteenth firing of Durocher at the New Yorker Hotel which followed.

On the next day, the 26th, all was forgotten and Larry and Leo put their heads together to lay plans on how to upset the Yankees in the Series.

September 29 was declared Dodger Day by the borough

president, John Cashmore. They hadn't seen anything like it since the armistice after World War I. Sixty thousand people marched in the parade with a long column of open touring cars carrying the players. Who were riding in the lead car, dressed in all their sartorial elegance but MacPhail and Durocher, basking in the glow of the festivities? It was a day to remember.

When approaching a World Series, one of the perennial discussions revolves around whether a team that has had an easy pennant race without the pressure of a close finish or playoff is better prepared for the Series than a team that has had to claw its way through every game in September and has finally won out in the end. Does the latter team have the advantage of the momentum that has carried them through the race, or the disadvantage of the letdown that occurs after the pressure of the bone-tiring race just concluded? It is a question for which there is no pat answer.

The Dodgers had had a tough race all the way, had won 100 games and their first pennant in 21 years. The Yankees, on the other hand, took their participation in the fall classic pretty much as a matter of course, and methodically prepared for the Series which opened on October 1. As it turned out, the outcome of the entire Series hinged on two breaks, one each in the third and fourth games.

Jam-packed Yankee Stadium had almost as many Dodgers fans for the opening game as Yankee rooters. Hilda Chester was there with her cowbell along with the four-piece Sym-Phony band. MacPhail's and Durocher's plans called for a few surprises. Wyatt and Higbe had each won 22 games and it seemed logical that they would start the first two games. However, their plans called for starting Curt Davis in the first game and saving Wyatt for the second.

Joe McCarthy, the Yankee manager, countered by starting his ace, Red Ruffing, in the opener and it was a fine pitching duel. Joe Gordon, who was to have a great Series, hit a home run in the second and, in the fourth, King Kong Keller walked and scored from first on a Bill Dickey double.

The Dodgers offset one of those runs in the fifth when Peewee Reese singled for the first hit off Ruffing and scored on a triple by Owen. Each team later scored one run and the final was a 3-2 win for the pinstripers.

Wyatt opposed Spud Chandler in the second game and, again, it was a 3-2 score, but this time the Dodgers came out ahead. The Yankees scored single runs in the second and third innings, but the Dodgers tied it up in the fifth. Camilli walked, Medwick doubled and Lavagetto walked, loading the bases. Reese drove in Camilli on an infield out and Medwick scored on an Owen single. In the sixth the Dodgers picked up the last run of the game when Camilli brought Walker in from third on a single off Fireman Johnny Murphy. The winning run was unearned because of a throwing error by Gordon but now the momentum had swung over to Brooklyn.

The Dodger clubhouse was jubilant! They were now no worse than even after two games at Yankee Stadium and were moving to the familiar surroundings of Ebbets Field. They had everything going for them and it was just a matter of finishing off the Bronx Bombers in the next three games. But, it was not to be, and the first of the two tough breaks happened the next day.

The third game saw another surprising starter for the Dodgers, Freddy Fitzsimmons. At that time he was the oldest pitcher ever to start a World Series game and he pitched his heart out. The Yankees gave their young southpaw, Marius Russo, the chance to face the Dodgers and it was a double shutout going into the seventh inning. Then fate stepped in.

With two outs in the top of the inning, Russo hit a line drive back to the pitcher and the ball hit Fitzsimmons on the kneecap bouncing up in the air to Reese for the third out. But, they had to carry Fitz off the field, cursing with pain and frustration.

Hugh Casey came in to start the eighth and, after retiring the first batter, was touched for two runs on consecutive singles by Red Rolfe, Tommy Henrich, Joe DiMaggio and Keller. Larry French came in to put out the fire, forcing Dickey to hit into a double play, but it was too late. The Dodgers did score one run in their half of the inning on Dixie Walker's first hit of the Series, a double, and Reese's run-scoring single, but the game finished in a 2-1 Yankee victory.

The fourth game was historic—the never-to-be-forgotten

dropped third strike by Mickey Owen—and really was the last gasp for the Dodgers. They literally had the game won and the Series tied at two games apiece when, incredibly, the Yankees were given one last chance in the ninth inning and, typically, took advantage of it.

It was Kirby Higbe against Atley Donald in game four, but Higbe was gone early, having given up one run in the first and two more in the fourth before French came in to relieve him and retire the side.

Things looked pretty dark for the home team but they made things happen in the bottom of the fourth. Suddenly, Donald couldn't find the plate and walked the first two batters, Owen and Coscarart, who was filling in for Billy Herman, out with a pulled muscle. Wasdell came in as a pinch-hitter for French and promptly doubled to right and both runners scored. Then, in the fifth inning, Walker doubled and Reiser hit a towering home run. The score was now 4-3, Dodgers, and the stands went wild.

The next three innings were scoreless with Casey shutting down the Yankees in fine fashion. Top of the ninth. Three more outs and the Series would be tied. Sturm, the first Yankee batter, hit an easy roller to Coscarart. One out. Rolfe then topped a come-backer to Casey who threw him out. Two outs. One more to go!

Henrich at bat. The fans sensed the end and were cheering with every pitch. Casey took extra time and pitched very carefully. Finally, the count went to three and two. One more strike and it was over. Casey reared back for something extra and threw a beautiful curve that cut the corner of the plate. Henrich swung and missed and the umpire yelled, "Strike three." The game was over—except for one small thing. Somehow the ball got by Owen and rolled just far enough away that Henrich, racing at top speed, beat the catcher's throw to first.

Everyone was stunned—the crowd, the Dodgers, Durocher, Casey. Rather than calling time to relax and regroup, they plodded on as if in a trance. But not the Yankees. They saw a flicker of light at the end of the tunnel. A man on first and the heart of the batting order coming up. First, DiMaggio, who quickly singled to right. Then up came Keller. With two strikes on him, he hit a drive that bounced off the right-field wall for a double. With two outs both runners were off with the hit and scored easily. The American Leaguers were now up by a run, but it was still not over.

Uncharacteristically, Durocher froze. He made no move to replace Casey who suddenly went wild and walked Dickey. Gordon promptly doubled and both Keller and Dickey scored. It was now 7-4 and that is the way it ended. Reese, Walker and Reiser went out one, two, three in the bottom of the ninth and, instead of the Series being tied at two games apiece, the Yankees were up three games to one.

In the clubhouse after the game, there was gloom and doom in every corner. MacPhail entered and tried to raise the spirits of the ballplayers. He went looking for Mickey Owen and found him trying to forget that dropped third strike under the full force of the water streaming out of the big showerhead in the shower room. Larry walked right in with all his clothes on and put his arm around the big catcher. With half the team looking on he said:

"Sure, this was a tough loss. A real tough loss. But it's not over yet. C'mon, let's go get 'em tomorrow."

But the heart had gone out of the Dodgers and the fifth and last game was strictly an anticlimax. Wyatt pitched a good game, but the Dodgers didn't put up much fight and Ernie Bonham beat them, 3-1.

It had been a great season. Brooklyn had drawn 1,200,000 fans into smallish Ebbets Field and another one million on the road. Now, the cry of "We'll get 'em next year" referred not just to the pennant but also the World Series.

10

Baseball and the War Effort

Could the finely tuned machine repeat? Larry had made a number of moves during his four years at the helm through trades and other means, including the acquisition of veteran ballplayers released by ball clubs building with youth. The sportswriters and the entire populace of Brooklyn thought they were a cinch to repeat. Was complacency starting to creep in?

There was one other external situation that was to have an increasing effect on the plans for '42—the war clouds over Europe and the Pacific. Pearl Harbor and December 7 were still almost two months away, but several ballplayers had already been taken from other clubs and the younger men on the Dodgers—Peewee Reese, Pete Reiser and others—were vulnerable to the draft.

First, Mungo, who hadn't contributed much during the season, had worn out his welcome and MacPhail released him to Montreal. Then, Larry picked up a couple of young pitchers— Ed Head and Max Macon. More patching and filling. MacPhail went back to his friend, Gerry Nugent, and picked up a journeyman outfielder, Johnny Rizzo, who had been making the rounds of the National League, having been with both the Reds and Pirates before the Phillies.

He had several other players in mind, including Johnny Mize. However, he lost Mize to the Giants, which was probably just as well since his acquisition would certainly have complicated things around first base with Dolf Camilli having had such a banner year.

Actually, although it was ridiculed by Stoneham and the Giants as sour grapes, MacPhail had called off the trade at the last minute. He and John McDonald had flown to Chicago to close the deal with Branch Rickey on December 7, 1941. As they heard the shocking news come over the wire that the Japanese had bombed Pearl Harbor, Larry lost interest and cancelled the trade.

He then began to plan on adjusting his team for '42 with an eye on who would be available to play all or most of the season and who was likely to be called for military service.

He then went after two other players, both of whom he landed. One, however, was Don Padgett from the Cardinals, a versatile hitter who could play first base, the outfield and also catch. Unfortunately, Uncle Sam stepped in and, before he could even don a Dodger uniform, he enlisted in the Navy.

The other, Floyd (Arky) Vaughn, the veteran infielder of the Pirates, proved to be a very valuable addition. It was a four-for-one trade that included Babe Phelps, a sulking catcher who had been suspended early in '41 for refusing to travel by air or even water to Cuba for the exhibition games there and had sat out the season at his home in Odenton, Maryland. The other three were Luke Hamlin, Pete Coscarart and Jimmy Wasdell. The wisdom of the trade was borne out when, even before the season started, MacPhail received a wire from Cookie Lavagetto telling him that he had just enlisted in the Navy.

An event occurred during the winter that had a tremendous effect on baseball's relationship with other segments of society and the sport's contribution to the overall war effort. Through a letter to Clark Griffith, President Franklin D. Roosevelt had given the "green light" to baseball and expressed his own desire that baseball continue during the war for morale purposes. However, none of the owners or others involved seemed to know quite how best to proceed and contribute.

The annual dinner of the New York Chapter of the Baseball Writers' Association was scheduled for February 1, 1942 at the Commodore Hotel. The early part of the evening was quite routine until Larry MacPhail got up to speak. Soon, not only his deep voice but also the content of what he had to say, quieted the crowd:

Before the 7th of last December, destructive criticism, vicious propaganda, mistakes and bungling, half-hearted efforts, and a complete lack of unity all but sabotaged the defense program.

That was before Pearl Harbor.

In the last fifty days mistakes are being remedied, labor and industry coordinated, the appeasers have crawled into their holes, criticism is constructive, the country UNITED.

What was responsible for the change overnight?

The driving force of an aroused public opinion.

As a result we are in the beginning of an all-out effort to win this war. Everything else is secondary.

That is what the Commissioner recognized when he wrote that letter to the Commander-in-Chief.

It was an all-out straight shooting question the Commissioner asked. It was an all-out straight shooting answer the President sent back.

There may be some who will interpret the President's "green light" signal to go ahead, as exempting baseball from its duties and obligations in the greatest crisis our country has ever faced.

I don't think so. But, if there are, I believe they will be in the minority when the two major leagues meet tomorrow.

We can't sit back on the cushions—now that the light has turned green—thank God for the President—and adopt any "Business as Usual" slogan for baseball.

There is no business in this country so completely dependent on the good will of the public as baseball.

We have one severe critic. . . . He is that fellow who digs down in his jeans and clicks the turnstiles in the 300 communities where professional baseball hopes to carry on in 1942.

He expects every individual in baseball to do his bit—whatever that may be—in living up to the obligations of citizenship. He expects us to do something more than provide recreation for 20 million workers. He expects us to work out a definite program of unselfish cooperation with agencies of government needing help.

If we keep the faith, he will agree with the President that baseball has its place in an all-out effort to win this war.

In that event, we need have no fear of the coming season.

We shall survive!

We have some problems and we should face them honestly and frankly.

The most important, in my opinion, is the necessity of understanding and agreement by baseball—its players, the press, and, especially, the public—of the obligation or duty of the player for service with the Armed Forces.

I've come across some pretty brutal statements which have appeared in various parts of the country in recent weeks. Here's one:

"Baseball owners and players are notoriously selfish. Baseball, as a group, had a poor record in World War I, and a poorer one so far in this one."

Here's another:

"Not a single player on the roster of the Dodgers, Yankees or Giants has volunteered to serve his country."

And, another:

"Professional sport has no place in the program. Baseball players, in particular, should volunteer."

These things have been said before. They will be said again. Constructive criticism does us all good. Unfair criticism should be answered.

Otherwise, you'll have leather-lunged customers hollering at some fellow who strikes out with the bases full, "Why don't you throw that bat away and borrow a rifle?"

No apologies are necessary for baseball's record in World War I.

Fifteen of the present day executives in the major leagues saw service in World War I. The list includes Phil Wrigley, Bob Lewis and Earl Nelson of the Cubs—Eddie Collins, Herb Pennock and Phil Troy of the Red Sox—Warren Giles and Tom Conroy of the Reds—Bill Benswanger, Branch Rickey, Gerry Nugent, Duffy Lewis, and others.

Of the managers and coaches still in the majors today, Jimmy Dykes, Casey Stengel, Del Baker, Muddy Ruel, Ray Blades, Bill Killefer, George Kelley, Hank Gowdy and others served with the army and navy.

In the spring of 1918 there were 264 players on the rosters of American League clubs. Of them, 144 saw service in the uniform of their country—and, a considerable percentage were overseas.

Considerably more than half of all the National League players—64% to be explicit—saw actual service with the army or navy; and, 59% of them volunteered before the conscription was put into effect.

Let any business or profession point to a finer record. It can't be done.

And, how about this war—and the suggestion that players ought to volunteer?

Baseball doesn't need to duck that question either. A little straight thinking is all that's needed.

A prominent baseball executive was quoted as saying the other day, that a player must be prepared to justify his deferment at the bar of public opinion.

I can't agree.

The decision whether any individual, including a baseball player, should serve with the Armed Forces—or carry on with his duties and obligations in civilian life—is not a decision for the individual at all, but a decision for the proper agency of the government.

The player's only obligation is to submit the facts—and accept the government's decision.

A baseball player is entitled to the same consideration as any other individual engaged in civilian activities—no more, no less. And instances where local draft boards have apparently discriminated against an individual simply because he was a professional athlete are to be regretted in a democracy.

If deferred by proper governmental authority, no baseball player is called on to offer any apology at the bar of public opinion (or to the standees at any other bar).

The criticisms directed against New York and Brooklyn players for not volunteering were brought, with Mayor LaGuardia's cooperation, to the attention of the Director of Selective Service in Washington—General Lewis B. Hershey.

I have a letter from General Hershey in reply. It is clear and illuminating and should clear up a lot of confusion. I'm glad to be able to read it:

"Dear Mr. MacPhail:

"You have requested my thoughts with respect to the matter of volunteering.

"In World War I all recruiting was finally stopped in August 1918. I believe that we should benefit from that experience and stop all recruiting at the earliest date.

"The entry of the United States into the war has

brought our people to a high emotional pitch. Men in all walks of life are trying to make an individual decision as to their part in the solution of the nation's problem. Many have reached that decision and the recruiting stations of the Armed Forces are crowded with men seeking to enlist. In many instances they are men who should stay in war production and civilian activities. Such enlistments tend to unduly disrupt essential activities. An appropriate agency of government should decide where the individual may best serve his nation in total war rather than to leave that decision to the individual who is not a free agent in the matter of such choice.

"The full utilization of our manpower in our present war effort requires that the selection of men for the Armed Forces or their deferment be determined by a systematic and orderly method of selection."

Sincerely Yours,
L.B. HERSHEY

The Selective Service System is selecting the men the government wants from the ranks of baseball. When this war is over, baseball will have made the same kind of a record it established in World War I.

Just a word or two about the PROGRAM.

On Christmas morning many of us received a telegram from the Commissioner of Baseball. Mine read something like this:

"IN THIS BLESSED SEASON, DON'T FORGET OUR MAIN JOB IS TO LICK HELL OUT OF THEM."

That sentiment could well be the theme song of our meetings.

In the last war the Ball and Bat Fund, conceived and managed by Clark Griffith, raised a grand total of nearly $200,000 to provide equipment for boys in our uniform wherever they were stationed. That is concrete evidence of what can be accomplished by one individual with energy and enthusiasm for a good cause.

The day war was declared the major leagues and the baseball writers appropriated $5,000 and borrowed another 20 grand from the Commissioner to start a similar fund. Equipment is already being distributed. The receipts from the All-Star game will go to this fund.

But, Mr. Griffith and Mr. Frick, who have been working on this with the Commissioner, tell me we will have
to have at least $150,000 this year, and, if the war lasts
through 1943, we will need close to half a million dollars.

All major league clubs give three days from their schedule for the All-Star game. Why not play two games instead
of one?

The first All-Star game might be played on Monday in
New York. Then an All-Star team of American and National League players might play an All-Star service team
in Cleveland, Detroit or Chicago on Wednesday. Such a program, if it can be worked out, might raise a quarter of a
million dollars for the Ball and Bat Fund.

We've cancelled a game with the consent of the Atlanta
Club to play Camp Wheeler on April 3rd with all proceeds
to go to their Athletic Fund. I understand other clubs in
both leagues are making similar arrangements.

Just one other suggestion in conclusion (you can't be arrested for making suggestions).

Mr. Connie Mack tells me the American League raised
over $400,000 for the Red Cross in the last war. This one
looks like it may be longer and tougher.

With the approval of the War or Navy Departments
(which I believe would be forthcoming), why not take a
small part of every admission in both major leagues and
use the total fund to buy an American Flying Fortress—
the biggest four-engined bomber that can be built in America this year—and turn it over to the Army or Navy, as part
of baseball's contribution.

It would carry our compliments overseas.

In recognition of devoted service to baseball that began
right after the last war—and, which will last through
this one—this American Flying Fortress should be named
KENESAW M. LANDIS. . . .

The audience responded with great enthusiasm. The sportswriters rushed to include the suggestions Larry made in their
columns the next day and, through the enterprise of Harold
Parrott of the *Brooklyn Eagle*, the verbatim text was preserved
in their office.

Almost every suggestion made in the speech was adopted
the next day in the meetings of the two major leagues.
Methods were set up for all employees of the ball clubs to

buy war bonds and stamps on a regular basis and they all subscribed heavily.

Two All-Star games were designated. Larry's suggestion of moving the first game from its scheduled location at Ebbets Field to the greater capacity of the Polo Grounds was accepted and a second game was played in Cleveland between an all-service team and the American League team, the winner of the first game. Although the Flying Fortress was never actually purchased, the major and minor leagues raised a total of $1,294,958.67 for the Army and Navy Funds.

11

He Had a Premonition

With these plans formulated, it was back to the preparation for the 1942 season.

Spring training again started in Havana but with America now at war it was a different Havana. In fact, the whole atmosphere was different from 1941. Discipline and conditioning seemed to become less important. After all, weren't they the National League champs?

The night life in the Cuban capital seemed to take on a greater degree of urgency. Enough so that, before he returned to the mainland, Larry had hired some Havana detectives to tail the more active revelers. John McDonald's notes on these escapades did not refer to the ballplayers by name, but by their uniform number for reasons of brevity as well as secrecy.

At the Havana airport, on the day of departure, one of the United States Customs officers, in examining McDonald's briefcase, happened to pull out a report that included the peripatetic trail of No. 15 who hit several of the more prominent nightspots, including Sloppy Joe's, and met up with No. 7 and several others. The officer was sure he had stumbled on an espionage ring and it took some time for John to finally convince the officer that he was merely the traveling secretary of the Dodgers and these were his ballplayers.

There was one other development that occurred with increasing frequency and one that greatly affected the team's fortunes—gambling. What had started out as penny-ante gradually grew into high-stakes poker. The favorite game was "low ball," in which the player with the poorest poker hand won the pot.

Starting in Havana and then through the rest of spring training and the entire season, there was a poker game going on before and after almost every game.

Durocher was in on most of the games and one of his favorite pigeons was Kirby Higbe. Leo would use the fact that Higbe owed him a couple of hundred dollars as an incentive in his next pitching start, telling him that he would wipe the slate clean if Kirby would win his game.

Their Florida camp was located at Daytona Beach and late in March an event of more than romantic interest took place. Peewee Reese and Pete Reiser were very close friends and the press had dubbed them the "Gold Dust Twins." Amidst all the veterans on the ball club they stood out as the two youngsters of the team. They roomed together and were almost inseparable. Peewee had been dating his fiancée, Dottie, for some time and invited her down to Daytona for a long weekend.

Pete had met his girl, Pat, in St. Louis over the winter and the plan was that Dottie and Pat would come down together and stay with Billy and Hazel Herman. However, Hazel's brother died and the Hermans went on to the funeral. So, other accommodations had to be arranged. Peewee felt that "it would look kinda bad if we put them up at the same hotel we were staying at," so they found another one nearby.

Their older teammates always took the "Gold Dust Twins" under their wing and now, with the two young ladies in tow, Dixie and Stell Walker invited the four of them out for dinner. According to Reese, "Stell Walker was a brilliant sweetheart of a lady and Dixie liked Dottie quite a bit."

Toward the end of the evening Stell said to Peewee:

"When are you and Dottie going to get married?"

After an exchange of glances with Dottie, Peewee said they would probably get married after the season. Spring training would be the worst time.

Stell answered, "Well, I don't know about that. The war is going on and you'll probably go into the service. Something may happen and you two will never get married and that would be a shame." She didn't direct any of her conversation to Pete and Pat because they had just met in the off-season.

One thing led to another and, before the evening was over,

not only did Dottie become Mrs. Harold Reese, but Pat became Mrs. Harold Reiser.

Peewee says, "It had to be Stell, because I never would have had the courage to do that, really. Well, it was the best thing that ever happened to me!" And, to this day, Peewee says that his mother-in-law still doesn't believe that it was not planned.

Reese adds, "Pat Reiser was a Jewish girl and Pete was a very strong Catholic. I remember we had gotten to Atlanta and Pete still hadn't talked to his father and mother in St. Louis. We called Mr. Reiser and they practically disowned Pete.

"I went and got Durocher out of bed. Pete was brokenhearted and almost broke down. Leo got on the phone, talked to Mr. and Mrs. Reiser—and this was not exactly the shank of the evening, it was late—and he straightened the whole thing out. You know, Leo could talk for half an hour to a bat standing over in a corner."

But, getting back to the day after their wedding night, Peewee and Pete got together the next morning and Reese said:

"Pete, damnit, we've got to tell Mr. MacPhail about this."

So, they went over to his office and blurted out the news.

Larry was shocked and looked out the window. Then, he looked back at both of them:

"Did you see that? Did you see that thing go by there?"

Reese and Reiser, with surprise and curiosity in their voices, said:

"No, we didn't see anything. What was it?"

"That was the goddamned National League pennant," screamed Larry, "it just flew out the window!"

The balance of spring training continued without much incident except that both Herman and Camilli went up to Johns Hopkins for checkups—Herman with some trouble with his hip and Camilli with a persistent cold.

Finally, the season got under way and they were off and running. They opened against the Giants at the Polo Grounds before 42,000 people and Curt Davis beat the great Carl Hubbell.

Everything was falling into place—when the pitching was a little erratic, the hitters came through. And, when the hitters grew cold the pitchers got the job done. They claimed first place as their own and proceeded to knock off all comers, including the Cardinals, through May and June.

The players they had been worried about in the Spring were starting to pound the ball—Camilli was hot and so was Herman. Even Medwick was hitting with consistency, having amazed one and all with a string of 27 games in which he got one or more hits. They were on a roll.

It was a cocky team that challenged everybody, not only with their hitting and defense but, more and more, with the bean ball. Soon they became the scourge of the league and every team was out to get them. It seemed every manager hated Durocher and instructed his pitchers to throw at almost every batter in a Dodger uniform.

Jimmy Wilson, manager of the Cubs, had a special hatred of Leo dating back to the time they were teammates on the Cardinals in 1933. The Dodgers came to Chicago in mid-July and Kirby Higbe was facing Hi Bithorn of the Cubs. Wilson claimed that Durocher started it by ordering Higbe to throw at Bill Nicholson.

Bithorn loved the challenge and went after the Dodger batters with relish. He was doing what he thought was a good job but apparently Wilson figured Paul Erickson could throw harder and with greater accuracy so he replaced Bithorn with specific instructions to go after Medwick and Herman. However, Herman's temper was sorely tested and he responded by hitting a home run.

There was a tragic event that also occurred in July, this time in St. Louis. One of the great careers of all time in the majors was ruined or at least blunted and shortened when Pete Reiser slammed into the center-field wall.

It had been a brilliant pitcher's duel between Whit Wyatt and Mort Cooper and was a scoreless tie in the last of the 13th inning. Enos (Country) Slaughter hit a rifle shot that went over Reiser's head. Pete, going full-speed, finally caught up to the ball in dead center but, just as it fell in his glove, Pete crashed into the wall. The ball trickled out of his glove and Slaughter circled the bases for an inside-the-park home run. The Cardinals won 1-0 but, much more tragically, Reiser never seemed to fully recover.

He was helped to the clubhouse but, just as he arrived there, collapsed and was rushed to St. John's Hospital where he was examined by Dr. Robert F. Hyland, team physician of the Cardinals and also a noted surgeon. He diagnosed the injury as a brain concussion.

In the heat of the pennant race Reiser may have tried to come back too soon. Headaches and double vision persisted and Pete was in and out of the lineup for the rest of the season. Before the accident his batting average was in the high .300s and even as late as August 1, it was .353. He finished the season at .310. Even though he played a few years after the war, Reiser never regained those lofty averages of the first few years or achieved the brilliance of a career that had held so much promise.

Peewee Reese had some interesting comments on the whole subject of Reiser's career:

"If he hadn't gotten hurt and run into so many walls, Pete Reiser, in my opinion, could have been one of the all-time greats. He played hard. He played damned hard! Talk about Pete Rose hustling—Charlie Hustle—Reiser out-hustled anyone. He would hit a ball, a one-hopper to the pitcher, and he would fly down that first base line. Most people would just jog down. Every time he would just run to the outfield (at the start of the inning) and then run back (when it was over). That was just the way he played. I don't know if he totally lacked peripheral vision or what but, when that ball was hit he had just one thing in mind, catching it. They didn't have any warning tracks at the time. In fact, I am sure he is responsible for warning tracks and padding on the walls.

"He led the league in hitting his first year up. Man, he could run, he could fly, he had a great arm. He could hit with power for a guy about my size.

"When we were at spring training in '42 at Havana I can remember Mr. MacPhail having a race to see what kind of shape we were in. There was a mile track around the ball park and he made everybody, even including Hugh Casey (who couldn't run 100 yards) run around the track twice for a two-mile run.

"I can remember Mickey Owen and Charley Dressen (God

bless him). He was a coach for the Dodgers and a great horse-man. They even put it up on the wall—Pete Reiser, early speed, will not finish—and, he put odds on everyone.

"Mickey Owen started running and he got way out in front of everyone. In those days I could run all day and I said, 'Hell, this guy isn't even going to finish.'

"Now, Pete Reiser was going to get out there and get them started, get them running fast and let them get going, and then I would come on and win the thing. Well, Mickey Owen had had a bad night the night before and he was running around that track at such a pace I thought he would even vomit at times. Anyway, by gosh, when I finally started to make a move on him, we couldn't catch him, Arky Vaughn and I.

"But, MacPhail was out there watching the thing. Every once in a while he would take part in spring training.

"That was really quite a ball club. And, they couldn't have had a better man to head that ball club than MacPhail, because it was kind of a rough-and-tumble outfit with Hugh Casey and Mickey Owen, Dolf Camilli, Whitlow Wyatt, Van Lingle Mungo. Wes Ferrell was on the ball club for a while. Johnny Allen came over to pitch for us. Now, he was a guy, a wild one. And, he got those types of people, Mr. MacPhail did. But, they had the reputation of being hard drinkers—that played hard, on and off the field. I couldn't think of a better guy to run that club. He probably loved those guys."

In the same series in which the Reiser accident occurred Hugh Casey broke a finger trying to stop a Stan Musial line drive. The Dodgers lost the series, but no one seemed to be particularly bothered by it.

August came around and the hatred of the Dodgers by the rest of the league continued to grow. Brooklyn and their fans loved it. The Dodgers went up to Boston for a series with the Braves and the bean ball war continued.

Wyatt was facing Manuel Salvo and the game got under way without incident. But, in the fourth inning, after he had an 0-2 count on Max West, Whit threw a fastball high and tight. West hit the dust and the battle was joined.

Wyatt came up to bat in the fifth and Salvo decked him, just missing his head. Things really opened up in the eighth when, with Wyatt up again, Salvo hit him and Whit responded by throwing his bat at the pitcher. The dugouts emptied and a melee was avoided only because the umpiring crew took quick control.

Ford Frick also took action from the league office, fining Salvo $50 and Wyatt $75. Apparently Frick figured the bat a more lethal weapon than the ball. Also, in his attempt to get control of the situation before it got entirely out of hand, the league president issued a stern warning to all National League managers: "You will be held fully accountable for all bean ball incidents and subject to an automatic fine of $200."

MacPhail reacted in typical MacPhail fashion, figuring that Frick's letter was directed specifically at Durocher and the Dodgers, an assumption which probably deserved great credibility.

Larry called a special meeting of the players and invited the sportswriters to join them. In his booming voice he accused all the other managers in the league of starting the war and that, regardless of the $200 fine (which, he said, the club would pick up, anyway), he wanted Durocher and his pitchers to "defend" themselves against these belligerent attacks.

He went so far as to call Frick the next day insisting that it was the other clubs who had started the war. Frick told him that the number of strong complaints from the other clubs would indicate otherwise. Nothing changed and the race continued.

In addition to the bad blood between the Dodgers and the rest of the league, MacPhail was doing some feuding of his own. Dan Parker, a sportswriter for the *Mirror*, had chosen Larry as his special target. His columns dealt increasingly with the head of the Dodgers and often would supply other names for Larry's initials. Instead of Leland Stanford he would refer to him as "Lucifer Sulphurious" MacPhail.

One time Parker did so was when the story of the "five hundred dollar bills" came out. One day Larry was heading for the track and found himself a little short for the betting window. He got Bill Gibson, the mild-mannered Dodger treasurer, on the intercom and told him to meet him in the lobby with five hundred dollar bills (meaning five one-hundred dollar bills). Thinking that he was complying perfectly, Gibby hurriedly and carefully wrapped five stacks of one hundred one dollar bills, each stack with a string tightly around it to hold it together. He rushed to meet Larry and present him with the money. When MacPhail saw the five packages he flung them in the air and stomped off cursing, with Gibby left to try to gather up the scattered bills floating in the air.

Another time, when Larry had oversold small Ebbets Field for a big game, Parker referred to him as "Letemall Standup" MacPhail.

One of the many firsts attributed to Larry MacPhail occurred about this time and, more rightly, should be credited to his daughter, Marian (later Mrs. Walsh McDermott, wife of a prominent New York doctor). For a while she was living with her mother and dad in New York.

One night Larry came home shaking with anger. He had scheduled the United States Marine Corps Band to play at Ebbets Field for a big celebration. Caesar Petrillo, president of the Musician's Union, insisted that he had to hire an equal number of union musicians who would receive their full pay for not playing. Marian related:

"Dad was just furious. I could see Mr. Petrillo's point, but I could also see Dad's side. We got to talking about it and I asked him why he didn't put in an organ at Ebbets Field. I told him that it was loud, had great volume and it took only one person to play it." And he roared:

"Who the hell ever heard of an organ at a ball park?"

Marian added: "So, that's the last I ever heard of it until one time I went to Ebbets Field and you know what they were doing—installing an organ. And they got Gladys Gooding, who became an institution and was there for years."

Came mid-August and the Dodgers were still riding high— in first place and cocky as ever. However, if they had stopped to look over their shoulder, they might have seen the St. Louis Cardinals moving up on the outside.

About this time, MacPhail called another meeting in the Press Club and again invited the press to join him and the ballplayers. Larry was always great copy and the sportswriters never missed an opportunity to listen to the "big mouth." However, they couldn't imagine why he had called this meeting. The Dodgers were ahead by 8-10 games. It was already the second half of August. Weren't they a shoo-in?

As usual, MacPhail got right to the point:

"You guys are going to lose the pennant."

Just like that! No ifs, ands or buts.

Whether he did that to shake up what he thought was a lethargic team, or whether he saw some things others didn't see we may never know. But he had a premonition that even with the big lead they were destined not to repeat.

MacPhail told them they weren't hustling, that they should be twice as far ahead of the rest of the league as they were, and that they were going to blow the whole thing.

Some of the players had a tough time suppressing their laughter. Others reacted with resentment and challenged him. Dixie Walker, who was not one of the gamblers on the team, but was often a spokesman for the rest of the players, said he would bet Larry $200 he was wrong and that they would win the pennant and go on to the World Series. MacPhail refused the bet. Some of the players and sportswriters thought he just didn't want to bet against his own team, but others thought his bluff had been called.

At any rate, MacPhail's prediction became prophetic. But, as Peewee Reese pointed out:

"We didn't exactly fold. After all, we won 104 games, 54 games over .500, and still finished second."

The Cardinals played like miracle-men. Of their last 43 games they won an incredible 37. The Dodgers even won their last eight games straight and, during that period, actually lost a half-game to the streaking St. Louis team.

In reality, the confrontation MacPhail had with the players may have goaded them into playing better ball. A couple of days after the meeting the Dodgers had a doubleheader with the Giants at Ebbets Field.

The first game was a dilly, with the score tied at 2-2 after nine innings. In the top of the 10th, Johnny Mize took great pleasure in hitting one out of the park with Mel Ott on base. The Giants were now ahead, 4-2, and just had to get three more outs to win. But, it wasn't to be. With the bases loaded in the last of the 10th, Camilli smashed a grand slam and "dem bums" pulled another one out of the fire. They also won the second game, beating their old teammate, Van Lingle Mungo, who had just been brought up from the minors.

It was a triumphant train ride heading for another western trip. The players even called it the "Victory Train" and were whooping and hollering the whole way, singing and telling stories and generally celebrating what they knew was to be their inevitable pennant. Of course, the poker game was in full swing and went on into the wee hours.

Their first stop was in St. Louis for a big four-game series. Billy Southworth had planned his pitching rotation carefully and led off with Max Lanier, who always had good luck against the Dodgers. This game was no exception.

The second game was the classic confrontation between Wyatt and Mort Cooper. It lasted 14 innings, but again the surging Cardinals won out, this time 2-1. The third game was another extra-inning affair and the Dodgers dropped another one, with Johnny Beazley out-dueling Max Macon.

The Cardinals were now looking for a sweep and Southworth came back with Max Lanier. Brooklyn countered with the old man of the staff, Curt Davis, who finally pulled one chestnut out of the fire, winning 4-1.

The next stop was Chicago where they broke even and then on to Pittsburgh where they took three out of four—not bad for the first three legs of the road trip.

Their pitchers were getting a bit overworked and MacPhail, always on the lookout for help in that department, picked up the well-traveled and voluble Bobo Newsom, who joined the team in Cincinnati. Befitting his reputation, he announced to his new teammates: "Have no fear. Old Bobo's here!"

The Dodgers won the first of the two-game series and, although he started and won the second game, Newsom proved to be a more disrupting influence on the team than the saviour he fancied himself to be. His eventual 2-2 record hardly justified MacPhail's expenditure of $25,000 to pick him up for "insurance" from the Washington Senators.

Now, they were back in Ebbets Field. Except for the loss of three out of four in St. Louis, it had been a successful road trip. The only trouble was that the Cardinals just would not ease up.

One other incident hit the papers with an exact quote. As

he had done on the Cardinals, Medwick was starting to wear out his welcome on the Dodgers, and for the same reasons. His total motivation seemed to be for his own benefit, never for the team, and it became more evident to the other players with each passing day.

Durocher had been his best friend on the Cardinals and they had remained close friends at Brooklyn. As things became more tense, Leo would be brought into an increasing number of arguments between Medwick and the other ball-players. Usually Durocher would side with his old buddy, a fact that became increasingly apparent to MacPhail.

One day, while he was sitting at the mahogany bar in the Press Room, Larry began mulling over this situation while sipping a couple of brandies. Down on the field he had just observed another of the altercations between Medwick and one of the other players. The color rose in his florid face as he became more and more agitated. Several of the sports-writers were observing the scene and watched as he grabbed a piece of paper and and a lead-pencil. He scribbled out a note and sent it down posthaste to Durocher in the dugout.

Noting how mad MacPhail had appeared and wondering about the subject of his wrath, one of the writers wandered over to the bar after Larry had left. He had been bearing down so hard on the paper that the impression of his note was still discernible when the light hit the surface of the bar at the proper angle. It read:

"Leo: Medwick is a nice fellow but why let him run the club?—Larry"

Another incident illustrates the growing tension on the club as the Cardinals moved ever closer to the top.

In the late innings of one game, with the Dodgers blowing another lead, Hugh Casey came on in relief. After they had finally retired the side, the Dodgers came back to the dugout. Pete Reiser handed Durocher a note and started up to bat. When Leo read the note he was fuming. It read:

"Casey looks tired out. Better get somebody warmed up and take him out."

Leo thought, "My god! Now, even one of my players is telling me how to manage" and he immediately called Pete on the carpet. The unsuspecting Reiser disclaimed any knowledge of what was in the note and told him that it had been handed to him by Hilda Chester who was sitting in her regular seat in center field.

The final denouement of the season happened during the three-day period ending on September 13. On the 11th the Cardinals came to Ebbets Field for two games with the Dodgers still in front, but only by two games. The first game was the usual battle between Wyatt and Cooper, with the latter winning again on a three-hitter, 3-0. Lanier pitched the next day and won another close one—this time 2-1. Now they were exactly even with all the momentum riding with St. Louis.

MacPhail tried to reverse the flow of events and told the team that it was now a new season since they were all even. "Let's go out and start winning again," MacPhail urged. "It's not over yet." But somehow they all knew he was whistling in the dark.

The Reds came in for a doubleheader and proceeded to take both games from the Dodgers. The scoreboard also told the fateful news that the Cardinals had beaten the Phillies, and now Brooklyn was a game and a half out!

The accuracy of MacPhail's dire prediction in late August was now becoming a reality. The Dodgers fought on gamely but, even with a great finishing kick, they could not catch the Cardinals. It was all over except for giving congratulations to St. Louis for a fantastic winning streak.

Actually, the importance of the race began to diminish for Larry during the last few weeks. There was a much bigger battle going on and, if there was one thing Leland Stanford MacPhail loved above all else, it was a good scrap. He was 52, but he couldn't see staying out of this one.

While he was preparing to reenlist, his final days were filled with sentiment and meetings with his team. Also, with his fellow members of the board of directors of the club. There had been rumors of dissatisfaction with his performance during the last year because of his spending money too freely but this was denied by all parties concerned.

Another theory about his decision to return to active military duty revolved around the idea, demonstrably quite ac-

curate, that what really made Larry MacPhail tick was building something from scratch. He loved the challenge and would
work night and day to achieve success in the current venture.
But when the goal was achieved he would lose interest and
want to get on with the next episode in his life.

This characteristic, which manifested itself a number of
times in his life, coupled with his strong patriotic feeling, was
probably the main reason for the change in his life at this
time.

At his final press conference at his office he was asked if
he were happy to leave. With tears in his eyes, he replied:

No, the five years I have spent here in Brooklyn have
been the happiest years of my life.

It is true that I have spent a lot of money around here.
I have spent about $1,000,000 for ballplayers and, this year
alone, I spent $250,000 on repairs at the ball park. But, I
leave the Brooklyn club with $300,000 in the bank and
in a position to pay off the mortgage on it. We have paid
off $600,000 we owed the Brooklyn Trust Company, and I
have reduced the mortgage—another $600,000 item—to
$320,000. I have sold the radio rights for 1943 for $150,000.
We have drawn a paid attendance of more than a million
at home in each of the last four years . . . and the future
of the club is bright, even under wartime conditions.

Another emotional meeting was the one at which the
players headed by team captain Dolf Camilli, presented Larry
with a watch and the sentiments that they all hoped they
could get back together after the war.

MacPhail was quoted as saying:

"Last year you fellows won a pennant. This year you have
won more games than any team in the history of the Brooklyn
ball club. I don't know which was the greater achievement.
It took a miracle team to catch you . . . Around the league
I hear there are clubs that don't like some of you fellows.
Well, that's O.K. by me and it's O.K. by four million fans in
Brooklyn."

Larry's swan song was at a luncheon he gave for the sportswriters. Smiling and, with a drink in his hand, he rose and
said:

There isn't a guy in this room that I haven't had an argument with, I guess, but I like to think I am not leaving any enemies among you. And at least it hasn't been dull around here, has it? I want to thank you for the support you have given me in the past five years and to ask you to give that same support to the directors and to my successor, whoever he may be . . . Now, I've talked enough. Let's have another drink.

One of the final tributes to Larry appeared in the *New York Daily Mirror* sometime after Branch Rickey had taken over the Dodgers. It was a poem over the by-line of Gowanus Geon (actually Dan Parker):

Leave us scrutinize da problem
Dat exists at Ebbets Field.
All the mob wears mournful kissers,
And da blood is sure congealed.

Dare no longer ain't da hoopla
From each feller and his skoit
And I have a sneaky feelin'
Dat dare feelin's have been hoit

We ain't peeved dat Lippy Leo
Had an eardrum on da fritz,
We are proud dat Petey Reiser
Is arrangin' for a blitz.

We are thrilled dat little Peewee's
Wearin' Uncle Sammy's Brown.
But, it's losin' Loud Mout' Larry
Dat has really got us down.

For, no matter how we razzed him
We wuz pals beneat' da skin.
And, it's tough to take a Rickey
When you've had a Mickey Finn.

12

World War II

Larry's two sons, Lee and Bill, were both in the Navy during World War II. Once, when Bill was questioned about his father, one of the queries referred to Bill's opinion of his father as a parent. Without much hesitation his answer was, "Miscast."

However revealing this viewpoint (and one which differed considerably from that of his older sister, Marian), he was equally decisive about his father's need to defend his country and enter any fray in which it was engaged.

Immediately after Pearl Harbor Larry wired the War Department that as soon as they needed the experience of those who had served in World War I he was ready and willing to return. His wire was acknowledged, but that was all that happened for many months.

Then, in May, 1942, Larry signed a new five-year contract as president of the Brooklyn Dodgers at an annual salary of $75,000, a lot of money in those days.

In August, a wire arrived from the War Department asking him to take a physical. No one in the baseball world was aware of this development or the fact that he passed the examination without any restrictions whatever. Shortly thereafter he received another wire asking him how soon he could report for duty.

Larry called for a family conference with his sons, Ensign Leland Stanford MacPhail, Jr., United States Naval Reserve, and Lieutenant William C. MacPhail, United States Naval Reserve:

"You are the guys who are going to be affected by this, so I would like to know what you think I should do."

Both sons were a bit surprised that their father had asked for their opinion and both knew what his decision would probably be regardless, but they told him they thought he should follow his own inclinations.

So Larry's answer to the War Department was that he would report for duty in September. He also made the decision to completely sever relationships with the Dodgers. He did not want to try to mastermind the operations of the club by long-distance telephone nor inhibit his successor by retaining any control that might be exercised after the war.

Larry reenlisted with the rank of lieutenant colonel and hoped to go overseas again by returning to the field artillery. Instead, he was assigned the job of "trouble shooter" for Lt. Gen. Brehon Somervell, Commanding General of the Service Forces.

After six months he had groused enough that he was assigned to the Command and General Staff School at Ft. Leavenworth, Kansas, for training to return to the field artillery and go overseas. Two weeks before graduation he was ordered back to Washington, this time to serve as special assistant to Robert P. Patterson, the undersecretary of war. He and General Somervell, as well as Undersecretary Patterson, visited many of the training camps in the states and the war fronts of Europe.

He and Judge Patterson were on the flagship of the invasion fleet that accompanied the landings in Southern France. Larry remembered an exchange he had with Winston Churchill on the bridge. Among other things, Churchill told Larry: "Young man, I have learned to make brandy my servant and never my master."

It was also just shortly before the southern invasion that he caught sight of his son's cruiser through his binoculars and was able to have a signalman wigwag a message between ships.

John Steadman, sports editor of the *Baltimore News American* in 1969 and close friend of Larry's, recalled two war stories MacPhail related to him from World War II.

Larry recalled being on a trip to Algiers when Charles de Gaulle, then chairman of the French Committee of National

Liberation, tried to catch a ride on a plane in which MacPhail was riding.

Larry said that de Gaulle was turned down "like a hitch-hiker you would pass by on the side of the road." He added:

"I believe only one of three men could have rejected de Gaulle's request to get on that airplane. It had to be either President Franklin D. Roosevelt, Prime Minister Winston Churchill or General Dwight D. Eisenhower. I doubt if history has recorded this incident and I wanted to ask General Eisenhower about it.

"I wrote the General when he was last in Palm Springs and told him I wanted to request a visit with him at his Gettysburg farm. He invited me to stop by. I was going to ask him to tell me who prevented de Gaulle from getting on that plane in Algiers and flying to London with us. De Gaulle was sizzling when they told him no. But, General Eisenhower was taken sick and never got back to Gettysburg."

According to Steadman, MacPhail did not tell many war stories, but one revolved about the time he was sent with General Somervell and Undersecretary Patterson to make a call on Pope Pius XII at the Vatican. The summer residence of the Pope had been bombed and it was felt that an apology was in order.

"I never saw so much pomp and ceremony in my life," Larry said, "I wasn't sure, not being a Catholic, how I was to act in the presence of the Pope. But, Archbishop Francis Spellman was in the procession and when he saw me, he said, 'Hi, Larry, welcome to the Pentagon.'

"I had known Archbishop Spellman when I was running the Brooklyn Dodgers. What a man he was. Well, anyhow, I met the Pope, kissed his ring and found him to be warm and unpretentious. Then, he asked me if I wanted him to bless the Brooklyn Dodgers.

"The Pope told me he knew about the Dodgers because he had once visited on Long Island when he was the Papal Secretary of State. I left some rosaries for the Pope to bless and went on back to Washington.

"Several weeks later, they told me that General George Marshall wanted to see me. I thought, 'What have I done now?' I went to see the General and he said, 'Are you mak-

Cameo of Larry's mother and father (Curtis W. and Katherine McPhail) and Larry in uniform at Staunton Military Academy in Virginia. Larry later added the first "a" in MacPhail to make it sound more Scottish.

At Beloit College.

Captain Leland S. MacPhail (on left) "somewhere in France" August 2, 1918.

Famous Kaiser's Ashtray – the only memento from the attempted kidnapping of the Kaiser in Holland in January, 1919.

Son Lee MacPhail pointing to his favorite picture of his father and Judge Kenesaw Mountain Landis at dedication of new Columbus Redbird Stadium in Columbus, Ohio June 3, 1932.

Larry and Powel Crosley whom Larry convinced to buy the Reds.

Larry and Burleigh Grimes, Hall of Famer and MacPhail's first manager of the Dodgers.

Larry holding court at Dodgers' offices in Brooklyn with Publicity Director John McDonald and members of the New York press corps. Left to right: Roscoe McGowan, New York Times; Jim Dawson, New York Times; John Drebinger, New York Times; Whitney Martin, AP; John McDonald, Dodgers; John Collins, Dodgers; Gary Schumacher, Journal-American; Pat McDonough, World Telegram; Tom Meany; Jimmy Murphy, Brooklyn Eagle.

Spring training in Havana. Larry is shaking hands with President Batista and Durocher is to the right.

With Whitlow Wyatt after clinching 1941 National League Pennant for Dodgers.

Showing proper batting stance at Brooklyn, 1942.

1942 – Dolf Camilli presenting Larry with Patek Philippe watch when he left Brooklyn to go back in the army in World War II.

Colonel MacPhail at time of purchasing Yankees.

Larry (in uniform) with Walter (Big Train) Johnson (on left) and George Weiss, after buying the Yankees.

Colonel L.S. MacPhail, Joe McCarthy and George Weiss cutting cake in celebration.

Larry with co-owners Del Webb (second from left), and Dan Topping (far right). Bill Meyer (seated) was manager of several top farm teams of the Yankees and later manager of the Pittsburgh Pirates.

With Joe DiMaggio and Joe McCarthy.

With Joe McCarthy.

Entering dressing room with Bobo Newsom and Dick Starr
after losing 6th game of 1947 World Series.

With Manager Bucky Harris after winning it all in 1947.

Presentation of silver service by Yankee team. Left to right: Bobo Newsom, Red Corriden (partially hidden), Charley Dressen, Ralph Houk (background), Tommy Henrich, Johnny Lindell (background), MacPhail, George McQuinn (background), Bucky Harris and Spec Shea.

Larry visits Charley Dressen and Bucky Harris at spring training of Yankees in March 1948.

Larry – Portrait.

With Presidential confidant , Bernard Baruch, at race track.

With Aly Khan (second from right) at French race track.

At Glenangus, looking out over estate through picture window.

With American League President, Joe Cronin, and son, Lee (future American League President), at Orioles spring training in Miami, 1960.

The Squire of Glenangus (after beating a heart attack and licking cancer twice).

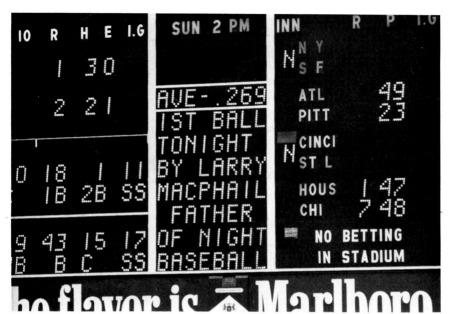

Scoreboard at Yankee Stadium during series with Oakland in 1974.

Larry and sons, Lee and Bill, at New York Baseball Writers dinner.

At Beloit College reunion.

At Larry's posthumous Hall of Fame presentation, August 7, 1978: William Schwartz (accepting for **Addie Joss**), Bill MacPhail, Lee MacPhail (who made presentation) and Eddie Mathews.

ing me your mail clerk?' Then, he broke out laughing and
handed me this package that had come to him from the White
House. It was the rosaries and medals from the Pope that I
was going to give to my Catholic friends."

MacPhail was convinced that General Somervell had done
one of the greatest jobs in the world of supplying everything
the army required with the exception of the specialized equipment required by the Air Forces. This latter, however, did fall
under the jurisdiction of Undersecretary Patterson and, therefore, as "trouble shooter," Larry performed services for both
men.

Colonel MacPhail made a speech which had originally been
intended as an introduction to General Somervell before the
Baseball Writers' Association at the Hotel Commodore on
Sunday, February 6, 1944. At the last minute the General had
been unable to attend and sent a wire to Larry which Mac-
Phail also read to the baseball assemblage:

> I regret more than you can realize my inability to be with
> you tonight. I wanted to tell you how important a factor
> baseball is in the winning of the war.
>
> It has been said that the successes of the British Army
> can be traced to the cricket fields of Eton. And, I say that
> the sandlots and big league ball parks of America have con-
> tributed their share to our military success.
>
> Nearly 70% of all major league players at the time of
> Pearl Harbor are wearing the uniform today and giving a
> splendid account of themselves. Besides, a million and a
> half kids from the junior sandlot teams sponsored jointly
> by the major leagues and the American Legion are in the
> Armed Services.
>
> They are good soldiers. They learned teamwork early.
> And it takes teamwork to win a battle or a war. It also takes
> realism.
>
> We never dare forget that a battle or a campaign can be
> upset by a ninth inning rally. We dare take no chances, we
> dare not slow down, we dare not relax until the last man
> is out.
>
> So far we have done well. We have produced munitions
> and supplies and we have trained our troops. We have
> shipped over two and a quarter million men and more than

forty million tons of arms, ammunition and equipment overseas.

In December alone, we built ten times the shipping tonnage that we lost. But, we have barely dented Hitler's fortresses of Europe. We have taken only a few far outposts from the Japs.

It will take millions of tons more, thousands more ships, many more divisions, much more sacrifice than we have experienced to bring about victory.

I call upon you to help your army and your navy by employing your skill and your knowledge in the maintenance of morale, both at home and among our troops. It is in your power to encourage both the workers and the fighters to give all they have to achieve the victory.

I am grateful for what you have done, for what I know you will do in the future.

Again, I regret that I cannot be with you in person.

Both speeches were received with great enthusiasm and applause. It was an emotional evening for Larry and the assembled baseball personalities.

There is a letter written by Larry about this time that appeared in a periodical called *Brief Items*, a somewhat occasional collection of pieces put out by an organization called the "Brief Items Committee" of the "Writer's War Board" in New York City.

The board was chaired by Rex Stout and included in its membership some of the most prominent names in the writing fraternity of that time, among them: Franklin P. Adams, Russell Crouse, Clifton Fadiman, Paul Gallico, Oscar Hammerstein II, John P. Marquand and William L. Shirer.

Larry's letter was addressed to the guys going "Over There":

You fellows going "over there" will be batting in a tough league. You'll be on the road all the time—the jumps are long—there are no Pullmans—the parks resemble ploughed fields planted with busted pop bottles.

The bunch you'll be stacked up against have as much conception of sportsmanship as sons of rattlesnakes who mass-married a pack of black widow spiders. If they can find a way to use rusty razor blades instead of spikes they'll have them on their shoes for tomorrow's game.

Every sack is "booby-trapped" and every bean ball that

skins your kisser didn't get there by accident—it was tossed that way, son, and don't ever forget it.

Those bastards you'll be up against aren't playing for pennants—nor even a decent cut of the gate. They're out after the gate, the parks, and anything else they can grab in every league, even including the hot dog stands. And, if they don't win this series, they'll start all over again next season—if you let them stay in the league.

Even the rookies just breaking in think their grandsons will be still cashing in on this series long after they start tripping over their beards!

The managers who call their plays from the bench know every lousy trick in the book. If they don't like the way the "ump" calls 'em, he just doesn't call 'em next time, 'cause you can't wave a man "out" if you're kind of dead! For their money a ball's a ball and a strike's a strike only if that's the way it adds up right for them.

Take a tip from the old timers who have seen a lot of ball played. When you step up to the plate in this game, take a real cut, and blast it out of the park. Anything short of straight over the center-field wall will be called a foul.

Oh—and just one more tip, son—carry that bat with you on the way 'round the bases. It might come in handy. The best of luck!

Of the many wires and letters of congratulations and expressed admiration Larry received when he reentered the service, the one from Branch Rickey seems to stand out:

I just want you to know that I have very deep admiration for the motive and purpose that lies back of your joining the United States Army. If similar opportunity for challenging service should come to me please know that I would have the same motive and purpose. I wish for you every good thing, always. From second to first division to a pennant in three years is a corking double play in anybody's league. You beat me last year, but surely not this. According to our wager, I am holding your seat in my box for the World Series games here in St. Louis. The Cardinals want, and may need, your turbulent support against the Yankees. Please come and, for the entire country's sake, wear your uniform.

Branch Rickey

Fate dictated that the man who followed MacPhail at the helm of the Dodgers was none other than the Mahatma himself. Dan Parker's poem reflected not only the opinion of the working press—"It's tough to take a Rickey when you've had a Mickey Finn"—but also that of the office staff.

Five, whose names are the most recognizable, were Buzzie Bavasi, Fresco Thompson, Branch Rickey, Jr., Ted McGrew, and Larry's private secretary, Jean Wanamaker. Jean left almost immediately saying that she and Branch, Sr. didn't get along.

With the two men, MacPhail and Rickey, being so diametrically opposed to each other in temperament and personality, it is not surprising that there would be a tremendous adjustment on the part of those closely associated with Rickey, after having worked for the swashbuckling redhead.

Bavasi, Thompson and McGrew all wrote letters to Larry, basically wishing that the change at the top had never taken place.

In January of '43, Buzzie wrote Larry that Rickey had told him that "the only job for me was the Durham operation (the Durham Bulls, in the Piedmont League), but in the next breath he said that it is almost impossible for the Durham Club to operate this season. So, that takes care of me, don't you think?"

Larry wrote him back with friendly advice:

> I am a little concerned about you. This experience you are going through is a damn good thing for Bavasi. You have had a good slant at one administration—its accomplishments, achievements, shortcomings and failures. You will get some good training in an entirely different setup with different ideas, and you will probably not only benefit thereby, but you will probably witness similar accomplishments, achievements, shortcomings and failures.
>
> From your experience, providing you keep your feet on the ground, a guy named Bavasi will benefit. If I have any advice to give you, it is to keep your ears and eyes open and your mouth closed. You did all of these things pretty damn well when you were working for me, and a pretty good job in addition. I don't think I ever had much time to tell you these things, but I think deep down in the bottom of your heart you knew I felt this way about it.

If I ever get back in baseball and Ted McGrew, Fresco Thompson, Bob Clements, Tom Downey, Malone and Hector Racine are available, I will be very happy. In a weak moment I might include Bavasi in this list.

The entire atmosphere at 215 Montague Street, the address of the Dodgers' office, was depressed and, when Branch, Sr., realized how bad it was, especially with the press and fans, he called Larry at the Pentagon and asked if he could have a meeting with him to discuss what he, Rickey, could do about improving his image. Larry took great glee in telling him that, if he could be at the Pentagon at 7:00 A.M., they could discuss the matter. Branch was there promptly and they spent most of the day on the subject.

In early 1944, Larry MacPhail was in the vanguard of another national effort. He was always concerned with the perception by the public of the role of professional baseball as it related to the war.

There was much discussion in both the executive and legislative branches of our government to pass some sort of National Service Legislation which would require active participation by the citizenry to make some sort of mandatory effort toward winning the war.

Larry wanted organized baseball to go on record as actively supporting this effort and, in a series of letters to Commissioner Landis and Judge Bramham, with copies to major league ball club owners, including Sam Breadon, Warren Giles, Leo Bondy, Tom Yawkey, Connie Mack and Clark Griffith, he proposed the following resolution:

> Everyone in this nation should have but one purpose—to help win the war as quickly as possible. For every month the war is needlessly prolonged, lives of many fine young Americans will be lost.
>
> Organized Baseball today has many men serving in our armed forces. It believes that it is the duty of everyone here at home to do his utmost, without stint of any kind, to support the men who are fighting for us.
>
> The President, in his message to Congress on the State of the Union and the Army and Navy, recommended the passage of a National Service Act which would impose on

every man and woman in this country the equal liability
to render personal service in the war effort. Organized
Baseball urges the adoption of this legislation and will do
its part. It's the very least we can do to bring the boys home
as soon as possible.

MacPhail felt that the legislation might or might not be
enacted, but that, in any event, baseball would find itself in
better position for having taken a positive and aggressive stand
in support of the war effort.

Prior to Larry's becoming interested in the Yankees in
early and mid-1944, he had an exchange of letters with Sam
Breadon, president of the St. Louis Cardinals. Breadon wrote
MacPhail that he missed Larry in the league meetings and
hoped he might return to the National League fraternity after
the war.

Sam highly recommended the Philadelphia franchise because, in his opinion, it was a "gold mine." He added, "with
your ability, it should pay for itself in two or three years."

Larry wrote back that he thought the directors of the
Phillies had really sabotaged the franchise, and that anyone
who might have been interested was no longer so inclined.
He felt that Postmaster General Jim Farley and half a dozen
others had been potential prospects, but not any more.

MacPhail told Breadon that "a hell of a lot of things would
have to be changed before I would want to be interested personally or before I would allow people who have asked my
opinion to become interested."

It was about this time he started thinking about the
Yankees. Sometimes, timing is everything!

13

Back to Baseball

Larry's return to baseball was done in typical MacPhail fashion—bombastically!

Col. Jacob Ruppert, the New York brewer, a bachelor and the owner of the New York Yankees, had died in 1939. His estate was left in two separate trusts—the Yankee trust and a residuary trust including all his other property. The only assets of the Yankee trust were the Yankee organization and its related properties, including Yankee Stadium and the farm clubs at Newark and Kansas City.

Ruppert's plan had been that, after the estate had been settled, the Yankee trust would be transferred to a trustee and the income paid to three women—his two nieces, Ruth McGuire and Helen Holleran, and a friend, Helen Winthrop Weyant. The trustee eventually appointed was the Manufacturers Trust Company of New York. The three women were to have no control over the trust, but only to receive the income from it.

By late spring in 1944 it became evident to the bank that the other assets of the estate were not great enough to pay the federal and state death taxes so that it became necessary to offer the Yankee organization for sale. Ruppert's personal debts exceeded one million dollars and even his interest in the brewery had to be sold as well.

It was a rare day indeed when a major league franchise became available, but when the most attractive of all was being offered on a must-sell basis, it naturally attracted individuals and groups from all walks and stations. Every few days a new proposed syndicate would appear as the likely purchaser. One group of negotiators who received the most publicity was headed by James A. Farley, Roosevelt's postmaster-general and an avid Yankee fan.

However, when a thorough analysis was made of the economics of owning and operating a big league franchise only one syndicate came forward with the money in hand and was approved by the bank—the one headed by Col. Leland Stanford MacPhail. His was a group of more than a dozen investors, the most prominent of whom was John Hertz, owner of not only a fleet of taxicabs in Chicago, but also a string of thoroughbred race horses.

The bank had questioned whether Larry could come up with the money, but when the investment banking firm of Lehman Brothers informed the Manufacturers Trust that, because of the involvement of Hertz, they would underwrite any deal signed by MacPhail, it appeared that the sale would be closed.

Now, it just remained to get the approval of the commissioner, Judge Landis. However, the judge was violently opposed to an owner of one of "his" baseball franchises being involved in any way with horseracing. This removed Hertz and his major financial backing from the syndicate and the whole deal fell apart.

Two of MacPhail's greatest attributes were his depth of research and his attention to details. On April 7, 1944, he had prepared an elaborate brochure covering a complete analysis of the operations of the Yankees and an evaluation of the total assets of the organization. This he had used to help put together the members of the syndicate. The bank was equally impressed.

Excerpts from this brochure covering a general description and an evaluation of the real estate holdings, franchise, players' contracts and farm system follow:

NEW YORK (AL) HOLDINGS

GENERAL

The principal assets are franchises, stadia, and players' contracts owned or controlled. New York and its subsidiary clubs own the franchises, land, stadium structures and equipment, and contracts of the players essential to the American League operation in the New York area; the International League operation in the Newark area; and, the American Association operation in the Kansas City area. These clubs also own or control the franchises and contracts of players of numerous minor league clubs, and a great number of players whose contracts are suspended for the emergency and who are carried on the National Defense Lists of Organized Baseball.

Appraisal of assets to be purchased for continued operations should be based primarily upon earnings and profit potentialities and not upon costs, book values, or even salvage values. Market values of these assets are a factor, however, because it may be advisable to dispose of certain assets in reorganizing operations.

Owing to their diverse nature, the stadia assets and operations (similar to those of real estate companies) and the franchises and players' contracts (pertaining exclusively to the baseball operations) are considered separately.

VALUE OF STADIA

The Yankee Stadium (New York) is a modern triple-decked plant with the largest capacity in baseball (78,000). Location, capacity, and adequacy of transportation makes its control essential to the American League, and an important factor as well in the promotion of professional and intercollegiate football and outdoor fights. The Newark and Kansas City plants are necessary to the operation of the two largest minor leagues in the United States, both of which have operated continuously for 40 years.

The land on which stadia in New York, Newark and Kansas City were built was acquired in an era of low real estate values and is carried at $748,239. Stadium structures have been depreciated to $1,586,877 or approximately $16 per seat. Construction costs for similar structures in the pre-war period would have been around $50 per seat.

The total present depreciated value at which these plants are carried is $2,235,116. This figure is considerably less than cost. It is about 70% of tax appraisal and about 40% of pre-war replacement figures.

FRANCHISE

Permanency of grant, freedom of threat of competitive invasion, and control of a stable commodity in a given market are characteristic of the New York (AL) franchise, but the value of the franchise is in proportion to its potentialities. The metropolitan population of the four largest major league cities, exclusive of New York, averages 2,947,000. The metropolitan population of the five smaller cities in the major leagues averages 1,218,000. The population of Metropolitan New York is 11,535,000—four times that of the average of other top-half cities—nine times that of the average bottom-half cities.

Schedules in all major league areas except New York are non-conflicting. The American League has only one franchise in New York. The National League, however, has two—one located in Manhattan and one in Brooklyn. As a result, the Yankees have schedule competition on about ten days in an entire season. The New York National League club, in comparison, faces competition for 75% of its home schedule. The Brooklyn National League Club has competition practically all the time.

Due to the population and character of the area—the location and capacity of the stadium—and the adequacy of the transportation facilities, the New York (AL) franchise is the most valuable franchise in "Organized Baseball." The book value of this franchise is $300,000.

PLAYERS' CONTRACTS

The New York (AL) Club owns or controls the contracts of more players of major league caliber or prospect than any other baseball organization. A large percentage of the players whose contracts are owned or controlled are serving at present with the armed forces.

The contracts of players owned could have been liquidated in pre-war periods for nearly as much as the figure at which all of the assets can now be purchased.

Any accurate appraisal of the asset value of the contracts of players owned is impossible because developments which will affect values cannot be predicted. The value of the players' contracts owned by the New York (AL) Club or subsidiaries are "hidden assets" and do not appear in the balance sheets. If a large percentage of these players become available for future operations—a bonus or profit on purchase of a large amount in the form of hidden values will result.

If the acquisition of new players in excess of ordinary replacement becomes necessary all major league clubs will be in the same boat. Clubs which have ample working capital will be in a position to finance the development of young players. The costs of such development can be expensed immediately and serve to reduce excess profits in a high tax period. The services of players developed would be available over a period of years.

FARM SYSTEM

Acquisition of players by purchase in a market where demand far exceeds supply is an expensive process warranted only when the purchase of a key player rounds out a strong club, and results in an immediate increase in income sufficient to justify out-bidding competing clubs.

Organizations which have been most successful in building strong clubs scout the sandlots and colleges for "prospects" and develop these players on their own minor league clubs. This is the so-called "farm system."

The New York (AL) farm system (franchises and players in the minor leagues, and personnel with ability and experience in this specialized field) has been built up over a period of years. It has been the major factor in producing 19 first division teams in 20 years—7 pennants and 5 World's Championships in 10 years. Surplus players in the five-year period immediately preceding the war were sold for over $400,000.

The intangibles of the farm system operation such as franchises, personnel, players' contracts, and players' contracts in suspense are "futures," difficult of accurate appraisal at this time, but values of importance in future operations. With the exception of certain franchises these "hidden assets," do not appear on the balance sheets. The exceptions are Newark—$27,796; Kansas City—$1.00; Binghamton $5,000; total, $32,797.

SUMMARY—BOOK VALUE OF ASSETS

The book value of all the assets of the New York (AL) holdings follows:

Plants and Equipment (less depreciation of $305,951 and Newark mortgage of $100,000)	—	$2,248,479
Cash, Bonds, Receivables, Deferred Charges (less current liabilities of $32,493)	—	528,984
Franchises	—	332,797
Players' Contracts	—	0
Total	—	$3,110,260

The book values above represent the net worth of the club, as the real estate mortgage bonds on the Yankee Stadium are owned by stockholders in proportion to their stock interest. The purchaser of 100% stock interest and the real estate bonds outstanding, therefore, is obtaining all the assets as listed above, free and clear of all liabilities as of December 31, 1943.

A final summary of the conclusions at the end of his elaborate document shows the extent to which he was able to put down on paper that which had defied analysis by others:

CONCLUSIONS

Baseball holdings which combine top franchises, and modern stadia with adequate capacities, have seldom been offered for sale. The necessity of partial liquidation of the Ruppert Estate to satisfy tax claims has forced the New York (AL) Club holdings on the market.

Low net profits in recent years; the "jitters" in baseball resulting from the loss of a great percentage of its personnel to the armed forces; and the lack of familiarity with baseball operations in financial circles—make it probable that these holdings can be aquired far below recent values.

The principal factors in the proposed deal which appeal to me follow:

(1) If all the assets can be purchased for approximately the liquidation or book value of the real estate—$2,235,116—there is an immediate profit of the present values of (a) franchises carried far below their liquidation values; (b) players' contracts which could be liquidated in normal times for nearly as much as the real estate; (c) good will—the "Yankee" name is almost as well-known as "Coca-Cola."

(2) A post-war net return on the proposed investment is a certainty as a result of stadium operations. If sound, modern, aggressive policies and management can achieve the potentialities in the baseball operation as I see them, a satisfactory net can be obtained on a valuation for these holdings in the range from four to five million dollars. The prospect for establishing these operations results and the "hidden asset" values within a reasonable time are good.

(3) Baseball in the United States is still in its infancy. Gross volume in the aggregate has shown steady increases without excessive ups and downs. World Series receipts in the 20-year period, 1903-1922 inclusive, totalled $6,350,000—in the period 1923-1942 inclusive, $21,500,000. Major league attendance held its own in 1943 in every metropolitan area except New York. The development of adequate illumination permitting night contests is resulting in a tremendous increase in market potentialities. There is every indication the increasing trends in volume and the value of franchises will continue.

In my opinion, the New York (AL) holdings are worth their book value of $3,110,260.

Operations for the duration of the emergency will be subject to the hazards which result from the shortage of manpower. Aggregate baseball income would be at its peak if sufficient players of major league caliber were available.

Discounting for this factor leads me to recommend purchase of a 100% stock interest and the real estate bonds outstanding at $2,500,000 as of December 31, 1943.

This would indicate the desirability of a trying offer for the 87% interest controlled by the Manufacturers Trust Company of approximately $1,750,000.

As far as Larry was concerned, that was that. He was stymied—at least for now. This was mid-1944 and the war effort occupied the mind and body of everyone. D-Day, June 6, saw the greatest massing of personnel and materiel in the history of the world. The allied invasion was on. Everything else was secondary.

However, in late fall the bank still had the problem of disposing of the Yankee organization and settling the Ruppert estate. When Larry was in Paris he received word from the Manufacturers Trust that they wanted to see him when he returned. When he got back to New York he went down to the bank and they ushered him in to the conference room.

This time they did not bother to ask him about the financing, apparently assuming that would be no problem. Without hesitation Larry signed the papers they shoved at him. He now owned the Yankees, but didn't have the slightest idea how he was going to raise the money to pay for them.

When MacPhail left the bank he went around the corner to "21," the famous watering hole, and ordered himself a drink to contemplate his challenging predicament. Shortly after he sat down at the bar who should come in the front door but Marine Capt. Dan Topping, home on leave from the Pacific.

Topping had been a tenant of MacPhail's at Ebbets Field before the war as owner of the Brooklyn Tigers Football Team. He was also a familiar figure in New York, both in the sports area and in the social world, having married the premier ice skater of the time, Sonja Henie. When the war had come and both of them enlisted, Dan told Larry that if MacPhail ever got back into baseball after the conflict he would like to be his partner.

Yes, Topping was just as interested as ever and definitely

wanted in the deal. However, this heir to a tin-plate fortune was still in the service and the sale price of $2,800,000 was more than he could swing right at the moment. He told Larry they would have to find another partner, and said, "What about Bing Crosby?"

They contacted Crosby who said that he would be interested, but that, since he owned Del Mar Racetrack, he would probably not be any more acceptable to the commissioner than was Hertz. However, he did suggest Del Webb, a friend of his and a contractor from Phoenix who had been building a number of airfields for the Army.

Webb had met MacPhail several years before and, in fact, had actually been part of the syndicate that Larry had put together originally. He knew Judge Landis and had, at the time of the syndicate formation, asked Landis his advice on whether he should join the group that was being formed to buy the Yankees. Landis' reply was:

"If, when you're making a putt, you want to worry; if, when you're having your dinner, you want to worry; if, before going to bed, you want to worry, well, then, go ahead and buy the Yankees."

Webb had been a frustrated pitcher in some of the "outlaw" California leagues as a young man. When he finally gave up this career he continued his work as a carpenter. In the words of a close friend of his, Arthur Nehf, the former star southpaw of the New York Giants: "He came to Phoenix without a dime and parlayed a saw and hammer into millions of dollars."

The sale price of $2,800,000 was first divulged in a scoop reported by Bill Corum, of the *New York Journal American*, during the last week in January, 1945. This price was confirmed by Larry and was broken down as follows: $2,500,000 to the Ruppert heirs for their 86.88 percent ownership, and the balance of approximately $300,000 to Ed Barrow for his 10 percent share. The remaining 3.12 percent was held by George Ruppert, brother of Colonel Ruppert; Ruppert Schalk, a nephew; and Mrs. Anna Dunn, a niece.

Further confirmation of this price came from Wilfred Wottrick, vice-president of the Manufacturers Trust Company, administrator of the estate. He said that the price for the Ruppert holdings was $2,500,000 and all cash. And he substantiated the statement made by Larry that negotiations with MacPhail had started originally as far back as the previous March.

Wottrick was also asked about how many offers had been received since 1941 when the bank became involved with the Ruppert estate. He said that no other bona fide offer had ever come from any other source.

MacPhail readily admitted that the price paid for the club was a bargain. He was anxious to take over, but was on active duty till February 10, and added that Ed Barrow would continue to be in charge until that time, continuing his contract negotiations with the players for the forthcoming season. Barrow was to remain on as chairman of the board of directors, but "Cousin Ed" was cast in an entirely different mold than the rambunctious redhead and there was no question that it was the end of one era and the start of another.

As great as the Yankees had been over the years, even they had had their good times and bad times.

In 1902, the recently formed American League had had teams in Chicago, Boston, Philadelphia, Detroit, Cleveland, Washington, St. Louis and Baltimore. Ban Johnson, president of the new league, had fought tirelessly for survival against the well-entrenched National League and now was determined that his league must have an entry in New York City. He was also convinced that Baltimore had lost its appeal as a big league sports area and so was prepared to sell this franchise when satisfactory buyers could be located.

A sportswriter by the name of Joe Vila, who later became sports editor of the *New York Sun*, had known Ban Johnson in the days when both had been cub reporters. He also had a wide acquaintance among sports personalities and introduced Johnson to an ex-saloonkeeper named Frank Farrell. Farrell, in turn, had a good friend, fellow Irishman William S. (Big Bill) Devery, whose background was similar to Farrell's in that they were both familiar with the lofty profession of bartending. Devery was also the retired chief of the New York police force.

Johnson then arranged for the sale of the Baltimore club to these two gentlemen for $18,000 and the transfer of the franchise to New York. Farrell and Devery agreed to build a new ball park, located on Broadway between 165th and 168th Streets, and to have it ready for the start of the season.

To make sure that the team would be able to compete for the attendance dollars with the popular New York Giants, Johnson also forced the other clubs in the league to transfer some of their greatest stars to the new club, dubbed the "Highlanders." Included in these were Wee Willie Keeler, whose record of 44 consecutive games in which he got one or more hits was later broken by Joe DiMaggio; Jack Chesbro, who had jumped the National League after he had led the Pittsburgh Pirates to the pennant in 1902; Herman Long at shortstop and John Ganzel at first. To lead them all he brought Clark Griffith, the best manager in the league, from Chicago.

Griff stayed as manager of the team for five and a half years, with two second place finishes, in 1904 and 1906, but more and more, the two owners could not keep from second guessing his moves when the team lost. Finally, fed up with the interference, he quit in the middle of the 1908 season and the team finished in eighth place.

The year of 1910 was really the high-water mark for the "Highlanders" under the ownership of the two ex-saloonkeepers. George Stallings, who later gained great fame as the "Miracle Man" of the Boston Braves when he took that team from last place on July 4 to the pennant in 1914, had been the manager of the New York team in 1909 and a good part of 1910. But, like Griffith before him, he, too, resigned because of the constant suggestions from the owners, and was replaced by the colorful and crowd-pleasing Hal Chase, the famous "Black Prince" of baseball.

They managed to finish in second place and, for the first time actually made a profit of $80,000. But, in 1911 they returned to mediocrity, winding up in sixth place with a .500 record of 76-76. By 1912 they hit rock bottom again in eighth place, while the rival Giants were winning the National League Championship under John McGraw. In 1913, with their tail between their legs, Farrell and Devery, now even bickering between themselves, had to move their team, now known as the "Yankees," out of their inadequate and outmoded ball park and become tenants of the Giants in the Polo Grounds.

Their last two years they finished seventh and sixth and, in 1915, gave up the ghost. They sold out to two wealthy men who also shared a love of baseball—the millionaire brewer, Col. Jacob Ruppert, and Capt. Tillinghast L'Hommedieu Huston, a soldier-engineer, for $460,000. Even with this amount of money split between them their debts must have been large. At their deaths Farrell left an estate of $1,072, and Devery debts of $1,023.

The two new owners had both been friends of John McGraw and had tried to buy the Giants. McGraw would have none of it, but persuaded them to make an offer for the Yankees. The negotiations did not last long and on January 11, 1915, they were the proud owners of a major league baseball club.

For the first few years the team hardly did better under the new ownership than it had done for Farrell and Devery. The main difference was that Ruppert and Huston could, at least, afford to indulge their fancies, spending freely to try to improve the product on the field. Their first manager had been suggested to them collectively by the sportswriters who had been following the team—a former popular pitcher for the Tigers named William E. (Bill) Donovan. He was there for three years but achieved only mediocre results and was let go at the end of the 1917 season.

Through the efforts of J.G. Taylor Spink, publisher of the weekly baseball bible, *The Sporting News*, Miller Huggins, then manager of the St. Louis Cardinals, reluctantly agreed to meet with Colonel Ruppert, president of the club. The two men hit it off immediately and Hug then started what proved to be one of the great managerial careers of all time which lasted until his death on September 25, 1929.

At the end of the season in 1919 an event happened that not only changed the fortunes of the Yankees, but had a tremendous effect on the whole baseball scene. Up in Boston, an orphan from Baltimore named George Herman (Babe) Ruth had been converted during spring training from the best left-handed pitcher in the American League to an outfielder by the manager of the Red Sox, Edward G. Barrow. Ruth was the talk of the baseball world, and finished the season with the phenomenal total of 29 home runs and a batting average of .322.

Ruppert and Huston were determined to get him if possible and, while they were discussing how much money it would take, the opportunity fell into their hands. Harry Frazee, the owner of the Red Sox, was also a heavy plunger in the theatrical world, and needed $500,000 to back some of his new stage productions. Ruppert agreed to a personal loan to Frazee of $350,000 with Fenway Park as collateral, and purchased Ruth outright for $100,000.

Other stars were to come in time, but, shortly thereafter, Ed Barrow also joined the Yankees as business manager. Barrow was the guiding hand for 25 years and compiled one of the greatest records of all time.

In 1921, the Yankees won their first pennant, repeating in '22 and '23. Amazingly, the Giants won the National League pennants in those same three years, so there were three consecutive subway series. The Giants won the first two, but the Yankees beat them out in 1923. In 1922 the Giants wanted the Polo Grounds to themselves and asked the Yankees to find other facilities.

Thus, Colonel Ruppert started construction of the most expensive and elaborate sports arena of its time, Yankee Stadium. In 1920, they had taken an option on property at 161st Street and River Avenue, and now were anxious to have their own facility and the finest park in the majors. Yankee Stadium was opened April 18, 1923 and the sportswriters soon dubbed it "The House that Ruth Built."

Shortly thereafter a rift developed between Ruppert and Huston and after some bickering and dickering, the Colonel bought out Huston's share for a reported $1,500,000 and on May 21 became the sole owner of the greatest franchise in professional sports.

To some extent complacency set in in 1924. By the time the Yankees got down to business and won 18 of their last 22 games it was too late. The Washington Senators were even hotter, nailing down first place and knocking off the Giants in the World Series. Ruth led the league in hitting with a .378 batting average and blasted 46 home runs.

The year 1925 saw the team sink to seventh place. But, this was the year Ruth tried to defy Huggins, saying that he would never play for him again. The Babe had been hitting all the night spots instead of the baseball and his batting average and run production suffered commensurately. Ruppert and Barrow backed up the little manager completely and the one-man rebellion was over. However, it was too late to change their place in the standings.

The only other event of note for the Yankees that year was that, on June 1, Wally Pipp, their first baseman, had asked Hug if he could sit out a game because of a headache. Huggins obliged him and thus started the longest consecutive game streak in the history of baseball as Lou Gehrig took over at first.

The next three years saw the Yankees in first place each year—1926-28. In 1929, the year Huggins died, they finished in second place. The following year, under Manager Robert Shawkey, they wound up third.

In 1931, Barrow hired Joseph V. McCarthy, who had been released as manager of the Cubs after the 1930 season. It was a most fortuitous choice because, in the next 14 years, from 1931 through the end of 1944, McCarthy led the Bronx Bombers to the incredible record of eight pennants, four second-place and two third-place finishes.

This, then, was the team Larry and his associates took over in January, 1945. Topping and Webb left the entire operation of the club in MacPhail's hands, but Larry knew that in the Yankee tradition, success was not hoped for—it was expected.

The Sporting News asked Ward Morehouse, who was the drama critic of the *New York Sun* and an avid baseball fan, to interview Colonel MacPhail, who was still in uniform, about his plans for the Yankees:

"So you're back in baseball," he said.

A grin spread over Larry's red face.

"I had a suspicion I would be. I knew I would have to work," he replied. "Hell, all I want to do is to turn out a fighting, aggressive, colorful club that will win ball games and will be the kind of club that the fans will want to see—a good team and a good ball park that will have an attractive atmosphere and courteous employees. I've always believed that the ball club belongs to the fellow who goes out there and pays his way in—to the fans. I've always tried to keep faith with the fans and I believe I've been fairly close to the fellow who sits out there in the bleachers.

"Now, I don't think it will be in the cards to win as many pennants and championships as the teams of the Barrow regime. Hell, that's something else. I doubt if the Yankees' records of the past 15 years or so will ever be equalled. And, as a matter of fact, I think in the postwar period all teams will start off much closer together than they have been in a long time. But, the Yankees should do all right.

"Yes, I'll eventually be moving into the 42nd Street offices. But, right now I'm in uniform—still in the army. Mr. Barrow will continue as operating head of the club for some time . . ."

"How about Joe McCarthy—and night baseball?"

He grinned.

"McCarthy will stay—sure. He's a great manager. We're damned fortunate to have him . . . Night ball? Well, I put in lights at Columbus in 1932, at Cincinnati in 1935 and Brooklyn in 1938. I think it is only a matter of time before all clubs will have lights and will be playing night ball, but I'm opposed to playing more than seven night games in any park in any season. If it comes to the question of whether baseball should be a day or a night game, that's something else again. But, if you start playing 14 or 21 night games a season, you're simply killing day baseball.

"The manpower situation is in a hell of a mess, isn't it? You can't be sure about baseball this year until everything jells in Washington. Do you realize that fully 80 percent of the men of baseball are in the service—and fighting? The other 20 percent are not in because the Army and Navy wouldn't let them in . . . Things being so damned uncertain right now, you really can't plan very much. My idea is just not to rock the boat right now.

"Sure, I'm glad to be with the Yankees. I'll be inheriting the nucleus of a fine organization. In Cincinnati I had a secretary and a bookkeeper when I started. In Brooklyn I didn't even inherit a secretary, whereas on the Yankees they have a good working organization. Brooklyn owed a hell of a lot of money; the same was true in Cincinnati. When I got there I got rid of all players but two on a list of 40. I kept Derringer and Lombardi. In Brooklyn, I kept only Durocher and Fitz-simmons of the original lot.

"It's different now. The Yankees don't owe any money and the organization has about 450 players. The greatest percentage of them have been loaned to Uncle Sam, but when the war is over—"

Morehouse then brought up MacPhail's relations with the press and their reporting of his feuds with Leo Durocher and his supposed hostility toward Dixie Walker.

"I always ask a man to be careful when he quotes me. The only thing I'm thin-skinned about is when the press gets a little careless in using quotes. . . . Take that Dixie Walker legend. When all other clubs waived on Walker, I bought him from Detroit. I bought him, kept him, paid him and raised his salary every year. As for Durocher, he has always been a good friend of mine. I suppose I've been his best friend. There was really very little to criticize about Leo when he was working for me in Brooklyn."

Another area in which MacPhail would be participating (and, actually one that he ended up eventually solving himself) was the election of a new commissioner. Landis had become ill in the late fall of 1944 and died of coronary thrombosis at St. Luke's Hospital in Chicago, November 25.

There was a meeting scheduled for February 3, during which the new owners of the Yankees would be approved by the American League. In addition, there was to be a discussion of the names of a potential successor to Judge Landis.

Since his "leave" from Army duties would not be up until February 10, Larry said he would attend the meeting but leave the official decisions of the Yankee organization in the hands of Ed Barrow. MacPhail felt that baseball should name a new commissioner as soon as possible. He added that his own personal choice was Ford Frick, but mentioned several other "fully qualified" men, including Will Harridge, Ed Barrow, George Trautman, Judge Bramham and Warren Giles.

At the February 3 meeting a commission was appointed to screen candidates for the job. The members of the commission included Alva Bradley of the Indians, Sam Breadon of the Cardinals, Philip K. Wrigley of the Cubs and Donald Barnes of the Browns. As is the case with so many similar commissions, very little was accomplished and by late April they had succeeded only in reducing the number of candidates.

At a meeting in Cleveland on April 23, representatives of all 16 teams were present. MacPhail was there and when he found out that it was likely the commission was going to recommend a further delay, he stormed out and tried to get a plane reservation back to New York. There wasn't a seat to be had. So, because of this delay, he was in attendance at the meeting the next day.

The meeting was held in the Rose Room of the Hotel Cleveland, and Barnes read the report. The list had been whittled down to six: Ford Frick, president of the National League; James A. Farley, former postmaster general; War Mobilizer Fred Vinson; Robert P. Patterson, undersecretary of war and, until recently, MacPhail's boss; Robert Hannegan, head of the National Democratic Committee; and, Frank Lausche, governor of Ohio.

MacPhail then suggested Senator Chandler of Kentucky. His name came out of the blue but, since there was no objection, his name was added to the list, making a total of seven to be voted on. Surprisingly, on the first ballot Chandler's name appeared among the top three on everybody's list, and either first or second on 13 out of the 16 ballots.

The other names were gradually eliminated and it finally came down to Chandler and Hannegan. On the first ballot thereafter Chandler received 11 votes and Hannegan 5. Horace Stoneham switched his vote on the second ballot and, on the third, Chandler was elected unanimously.

What insignificant things can affect major decisions! Like the fable of the kingdom that was lost for want of a nail for the horse's shoe, who would have been named commissioner had Larry been able to get the plane reservation and return to New York the day before?

A fully-booked plane led to the election of Albert Benjamin (Happy) Chandler whose decision in the Durocher case in 1947 altered the events of that momentous year in major league baseball.

14

The New Regime
Takes Over

Meanwhile, the day-to-day operations continued under Ed Barrow, at least for the time being. The new training site he had selected was Atlantic City. The backbone of the team that still remained was built around Ernie Bonham, Nick Etten, Hank Borowy, Snuffy Stirnweiss, Johnny Lindell, Atley Donald and Frank Crosetti.

The team that McCarthy was able to field had Etten at first, Stirnweiss at second, Crosetti at short and a third-baseman named Don Savage. In the outfield he started the season with Lindell, but he, too, was claimed by the Army during the season and was replaced by Russ Derry. The balance of the outfield was made up of Herschel Martin and Bud Metheny. The catching was handled by Mike Garbark and Bill Drescher and the pitching staff was made up of Bonham, Borowy, Floyd Bevins, Donald, Joe Page, Walter Dubiel and Al Gettel.

As the season started it became more and more evident that there was really only one person running the show. The quiet and talented Barrow, newly elected to the title of Chairman of the Board, became extraneous and pretty much a figurehead. In reality, it was no one's fault. When MacPhail was involved in an enterprise, especially when he was an owner of a third of that enterprise and its president, there was really not much authority left to go around.

Larry never did move into the offices on 42nd Street. In July, he closed those offices and moved into more lavish quarters in the Squibb Building, on Fifth Avenue and 58th Street.

171

Barrow seemed like a duck out of water, and his visits to the new headquarters became less and less frequent.

In the meantime, the team seemed to be playing lackluster ball, winning a few, then losing a few. Then, in late July, McCarthy became ill when his chronic stomach problems acted up again. He returned to his home in Tonawanda, New York, to recuperate and left the team in charge of Arthur Fletcher. Shortly thereafter he resigned and the sports pages were filled with, "There, I told you so! He isn't really that sick. There just is no way McCarthy can work for MacPhail."

Larry vehemently denied any interference with McCarthy and rushed to Tonawanda to persuade him to reconsider the resignation and return to run the Yankees. He was successful and Joe came back to pick up the reins again.

Probably because he felt the team was not playing up to their capability and wanting to shake out the lethargy, Mac-Phail then shocked the New York baseball community, and the American League in general, by selling his best pitcher, Hank Borowy, to the Chicago Cubs for $100,000.

No one could understand it. Did the Yankees need the money? Larry said that was not the case—that they had cash on hand of $519,000. When pressed he answered that Borowy had never done well in August and September and that, in addition, McCarthy had sanctioned the sale.

Clark Griffith, owner of the Washington team, was especially vehement. Larry had commented, "Griffith wouldn't have paid $100,000 for Borowy with the Queen Mary thrown in."

Sportswriter Shirley Povich, in the *Washington Post*, quoted Griffith as responding:

"He was a failure at Cincinnati and a flop at Brooklyn and the fact remains he sold the Yankees' best pitcher at a time when the Yankees needed pitching. Nobody pays any attention to what MacPhail says." He added:

"We ought to keep our stars in our own league. That's what makes our league prosper. Every club owner has a certain equity in all the league's players because, without stars, we'll have a cheaper league, and the National League will be laughing at us."

Griffith was always supersensitive about the relationship

between the two leagues, ever since he left the Cubs and helped form the American League over 40 years before.

One other possible reason for the sale of the Yankees' best pitcher, at least a possible contributing factor, was that Larry might have felt some indebtedness to the Cubs for the very one-sided trade he had made with them for Billy Herman back in the Brooklyn days.

The amazing thing about the whole deal was the fact that all the other American League teams had to have waived Borowy out of the league to enable MacPhail to sell him to the Cubs. Coincidentally, it was pointed out to Griffith that he had virtually done the same thing in 1942 when he got Bobo Newsom waived out of the American League. No other team in that league would come up with the waiver price of $7,500 for him, whereupon Griffith sold him for $45,000 to this same MacPhail and the Brooklyn Dodgers. Clark maintained it wasn't the same thing, but the facts do not seem to back him up.

The '45 team was still in transition. Countering the loss of Lindell to the army and the sale of Borowy was the return of Red Ruffing, Aaron Robinson, Charley (King Kong) Keller and Spurgeon (Spud) Chandler from the service. However, they couldn't shake out of it enough, and the best they could do was to finish fourth.

Incidentally, MacPhail was a bit premature in his assessment of the decline of Borowy. He went on to win 11 and lose 2 with Chicago and greatly helped them in winning the National League pennant. They also came close to beating the Tigers in the World Series. The next year Hank had only a so-so record, finishing 12-10, and he never had another winning season.

Now, the '45 season was over and Larry had great plans for '46. First off, as he had before in Columbus, Cincinnati and Brooklyn, he went after the physical plant with a vengeance. One of his primary considerations was always the comfort and entertainment of the fans—how to increase their "fun at the old ball park."

Barrow had always opposed night baseball. With the new regime, however, this was an integral part of expanding the appeal of the Yankees and MacPhail announced that there would be lights in Yankee Stadium for the 1946 season. In addition, he made many other changes in the structure of the ball park. He then ripped out a portion of the grandstand and increased the number of box seats with his first Stadium Club. This was on a membership basis and brought in $500,000, all up front before the season even started. He built a new clubhouse for the team and greatly enlarged the facilities for the catering firm. He was now in high gear.

Larry also revolutionized the whole idea of spring training, at least as far as the Yankees were concerned. Normally, spring training was not only necessary, but also quite costly. Most teams lost between $20,000 and $40,000 getting their teams ready to start the season. Not MacPhail.

He planned a pre-spring training in Panama and, for the first time, flew the entire team to Balboa in the Canal Zone. The Panamanians had guaranteed Larry a minimum of $30,000 which more than paid for the costs. Actually Stirnweiss and Ruffing did not join the team for this portion of spring training—Stirnweiss holding out for a better contract, and Ruffing just refusing to fly across the water.

Eventually, even the reluctant McCarthy was reconciled to the idea when he saw how well conditioned his Yankees were. When they returned to St. Petersburg they were in much better shape than the teams they played and proceeded to run all over the Red Sox, Indians, Cardinals and Reds. It was to be said by some of the sportswriters later in the season, however, that maybe the Yanks left some of their victories in Panama and Florida.

The balance of spring training was so successful at the gate that Larry took in almost two and a half times as much as the best previous year and, for the entire spring training, cleared over $65,000.

MacPhail further shocked his more staid counterparts in the ivory towers of baseball ownership by doing the unthinkable and revealing to the public at large the numbers involved in the operation of a major league baseball club. He published the consolidated operating statement and balance sheet for the entire Yankee operation in 1945. It showed a net profit of $201,881.

The war was now over and the veterans had returned.

Down the middle they were in great shape. The 39-year-old veteran catcher, Bill Dickey, was behind the plate. The keystone combination was made up of Joe Gordon at second and Phil Rizzuto at short. Rizzuto had originally been discovered at one of the Yankees' annual two-day tryouts and then had come up through the system.

In center field was one of the greatest ballplayers of all time, Joe DiMaggio. The Yankees had actually acquired Joltin' Joe through the faith and perseverance of one of their best scouts, Bill Essick, a man in whose judgement Ed Barrow had had a lot of confidence. After DiMaggio had been burning up the Pacific Coast League in the early '30s most of the major league teams got in a bidding contest to buy him from Charles Graham, owner of the San Francisco Seals.

However, Joe had a knee that popped out and most of the other teams lost interest right away. Essick convinced Barrow that he should follow Joe around the league to determine how serious the condition was. When he became convinced that the knee did not affect DiMaggio's play at all, Joe became one of the greatest steals of all time—at $25,000. One condition of the sale was that Joe should stay with the Seals for the year of 1935 and then report to the Yankees for their spring training in 1936.

So, the team was solid where it counted most, behind the plate, around second base and in center field. Stirnweiss, after he signed a more lucrative contract, was moved over to third and they still had Nick Etten at first. Flanking DiMaggio in center were two other fine ballplayers, both real sluggers and good fielders, Charley Keller in left and Tommy Henrich in right. Dickey, Henrich, Keller and Etten were all left-handed hitters and adept at depositing the home run ball over the short right-field fence at Yankee Stadium.

The only weak area, if there was one, seemed to be the pitching staff. Spud Chandler was their ace, but there were some question marks after him. Nonetheless, the consensus of the sportswriters, especially in New York, was that the Yankees should win the American League pennant.

There was a new election of officers, with Topping, Webb and George Weiss, the extremely capable head of the farm system, being reelected vice-presidents. In recognition of the great job he had done over the years, Weiss' job was even expanded.

The season got under way. On Opening Day, Chandler shut out the Athletics and, apparently, they were off on their quest for the brass ring. Oddly enough they fell out of first place on April 27 and were never able to regain the top spot throughout the entire season.

At the start of their first western swing in Cleveland, McCarthy's stomach ailments returned and he was confined to his hotel room. Although he did make the trip to Detroit, after two days he again returned to his home in Tonawanda. This time it was for good.

He had left the team in charge of Johnny Neun, a coach and former minor league manager in the Yankee organization. Neun had replaced the popular Art Fletcher who had recently been forced to retire with a heart condition.

McCarthy had retired with grace, but again the wags were convinced that his physical problems were exacerbated by the change in ownership of the team. Regardless of the cause of McCarthy's resignation, MacPhail accepted it reluctantly, noting that Joe had been one of the great managers of all time, having won eight pennants and seven world championships in 16 years at the helm.

The team flew on to Boston where Larry met them. Naturally, there was a need for an immediate replacement for McCarthy, and MacPhail made the very popular choice of Bill Dickey, who was not only a favorite of the fans, but also well-liked by the players. However, the relationship he had with the rest of the team when he was looked up to as one of the veteran players turned out to be different when he became manager. Things didn't seem to be quite the same.

The team muddled on through most of the summer but never rose to the heights expected of them. An event of indeterminate significance at the time occurred on September 9. Larry announced that he had hired Stanley (Bucky) Harris in an executive capacity. Harris had been the Boy Wonder who, in 1924, had been the manager of the Washington Senators, the team the Yankees had been unable to catch for the American League pennant that year. He also led them to a dramatic victory over the Giants in the World Series.

There was much speculation as to what MacPhail had in mind for Harris. At Larry's direction, Bucky went on to Detroit to look the team over. Dickey, probably feeling insecure about the whole situation, told Harris he did not want to be considered for the manager's job again for 1947. MacPhail then appointed Neun as manager for the balance of the '46 season.

With all the upheaval the Yankees staggered to the finish in third place, 17 games behind the Red Sox and 12 behind the Tigers.

Artistically, it was a disappointing end to the season but with all kinds of promotions and fanfare they set fantastic new attendance records, exceeding the supposedly elusive goal Larry had set for himself of two million fans. Actually, a total of 2,309,029 passed through the turnstiles at Yankee Stadium, 683,744 for the night games. On the road they attracted 1,269,697 and, including the 316,946 fans that saw their exhibition games in the spring, the amazing number of 3,895,672 people saw the Bronx Bombers in 1946.

The dismal finish in '46 presaged a number of changes if there was to be improvement for '47. Some of these changes started immediately after the end of the season and at the World Series at Fenway Park in Boston.

First, Johnny Neun resigned to take the manager's job at Cincinnati. Their field manager, Bill McKechnie, decided he didn't want the pressure of the job any longer and signed to be one of Lou Boudreau's coaches with Bill Veeck's Cleveland Indians.

Then, Larry ran into Veeck at Fenway and suggested they make a deal. Now, these two liked nothing better than making a trade, whether it was one with some significance or one bench-warmer for another. Bill told Larry he would stop over at his seat and discuss things with him after an inning or two. He remembered a trade they had made when Veeck had the Milwaukee team in the American Association in late 1942 and MacPhail ran the Dodgers and had not yet gone back into the service.

Unfortunately as was often the case with Bill in his swashbuckling days as a baseball club owner, he had been operating on a shoestring in Milwaukee. He had an outfielder named

Hal Peck who was having a big year for the Brewers. Veeck had already agreed to sell him to the White Sox for $40,000 when he received a frantic phone call from Peck's wife, sobbing that Hal had shot his leg off. What had actually happened was that Hal had accidentally shot off the second and third toes on his left foot.

Bill figured there was only one man in baseball with enough guts and imagination to buy a three-toed outfielder and that was Larry MacPhail. Veeck flew to New York and, after several vehement refusals by MacPhail, finally sold Peck to him at the racetrack when he caught Larry in an expansive mood after betting on several consecutive winners.

Incidentally, as evidence that the loss of the toes did not materially affect Peck's potential ability, Veeck was later to reacquire the outfielder from MacPhail and the Yankees before the start of the '47 season, and Peck had three fine years for Veeck at Cleveland. However, the return of Peck was not the first trade Bill was to make for his new team. That trade was a much bigger one.

About the fourth inning Veeck went over to MacPhail's box to see what the redhead had on his mind. It turned out to be one of those great trades that actually helped both sides. Larry needed pitching and Bill needed a crackerjack second baseman to complete the double play with Boudreau. Veeck offered MacPhail a choice. He would trade right-hander Allie Reynolds for Joe Gordon and a rookie third baseman named Ed Bockman. Or MacPhail could have Red Embree, a good pitcher who was especially tough on the Yankees, even up for Gordon.

Gordon had just come off his poorest year, so Larry was willing to part with him for good pitching. He was on the verge of making the Gordon-Embree swap when he decided to talk over the choice with Joe DiMaggio who was sitting in another box further down. When he returned he told Bill that DiMaggio told him he was nuts if he didn't take Reynolds. So, the blockbuster deal was made and scribbled out on a hotdog napkin.

Gordon had three good years for Cleveland, helping them to the pennant, and Reynolds had eight highly successful seasons for the Yankees, with his best year being 1952 in which he posted a 20-8 record. He, too, helped the Yanks to American League pennants and finished with a 7-2 World Series mark.

A month and a half later, the two owners completed the trade in which Peck was returned to Veeck. MacPhail, in need of bench help in the infield after having traded Gordon, was interested in Ray Mack. Although these two were the ones who sparked the trade in the first place, the "throw ins" turned out to make more of a splash later on. The Yankees also received a rookie catcher named Sherm Lollar who later had many good years with the Browns and White Sox, being a pivotal part of the Sox pennant-winning team in 1959, their first pennant in 40 years.

Veeck received two pitchers along with Peck—one, Al Gettel, never did much for him, but the other, Gene Bearden, had one fantastic season, 1948, in which he went 20-7. He also won the playoff game against the Red Sox, pitched a shutout in the Series and recorded a save in the final game. Oddly enough, that was really the only good year Bearden had in the majors.

Larry was to make one other very significant move before the end of the year. George McQuinn had been released by the Athletics and was signed as a free agent. This is the same George McQuinn who had replaced Jim Bottomley with MacPhail's Cincinnati Reds in 1936. At the time he didn't fill the bill at first base and had been shipped on to the Browns. Now a Yankee, he went on to have a great year in the pennant-winning season of '47, batting .304 and driving in 80 runs as the Yanks' regular first baseman.

Two other changes occurred in the pitching staff before the start of the season. Ruffing had finally reached the end of the line and was released outright and Ernie Bonham was waived out of the league and moved on to the Pirates.

These changes all involved the playing personnel. But, who was going to manage the Yankees in 1947? Neun was only an interim manager and had since moved on to Cincinnati. There was some speculation that it would be Billy Herman, but he signed to manage the Pirates. Many people thought it was inevitable that Leo Durocher would rejoin Larry in the Bronx, but he decided to stay on with Rickey at Brooklyn.

However, two of Durocher's coaches, the colorful Charley Dressen and Red Corriden, moved over to MacPhail and Rickey was livid. He was furious because, according to Rickey, Dressen said he would leave the Mahatma only if he were offered the job of a major league manager. MacPhail said he had no plans to offer Charley that job and also made it known that he had no interest whatsoever in Rickey's comments on the matter.

It seems that when MacPhail hired Harris neither of them had really determined in what capacity he would serve the organization. It had not been Harris' intention, nor probably Larry's either, to have him run the team on the field. However, a phone call in late autumn from Walter (Spike) Briggs, owner of the Detroit Tigers, started a scenario that not only resolved the dilemma, but also gives great insight into the character of both Harris and MacPhail.

Briggs called Larry and asked him for permission to talk to Harris for the purpose of signing him for the position of general manager of the Tigers. MacPhail reacted in typical fashion, almost coming through the phone:

"Don't you dare tamper with any of my players or others in my organization or I'll have you up before the commissioner!" Larry screamed. "Have you talked to Harris?"

Briggs mumbled something or other and declined to answer the question. MacPhail slammed down the phone and began to think about it. He had had three managers during the past year—McCarthy, Dickey and Neun—and knew that he couldn't continue on that pace with any degree of success. So, he immediately sought out Harris.

"Has Spike Briggs been after you to offer you the general managership of the Tigers?" Larry never beat about the bush.

Bucky was never one to equivocate, either.

"I suppose I could lie to you, Larry, but that isn't the way I do things. Yes, he called me about it and offered me a five-year contract at $50,000 a year."

MacPhail was still steaming.

"Well, you can't take it. You're still under contract to me!" Larry answered, and stomped out of the room.

Then, when he had calmed down a bit and got to thinking about it, his conscience starting hurting. There are really few jobs like this one that ever become available to anybody. Could he really stand in Bucky's way when such a great opportunity arose? After all, this job was the general managership of one of the best organizations in baseball.

So, he returned and told Harris:

"Bucky, I've been thinking about it and I'm wrong. It's too good a chance for you and I'm going to release you from your contract . . ." Then, all of a sudden he started laughing. "Contract? What am I talking about? You have no contract. You can go ahead and sign up right now. Congratulations!"

Harris shook his head.

"No, Larry, I gave you my word, and that's more important to me than a contract. If it hadn't been for you I would still be managing in the minors and I owe that much to you."

It then started to become comical, Larry insisting that Bucky take the job and Harris insisting that he owed MacPhail too much not to stay.

Finally, Larry, getting mad all over again, yelled:

"Bucky, you're nuts. It is the chance of a lifetime. You've got to take it! Tell you what. You go home and sit on it for 24 hours. Talk it over with your wife. And, then, take the job. You've always wanted to be in the front office and swore you would never want the pressure of being a field manager again."

Harris agreed to wait till the next day. The following morning he came back to Larry's office. Before he could say anything Larry said:

"Wait a minute. I want my partners to hear your decision, too." Topping and Webb were both in town and came into Larry's office.

"Okay, Bucky, what have you decided?" he asked.

"Well, gentlemen, I won't kid you. I'll confess, it has been a tough decision. It's the kind of a job I've been working for. But, I've always felt that my word was my bond. I called Briggs before coming here and told him that I was turning it down. I am staying here."

On November 5, Bucky Harris was named manager of the Yankees for 1947.

15

He Wins It All in '47

In January, an announcement to the press made official what had been de facto for some time—the resignation of Ed Barrow as chairman of the board of directors of the club. It had been inevitable and, actually, Barrow had seldom been seen since MacPhail had taken over.

As far as the team that would take the field, MacPhail and Harris started to lay their plans. Frank Crosetti was coming to the end of the line and signed a contract as a player-coach. DiMaggio had a troublesome spur on his left heel and went into a hospital to have it removed.

Larry had been delighted with the financial success of the Panamanian portion of the previous spring training and planned in great detail an even more peripatetic trip for 1947, including: San Juan, Puerto Rico; Caracas, Venezuela; Havana and then on to St. Petersburg to conclude the training period. This did not meet with the greatest degree of enthusiasm from Harris and the players but, nonetheless, on February 15, a contingent took off for San Juan for the first leg of their travels.

Bucky had to make a number of decisions about who would play where, and this was not made any easier by the fact that while he and many of the veterans were flying around the Caribbean all the rookies were up in St. Petersburg. This meant that he could not pass judgment on their potential value since he wasn't there to see them perform.

One question mark was George McQuinn at first base. He had enjoyed a good season in 1946 but there were doubts that he could do it again. Another question that had to be decided was where to play a rookie named Lawrence (Yogi) Berra, who grew up in the Italian section of St. Louis known as The Hill, and had been a power hitter for their farm club in Newark. MacPhail did not know very much about him except that he had been offered $50,000 over the winter for him by his old rival, Horace Stoneham. Larry had turned the money down out of hand, figuring that if he was worth that much to the Giants, he must be worth that much to the Yankees. When MacPhail met the burly, squat Berra for the first time he couldn't believe he had passed up that amount of money for this rookie who didn't look anything like a ballplayer.

Then, on the pitching staff he had just acquired Allie Reynolds from Cleveland and there was a rookie, Frank (Spec) Shea, whom he had never seen.

Spec was from Naugatuck, Connecticut, and is now superintendent of Parks and Recreation there. He had served in the Army in Europe for three years and had been released during the winter of 1945-46. He remembers an incident with Larry:

> I had the good fortune to go to spring training in 1946, having just gotten out of the Army. I worked very hard trying to get a job on the club, and had the starting assignment to pitch the Opening Day game of the spring in Panama. That night I got sick and it ended up that I couldn't pitch. I had a ruptured appendix and had an emergency operation. Infection set in and I was laid up in the hospital for three weeks.
>
> When I tried to get out of the hospital they said I had to pay my bill before I could leave and that the Yankees would not pay my bill (sic). I paid the bill and, when I joined the club in New York, he [MacPhail] still wouldn't pay me. In May, I was sent to Oakland in the Pacific Coast League where Casey Stengel was my manager. In June or July, Mac said he wanted me to rejoin the Yankees in New York. I had told Casey about the (hospital bill) situation and he told me to hold out until he paid me the money for the operation, which I did. The news got out, and when UPI printed it, Mac went nuts. The next day I got a call, the bill was paid and, seeing that we were in a fight for first place, I stayed with Casey at Oakland. And, from then on we got along okay, Mac and I.

Incidentally, Shea ended up with a 15-5 record for Casey that year, but Harris had never seen him pitch and was anxious to remedy that situation.

Things started off well in Puerto Rico where the weather was perfect and the veterans got in condition quickly. That is, all except DiMaggio whose heel was not healing properly. Dr. Marvin A. (Mal) Stevens, a noted surgeon in New York, and formerly a coach for Yale and New York University football teams, had been appointed team physician over the winter. He had not performed the operation on DiMag's heel, but advised that Joe be sent to Johns Hopkins Hospital in Baltimore for a skin graft. The rest of the team enplaned for Caracas, but DiMaggio went back to Maryland.

The Yankees had three games scheduled with the Dodgers in the Venezuelan capital. Larry and Jean were staying at a lovely hotel and the Dodger hierarchy in an old flea-bag reserved by Rickey for his two partners.

The year that MacPhail, Topping and Webb had bought the Yankees was the same year that there was a change in ownership with the Dodgers. Walter O'Malley had been a lawyer closely associated with George V. McLaughlin of the Brooklyn Trust Company and became involved with the Dodgers in 1943. John L. Smith was president of the Charles Pfizer Company, a prominent manufacturer of pharmaceuticals. In 1945, each of the three of them—Rickey, O'Malley and Smith—had purchased a one-fourth share of the Dodgers. The other share was owned by Dearie Mulvey but the other three ran the show.

Actually, there was no love lost between O'Malley and Smith toward Rickey. Larry had invited the two Dodger owners to his suite for dinner and, when the two of them saw the lovely furnishings the MacPhails were enjoying, they were livid at their parsimonious partner.

The promoter of the Yankee-Dodger weekend series became very difficult, trying to force the Americans to stay over for more games. They ended up playing only one, which the Yankees won 17-6. Jean says the ride to the airport was one of the most harrowing she has ever experienced. The road was narrow and winding and they kept passing white wooden crosses tilted at different angles at almost every bend in the road. Each represented the death of someone who was not able to negotiate that turn. The driver of the car was the promoter, who was enraged that the Americans insisted on leaving and was taking his vengeance out by roaring and skidding around every turn.

They flew into Havana for two games with the Dodgers on March 9 and 10. An incident occurred at the first game that seemed insignificant at the time, but caused a verbal donnybrook in the papers between the MacPhail and Rickey forces that eventually brought on the year-long suspension of Durocher.

A daily article in the *Brooklyn Eagle* appeared over the byline "Durocher Says." The column was actually written by Harold Parrott who was now the traveling secretary of the Dodgers. Parrott and Durocher thought enough alike that it seemed to make little difference whether Leo read it before publication or not.

Probably as much to encourage the rivalry and hype the attendance during the dull days of spring training as anything else, Parrott's articles were very acerbic. One appeared with a dateline from Caracas virtually challenging MacPhail and the Yankees. It helped swell the gate to more than 10,000.

Then, the fat went in the fire. In looking around the crowded stands, Durocher happened to locate the MacPhails in their box. He also noticed two men with the Damon Runyon type names of Memphis Engelberg and Connie Immerman, one a gambler who, when asked his occupation prior to induction in the army, had answered "handicapper," and the other the manager of a casino in Havana.

Durocher had continually been in hot water because of his association with known gamblers, including George Raft. He had even lived with Raft both in California and New York. He had also been specifically warned by Commissioner Chandler not to be seen with Engelberg.

When Durocher saw him sitting with Immerman, he mistakenly thought both men were also sitting in the same box with the MacPhails. Leo screamed there was a double standard—one for him and one for everybody else in baseball. Rickey also reacted with typically righteous indignation.

Naturally, the press, sensing a good story and happy to exacerbate the feud, followed up by approaching Larry. Actually, the two gamblers were not sitting in the MacPhail box, but in a box directly behind them, with the aisle separating them.

Dick Young of the *Daily News* went to MacPhail immediately, told him of Durocher's remarks, and asked Larry if
the two men were guests of his. MacPhail raged:

"First of all, it's none of Durocher's damned business who
I have as a guest. And, secondly, I had nothing to do with their
being there."

After the two-game series the Yankees resumed their
schedule and flew on to St. Petersburg and the Dodgers headed
on to the Panama Canal Zone. However, it was just the lull
before the storm. Neither MacPhail nor the press was about
to let the matter rest.

With the New York newspapers printing indignant comments by Rickey and Durocher about the inequities of the
situation, Larry proceeded to file formal charges with the
commissioner:

> I am attaching a summary of quotations attributed to
> Branch Rickey and a summary of statements appearing in
> the articles signed by Durocher.
>
> These articles, appearing in the *Brooklyn Eagle*, are
> allegedly written and/or publication-authorized by officials
> of the Brooklyn Baseball Club. Either the president of the
> Brooklyn Club made the statements attributed to him or
> he has been misquoted.
>
> In any event, the charges are either true or false. If true,
> they should properly have been communicated to the Com-
> missioner of Baseball. If false, their utterance and/or pub-
> lication constitutes slander and libel and represents, in our
> opinion, conduct detrimental to baseball.
>
> For these reasons the New York Club requests the Com-
> missioner to call a hearing to determine responsibility of
> the statements and then whether they are true or not.
>
> When these matters have been determined, the New
> York Club takes it for granted, in view of the publicity
> which has followed these charges, that the Commissioner
> will make his findings public. Mr. Will Harridge, president
> of the American League, joins me in making this request.

One of Larry's strongest drives was that he must win any
battle he entered, regardless of its triviality. It mattered not
how inconsequential the affront.

One lawsuit in his later life lasted over 20 years and was

actually settled after his death. It concerned a horsebreeder who had determined to leave his stallion for stud at Larry's farm and had become dissatisfied with the number of brood mares that had become available for his animal to service. He became so obnoxious about it that Larry told him to take his horse and get off the property.

He then sued and, although MacPhail won the suit at every level, the case was appealed time after time. As in so many such lawsuits, only the lawyers profited and the entire matter became more and more bitter.

The lawsuit started in the neighborhood of 10 to 15 thousand dollars and, by the time it was finished, almost $250,000 was involved. Before it was settled MacPhail, the plaintiff and even the horse had all died. His daughter said:

"It was absolutely incredible! One dead man sued another dead man over a dead horse!"

What it came down to was that Larry MacPhail really relished a good fight—be it physical, a world war or just a legal battle to determine right from wrong. He was not interested in hurting anyone, especially after he cooled down, but winning was paramount.

One night in 1945, shortly after V-E Day, Bill MacPhail returned to the States on his ship, the cruiser U.S.S. Philadelphia, which entered the harbor of the city after which it was named. Larry and Jean were at their farm in Maryland and Larry wanted to call Bill. Jean put in the call and, since wartime rules still applied, she was asked by the operator:

"Is this an emergency?"

Jean's knee-jerk reaction was that it was, indeed, an emergency and, when pushed for an explanation, replied on the spur of the moment, and unconvincingly:

"I'm pregnant!"

The call went through, but the suspicious operator, listening in, determined that it was not an emergency, pulled the plug and Larry was left holding a dead phone.

Well! Larry and Jean raced down to the phone exchange and the rambunctious redhead blew his stack. When he wanted to emphasize a point, Larry had a habit of poking the person he was talking to with his index finger. The operator who had cut him off in his phone conversation was amply endowed and later claimed that Larry had jabbed her repeatedly on the bosom.

She, too, sued, and it was only after several appeals that it was thrown out of court by a judge who said that it was only because of the prominence of the president of the New York Yankees that the case had gotten that far. But, it was typical MacPhail.

Another case in point was a fight he had with Red Patterson of the *New York Herald Tribune.* They got into a real rhubarb one night and started slugging each other. The next day it was all forgotten. MacPhail was not one to hold grudges. Patterson recalls the story:

> Larry said something I didn't like and we got to punching each other out. But, I was one of the first ones he hired when he got the Yankees, so I guess he forgot the fight.
>
> I had been working for Ford Frick at the National League Office as a publicity man for the league when Larry asked Ford if he could talk to me about joining him with the Yankees. There was a lot of entanglement in it.
>
> I had been Chairman of the Baseball Writers' Association and had just returned from a USO tour that had played in China. Frankly, I had joined the National League Office because there seemed to be a good chance that Ford Frick would be named the new commissioner and, if so, there was also a chance that I would take his place as president of the National League.
>
> Since Chandler had been named commissioner (and Larry handled that, too) I was willing to make the move to MacPhail and the Yankees. So, I called him and said:
>
> "Yeah, I want to come over and what are you going to pay me?"
>
> I had just been raised to $7,500 with the league office and Larry asked me how much I was making. I told him and he said that he would give me the same amount. I countered:
>
> "Wait a minute. This isn't my idea at all. You're taking me away from a good job."
>
> He allowed as how that was true, but that I would be getting chances that I wouldn't get anywhere else.
>
> The reason I remember so good was that he was just stepping out of a shower in Chicago. He's all naked and I'm dressed trying to make my best appearance and this is how

we're negotiating. He also ended up giving me a naked salary, too. And, I never got a raise from Larry.

I got the $7,500 each year that he was there. We had a big competition with Cleveland and we drew over 2,000,000 people each year and had a fantastic spring training both years and he never gave me a dime.

Larry had a reputation for having been a guy who really put out for the clubs, so, in my case, and I guess in a lot of other cases, he stuck close to his old money. He made plenty himself. I didn't regret it because it started me on a completely new path.

Getting back to the Chandler hearings, it must be remembered that the long and dictatorial reign of Judge Landis as commissioner of baseball would have been a tough act for anybody to follow. In personality, goals and almost any other way, the two commissioners could hardly have been more diametrically opposed to each other.

Chandler had moved the Office of Commissioner from Chicago, the second largest city in the league, to Cincinnati, the smallest city in the league and the one nearest to Happy's home in Versailles, Kentucky. This, however, removed him geographically from being in a very good position to defend himself against the vilifying press in New York who were constantly comparing his style to that of Landis. Thus, Chandler was looking for any possible opportunity to change his image and take a strong and forceful stand.

The first hearing was called by Chandler for Monday afternoon, March 24, 1947 in Sarasota, Florida. Rickey was unable to attend since, over the weekend, Mrs. Rickey's brother died and the Rickeys attended his funeral in Lucasville, Ohio.

A former newspaperman, Arthur Mann, who at the time was a confidential assistant to Rickey, felt the story important enough to write a book on the subject of the hearings and Chandler's decision. In it he refers to MacPhail producing a copy of the "Durocher Says" article Parrott had ghosted for Leo in Caracas. Durocher took full responsibility for the content of the article and in the hearing explained:

"It seemed just another rhubarb. We went on like that, Mr. MacPhail and I, for years. Why, he fired me many times after such arguments and hired me back. But, we always laughed it off.

"If I've said anything in that article to hurt Larry's feelings, I'm sorry, and I apologize."

As reported by Mann, MacPhail then got up, took Leo's hand and said:

"That's good enough for me," and sat down.

However, it was not allowed to end there. MacPhail was obviously disturbed by the hornet's nest he had shaken and, had he known the eventual outcome and the effect it would have on Durocher, he would not have filed the charges in the first place. But, it would appear that Chandler, having started the hearings, was determined to conduct himself in a manner designed to change his image in the press to one of strength and toughness.

Chandler continued the interrogation from several other angles, mostly involving gambling. When he was through, he told Durocher he was dismissed, but that he had to remain absolutely silent about anything that had transpired in the secret hearing. Chandler then scheduled the second meeting, with Rickey present, for Friday, March 28, in St. Petersburg.

This second hearing was also conducted behind closed doors, with MacPhail and Rickey giving further testimony. At the end of the inquisition Chandler said he would reserve judgment and, again, swore all participants to secrecy.

In Cincinnati, on April 9, just six days before the Dodgers' opener, Chandler rendered his decision. Harold Parrott was fined $500 and ordered to discontinue his "Durocher Says" column. Charley Dressen was suspended for 30 days without any specific incident being cited. It was generally assumed that his strong interest in betting on the horses was the reason. The New York Yankees and Brooklyn Dodgers Baseball Clubs were each fined $2,000, but the big bombshell was that Durocher was suspended for the entire year of 1947. The written verdict concluded with the terse admonition:

"All parties to this controversy are silenced from the time this order is issued."

All parties with the exception of Larry MacPhail abided by the edict of silence. On the next day, April 10, he called a press conference. He started off by saying:

Under baseball law, the Commissioner is prosecutor, judge and jury. There is no appeal from his decisions. That does not mean, as we understand baseball rules, that the Commissioner has any right to prohibit the release of factual information regarding any matter in which the press and the public are concerned. This club will continue to release to the press any factual information pertinent and proper.

If we violate any baseball law, and go outside our own prerogatives, we will accept the responsibility.

Larry also added that he would back up Dressen if he appealed. Charley did not choose to do so.

The daily papers and the weekly *Sporting News* were filled with reactions to the decisions. They ranged the entire spectrum—from total defense of Chandler's action and that it was about time Durocher was "handled," to criticism that the punishment given to Durocher was excessive in the extreme.

Rickey's reaction was one of shock and disbelief. However, he did not fight it. Several times Leo had gotten out of hand and Branch may have felt that Chandler had actually done him a favor by his action, albeit severe, in punishing Durocher.

The *Sporting News* carried five full pages on the subject, including comments by 36 different sportswriters in all the major league cities as well as other parts of the country. The weekly sports bible itself had long backed Chandler as commissioner and was equally anti-Durocher for his many peccadilloes over the years and their editorials reflected these sentiments.

Finally, at long last, the attention of the sports fan was switched from the distractions of the legal battles involved in the front offices to the playing fields themselves.

In 1946, the Boston Red Sox and St. Louis Cardinals had won their pennants and, as is often the case, were established as early favorites to repeat.

The Yankees were scheduled to open the season on Monday, April 14, against Washington in the nation's capital. President Harry Truman was ready to throw out the first ball. However, a drizzle greeted the packed stands and it gradually increased to a downpour, so the opener was postponed.

The Yankees returned to New York where they opened the

season against Connie Mack and his Athletics. It was not an auspicious start, since Philadelphia won 6-1, with Phil Marchildon outpitching Spurgeon (Spud) Chandler.

The Opening Day lineup had an infield made up of George McQuinn at first base, Snuffy Stirnweiss at second, Phil Rizzuto at short and Billy Johnson at third. Harris had to get Berra's bat in the game, so started Yogi in right field, with Johnny Lindell in center and Charley Keller in left. Joe DiMaggio was on the bench with his heel still not quite mended. Aaron Robinson was behind the plate.

The second game against the Athletics was won by the Yankees, 2-1, with Bill Bevens going all the way. Then, on Friday, New York returned to Washington for the opener. Truman showed his ambidextrous abilities and threw out two balls, the first right-handed and the second as a southpaw. However, the partisan crowd was disappointed as the newly-acquired Allie Reynolds pitched a shutout and won, 7-0.

Red Barber pointed out an interesting bit of trivia in regard to this game. Truman was the fifth president to throw out the first ball for an opening game in which Bucky Harris was the manager. He had been the field manager for the Senators for four previous openers in which Presidents Warren G. Harding, Calvin Coolidge, Herbert C. Hoover and Franklin D. Roosevelt had started the festivities.

The next day DiMaggio pinch-hit and, although he grounded out, it was great to have him back. He led by example and had a way of lifting the team with his leadership. The following day he started the first game of a doubleheader against the Athletics and the Yankees swept both games, with Joltin' Joe slamming a home run with two on his second time at bat in the first game. Although he sat out the second game, the Yankees won that one too, 3-2.

Next came a three-game series with Ted Williams, Rudy York and company as the Red Sox moved into Yankee Stadium to begin defending their American League pennant. Bill Bevens won the first one, 5-4, and Reynolds pitched his second straight shutout in the second. Frank Shea lost a tough one, 1-0, when Tex Hughson allowed only two hits, but the Bronx Bombers still had a half-game lead when Washington came in for the next series.

On April 26 the story broke that Commissioner Chandler had ordered MacPhail and his two partners to come to his office in Cincinnati the next week. No reason was given, but there was no doubt in Larry's mind that the commissioner would try again to silence him about the Durocher suspension and related matters. Topping and Webb were out of the country so it was set that MacPhail would meet with Chandler on May 1.

In the meantime, on Sunday, April 27, one of the greatest celebrations in the history of baseball was scheduled in Yankee Stadium—Babe Ruth Day. The Babe was in failing health, suffering from cancer of the throat, and Chandler had declared this day in his honor in "the house that Ruth built."

MacPhail and "Red" Patterson planned the festivities with meticulous care. Before the start of the season Larry had sold the local TV rights to all Yankee home games to Dumont for $75,000, so, although the number of sets was limited, the "Day" was televised locally. The game was broadcast on radio throughout the country.

The stadium was festooned with pennants and bunting that made it look like the start of the World Series. The list of dignitaries included Commissioner Chandler, Cardinal Spellman, American League President Will Harridge, National League President Ford Frick, all of whom were to speak at home plate, and many others.

The front pages and sports pages of not only the New York papers, but many across the country, carried a picture the next day of probably the greatest player ever to don a baseball uniform, now tragically hunched over and bundled up in a warm camel's hair coat. Speaking in a rasping voice to a crowd of over 58,000, hushed with the drama of the event, Ruth said:

"Thank you very much, ladies and gentlemen . . . you know how bad my voice sounds . . . well, it feels just as bad."

In the last few years the Babe had interested himself in American Legion ball and, therefore, had a few more glowing words to say about "the greatest game" of baseball in general and the sport at the Legion level in particular. Slowly he returned to his seat and was forced to leave the stadium before the end of the game. Slightly more than a year later he died in Memorial Hospital in New York, August 16, 1948.

Before the May 1 meeting with the commissioner in Cincinnati MacPhail held court again, stating that this was the first time that a man had been suspended without the specific charges having been spelled out. Larry added that it was patently unfair and that "sooner or later baseball would have to redefine the powers of the commissioner."

There was no doubt in the minds of the dozen or so sportswriters who congregated outside the commissioner's office that there would be further interesting stories to write after what they assumed would be a brief exchange between MacPhail and Chandler. They were nonplussed when the conversation lasted over six hours and then Larry emerged to tell the assemblage that he was sorry but he had nothing to say about the meeting and that any information about the conversation would have to come from the commissioner's office.

They also ran into a brick wall there when they were told that the commissioner had nothing to say to the press and would not answer any questions whatsoever. Period.

Meanwhile, the Yankees were having their ups and downs on the baseball field. They were in and out of first place during a five-city trip through the West. The weather had been deplorable with the entire series in Cleveland having been rained out, and when they limped into Boston they brought with them a four-game losing streak.

Aaron Robinson was suffering from a bad back and more and more frequently Bucky Harris was using Berra behind the plate. In the first game, Yogi went three for five and the Yankees won, 9-6, with DiMaggio, his heel now comfortably in a regular baseball shoe, collecting two hits. Joe's favorite ball park was Fenway with its short left field and high wall known as the Green Monster.

This brings to mind a trade that almost came about—one that allows the mind to wonder about "what might have been." Two of the greatest hitters of all time played half of each season in a park designed to thwart their natural talents. Imagine DiMaggio, a great right-handed pull hitter eyeing that left-field wall at Fenway four or five times a game for 77 games each year. Now, imagine Ted Williams, the Splendid Splinter who swung from the other side of the plate, looking out at the short porch in right field at Yankee Stadium for the same number of games each season. It almost happened!

One night MacPhail and Tom Yawkey, owner of the Red Sox, got to hoisting a few and Larry proposed trading the two best players in the American League even up. He pointed out some of the advantages to Yawkey and the Red Sox. Williams had had frequent difficulties with the Boston press, whereas DiMaggio was always good copy and well-liked by the members of the fourth estate. Joe would be a real hero to the huge Italian population of Boston and the surrounding area. Think what he would do to the Green Monster. Larry did not dwell on the records Williams might set at Yankee Stadium.

As the evening wore on, the deal became more attractive to both owners with each additional highball. As they parted company for the night they shook hands on it and consummated the deal. However, in the clear light of the next morning Yawkey started to have misgivings. Although he was a man of his word, he told MacPhail that he just couldn't go through with the trade—that he would have to call it off. Larry laughed and they cancelled the deal, but it does conjure up what might have been!

Although they had won the opening game of the series, the Yankees were not so fortunate in the next two, dropping both and returning to New York, having lost seven out of nine on the road trip.

The White Sox came in for the first night game on May 15. It also marked the return of Charley Dressen to the third-base coaching box, after he had served his 30 day suspension. Chicago was not very hospitable and smothered the Yankees, 8-2. However, there was a big doubleheader with the Pale Hose on Saturday and New York swept both ends by identical scores of 4-3 before 66,666 people, including over 12,000 screaming youngsters on Yankee Junior Day.

Sunday brought Bob Feller and the Cleveland Indians to the Stadium and the Yankees dropped three straight. This first encounter between the two teams since the Reynolds-Gordon trade made Veeck look like a genius. Gordon got three hits and two walks in five times at bat in the opening game of the series and Feller beat Reynolds, 5-3. New York was now four and a half games behind league-leading Detroit who came in for the next series.

They opened with the second night game and Frank Shea pitched a shutout, winning 5-0. Another rookie, Ralph Houk, was behind the plate as Berra moved to the outfield. The next game was rained out, but things did not remain quiet at the Stadium.

For whatever reason—whether just to be feisty or for some other motive—MacPhail decided to fine DiMaggio $100 and several others lesser amounts for failure to participate in a photographic session for an Army publicity stunt. He also fined Lindell and Johnson for not having attended a dinner to which they had been invited. The requirement of cooperation with the club in promotional activities was part of the standard player's contract at that time, but the fact that they had fallen to sixth place might have had something to do with Larry's mood.

There was also a rhubarb developing about traveling by air. Most of the players went along with it, but a few insisted on going by train. This was just another thing to grouse about. Then, the Red Sox came to town for a four-game series. There is nothing like winning to calm things down a bit.

The Yankees humiliated the defending champions and swept all four games. Now it was MacPhail who looked like the genius. Allie Reynolds, the Superchief, was unbeatable. Once, when he was with the Indians, Reynolds had said, "there are only so many pitches in this arm of mine." He later revised that and knew that he could come up with something more when he needed it.

New York was hot. The sweep put them in second place, only three games behind the league leaders, Detroit, and the fans of Gotham started to take the Yankees seriously. They had won eight out of their last 12 games, a .667 percentage, and the fans felt the excitement. The Monday night game against Boston drew a crowd of 74,747 and refunds had to be handed out to 1,140 fans who couldn't get into the jammed stadium.

Bucky Harris had been trying to sort out his pitching, both starters and relievers, and this series went a long way toward solving both situations. Reynolds had pitched the opening game and had recorded his third shutout, 9-0. Spud Chandler won the second game on a two-hitter and Bevens swamped the Red Sox, 17-2, the next day. When the starting pitching faltered it became more and more evident that Joe Page was just the cure the doctor ordered for the bull pen. He saved the last game, 9-3. Bucky was now getting the consistency he needed in both areas.

That fourth game may have been the turning point of the whole season. Shea was knocked out in the third inning, the first time he had been taken out of a game in his rookie year. Page came in with two on and nobody out and all he had to do was to face Ted Williams, Rudy York and Bobby Doerr as the first three batters.

Williams hit a grounder to McQuinn for what could have been a double play, or at least the first out, but wasn't as the first baseman bobbled the ball. Bases loaded. Nobody out. The right-handed hitting York came to the plate to face the left-handed fireman. The first three pitches were wide of the plate. One more would force in a run. Any kind of a hit could put the game away. But, Joe came right down the middle three times and Rudy missed three times swinging. Then he struck out Doerr, the Boston second-baseman, and got Eddie Pellegrini on a fly to Tommy Henrich. The stands went wild and, in the fifth, DiMaggio hit one out with two on.

Actually, incredible as it seems today, Harris said afterwards that Page was one pitch away from being exiled to the minors. If that fourth pitch to York had been a ball, Harris had already decided that he would pull Page and send him down the next day!

Joe Page was not the first pitcher to have been used exclusively in the relief role, but many people think of him as the prototype of the great ones of today.

He had an overbearing confidence when he headed for the mound that would intimidate even the best hitters. Ted William once remarked:

"When that big baboon comes out of the bull pen, he sneers at you. He just defies you to hit him."

Yet, in the three previous seasons Page had done little to

recommend him for the future greatness he enjoyed. His activities in the wee small hours did not help and Harris had just about seen enough.

But, this game seemed to make Page realize his potential. At the end of the year he had won 14 games and had saved 20 more. It was a magnificent season for the handsome left-hander and it also turned out to be a rewarding one.

At the start of the season, Larry had been tough to deal with in negotiating Page's contract. He knew of the pitcher's nocturnal habits and decided to give him incentives which required checkpoints as well.

Finally, he told Page:

"Sign this contract, Joe. At every payday, I'll go to Bucky. If he says, 'Page is my boy!,' I'll give you an extra $2,500 in $100 bills—on the line."

Eight times out of 11 paydays, Harris gave MacPhail the same answer.

"He's my boy, Larry," said Bucky, "I cannot tell a lie."

Because of the originality and inventiveness of the incentive clause MacPhail had used as the carrot for Page, the talented southpaw earned an extra $20,000.

The Yanks took two out of three at Washington, with Spec Shea winning his fifth game of the young season. Even though Chandler and Bevens lost double shutouts in Philadelphia, New York rose to the occasion when they beat Feller and the Cleveland Indians, 8-4, again behind the relief pitching of Page. They were three and a half games behind the Detroit Tigers. The next day was a slugfest with DiMaggio getting four hits, two of which were home runs. The second was a grand slam and they beat Cleveland, 11-9. Now, this team of destiny moved up to Detroit for the next crucial series against the league-leaders.

It was now June and the team was pretty well set. The infield was solid with McQuinn having a good year at first base, Stirnweiss at second, the redoubtable Rizzuto at short and Billy Johnson at third. The outfield was even stronger with Keller in left, Joltin' Joe in center and Tommy Henrich in right.

However, there was one fly in the ointment. Keller was having frequent back spasms and went to the hospital for an examination. They found a crushed vertebra and on June 5 it was removed. It was thought that he would be gone for about six weeks but, actually, he was out for the season. Johnny Lindell had been riding the bench most of the time and now took Keller's place in left and played very well.

Berra had virtually taken over the catching duties. Harris used a four-man rotation most of the time, consisting of Allie Reynolds, Frank Shea, Spud Chandler and Bill Bevens. Then, for spot starting and occasional relief there were Randy Gumpert, Don Johnson, Karl Drews and Charley Wensloff. More and more Bucky relied on Page to clean things up and close them out. Many people today still think that Joe Page was the greatest relief pitcher of all time, and, with the job he did in '47, it is a claim that has some merit.

In Detroit, the Bronx Bombers took three of four and their confidence was overflowing. At every park in the league the New York Yankees were setting new attendance records and at home they drew over one million fans in the first 28 games. By the end of the month they had a four and a half game bulge on the league.

On June 29, in the second game of a doubleheader, the Yankees started a streak that left Boston and Detroit in their dust. They weren't beaten for 19 straight games! This tied an American League record that had been set by the Chicago White Sox 41 years earlier when the Hitless Wonders had taken the pennant in 1906.

The only physical difficulties that showed up during this stretch were some sore arm problems with Bevens, Shea and Chandler—nothing too serious but enough so that they would miss occasional starts. However, it was consistent with MacPhail's attention to detail that he would, first, recognize the problem and, second, do something about it.

On July 12, he brought in two pitchers who really picked up the slack—one, the well-traveled Bobo Newsom whom he had purchased from Washington back in '42 to help the Dodgers. Larry had paid a lot of money for him at that time and Bobo had been rather mediocre, winning two and losing two.

Larry picked him up on waivers, again from Washington, and, this time he was really a big help. After he had announced his usual, "Have no fear. Bobo's here," he won the 13th and 18th games of the 19 game winning streak and his next two starts after that.

The other was a can't-miss rookie named Vic Raschi, who had already won eight and lost two for Portland in the Pacific Coast League. He, also, won two games in the streak and was a tremendous addition the rest of the way.

The Yankees were seven and a half games ahead by July 4 and, a month later, had increased this lead to 13 full games. By the night of September 3 they had clinched the pennant.

During this stretch there was the beginning of the tragic ending to a career that had held so much promise—that of Spurgeon (Spud) Chandler. His sore arm proved to be of more than passing significance. On July 4 he had won the first game of a doubleheader against Washington, 7-3, and had contributed a home run to his own cause. That turned out to be his last victory, not only of the year, but of his entire career.

Spud, who is now connected with the Minnesota Twins, remembers his association with MacPhail with fondness:

"I first met him just after getting out of the army in 1945. It was a pleasure talking with him, especially during contract time in the spring of 1946.

"He often visited us in the clubhouse and gave the players nice gifts, such as an order for a suit of clothes or a sterling silver humidor with all the autographs of the players on the club. He made a positive effort to get along with all of us, in which, in my book, he did a great job."

Chandler continues, "I have wished many times that he had joined the Yankees years before he did. I was very fond of him and our dealings were never harsh, but very appealing. I was a bush shaker scouting for the Yankees and I still regret losing Herb Score and Frank Lary. Both were Yankee-type pitchers. Mr. MacPhail had retired at that time and George Weiss would not give me the money to sign them."

The last two games of the streak were vivid testimony to MacPhail's attention to detail and the performance of his job. It was a doubleheader at Cleveland and the two newcomers to the staff were the winning pitchers. Newsom won the

200th game of his career in the opener and Raschi won the nightcap. They were stopped the next day in Detroit on a two-hitter by Freddy Hutchinson, but it had been a thrilling streak that the whole country had been watching with awe.

The players were fully aware of the job Larry had done in patching up the bone-weary and sore-armed pitching staff. They had taken Jean MacPhail into their confidence and asked her what she thought he might like as a tribute from the team. She had suggested a tray with all the players' names engraved on it, and they went one step further.

On the Friday of the last series of the year "the boss" was surprised when he was called to home plate before the game. For one of the few times in his life Larry MacPhail was speechless. Tears were streaming down his ample red cheeks when the players presented him with a full seven-piece sterling silver service. The tray had all their names inscribed on it along with this message:

"To Larry MacPhail, greatest executive in baseball, whose zealous efforts were a major factor in our 19-game streak, and the winning of the American League pennant. From his Yankees, 1947."

The tumultuous season was over. Now, for the World Series against his old Brooklyn Dodgers and old adversary, Branch Rickey. What a series it would be!

16

The Other Side of the Jackie Robinson Story

Before jumping into the excitement and events of the historic World Series of 1947, a story of much greater social significance must be told.

There was a development that had been brewing for years, one that culminated during spring training of 1947 at the camp of the Brooklyn Dodgers and was to affect major league baseball from that point forward for the rest of its existence—the breaking of the color line.

Many books have been written about the courage and humanity exhibited by Branch Rickey when, against almost insurmountable odds, he signed the first black, Jackie Robinson, to a major league contract.

These books also detail the trials suffered by and the abuses heaped upon this gutsy leader of his race in pioneering the way on the baseball field for all the great black athletes that were to follow in his footsteps.

No attempt is made here to minimize the importance of these accomplishments. They have been well chronicled. There is, however, another side of the Jackie Robinson story that deserves to be told—one that would indicate that the Mahatma's motivations were not entirely altruistic.

Despite the bigotry in many areas of baseball ownership and the public in general, it was becoming increasingly apparent that the not-too-distant future would see the entry of the black athlete into organized baseball. How could this best be accomplished?

There were four Negro leagues—two major and two minor—that had been in business for many years. Should not these owners be considered in whatever decisions were made? How about compensation? Would their teams and leagues be completely destroyed?

These four leagues employed 400-500 ballplayers. If the major leagues skimmed off only the cream of these players how long would the individual teams and, shortly thereafter, the leagues themselves be able to operate? Then, of course, as a consequence, would this not necessarily throw several hundred black ballplayers out of work?

In addition to the question of integration there were many other problems that were becoming increasingly thorny to major league baseball and that had to be faced.

The Mexican leagues had been raiding the majors and paying, or promising to pay, what were then huge salaries to those ballplayers who would play "south of the border." Concurrently, there had been attempts to form a union of major league ballplayers. It seemed vital at this time to do something about these many questions.

Therefore, on the 8th of July, 1946, the American and National Leagues together appointed a joint committee "to consider and test all matters of Major League interest and report its conclusions and recommendations."

The committee was composed of six members and included both league presidents—Will Harridge of the American and Ford Frick of the National—Larry MacPhail of the New York Yankees, Tom Yawkey of the Boston Red Sox, Phil Wrigley of the Chicago Cubs and Sam Breadon of the St. Louis Cardinals. They elected Larry chairman.

Under his leadership this committee, unlike so many other such groups, was an active one. They met seven times during the next month. MacPhail planned to prepare a report of their activity and recommendations for presentation at the meeting of the major league owners in Chicago in August.

The purview of subjects to be tackled was wide-ranging—player pension plans, possible rule changes, bonuses for first-year players, how to handle attempts to organize the players into a union, the raids by Jorge Pasqual of the Mexican League, and the more mundane subjects of ticket prices and schedules.

In addition to this long list of subjects Larry was determined to get into the "race question." It was the type of project that Larry approached with relish and with his usual degree of thoroughness.

The meetings were held in three different cities—Boston, Chicago and New York. For the first time a genuine effort was made to listen to the opinions of the players concerning the problems facing organized baseball and three players from each league were selected by the players to sit in on the discussions.

The National League players selected Fred "Dixie" Walker as their spokesman and Johnny Murphy, the great Yankee fireman, was picked by the American League players.

MacPhail was instrumental in getting the committee to agree to give an assurance to the players that before the start of the next season the owners would approve a plan that would include setting a minimum salary and providing expenses for spring training.

Larry was also determined to lay the groundwork for a major league players' pension fund. Toward this end the committee asked the well-respected Cardinal shortstop, Marty Marion, to join them in preliminary discussions.

The legal climate and overall fear of possible court action was such that MacPhail and his committee had little trouble getting through a few other provisions that would benefit the players.

The standard player contract with a major league team contained a 10-day clause that allowed a ball club to sever connections with a player after 10 days' notice. At MacPhail's suggestion it was recommended that this period be extended to 30 days.

There was also, at that time, no limit to the amount a player's salary might be cut at the time of his contract renewal during an option year. Again, MacPhail suggested, and the committee agreed to, the recommendation of a maximum of a 25 percent reduction for the option year.

Shortly before the first of August most of the committee's recommendations were given to the press. One of the milestones of all future contracts was the establishment of a minimum salary. Although the amount was only $5,500, it had laid down the principle of a floor beneath which no major league salary could be negotiated. From thence forward the minimum could only go up.

A second provision covered a spring training allowance of $25 a week.

Probably the most revolutionary and important recommendation of all was the establishment of a players' pension fund to be set up by the owners with additional contributions from the players. This was a tremendous breakthrough. Now, ballplayers had something to assist them in their old age.

In this first step, all veterans of five years or more in the majors who had attained the age of 50 would start participating. The fund would grow with each passing year, through contributions from the annual All-Star games, World Series and other events.

With these basic principles established there was still another most important area of controversy to be confronted—how to bring the black athlete into organized baseball.

The Negro leagues were pretty much a catch-as-catch-can proposition. Sam Lacy, a black sportswriter who was a champion of integration, wrote that he thought there were few, if any, complete black ballplayers who could play in the majors because of the lack of the teaching of the fundamentals of hitting, fielding, and baserunning.

Nonetheless, there were talented young players in the Negro leagues at that time who could be nurtured in the minor leagues if a way could be found to gradually integrate the minor leagues and, eventually, the majors.

But MacPhail was very sensitive to the consequences if the major leagues simply took the top black athletes from the Negro leagues. Wouldn't this cause those Negro leagues to fold? Wouldn't it then follow that all but a small handful of black athletes would be thrown out of work? Thirdly, shouldn't the owners of the Negro teams be adequately compensated for the loss of their top stars if the major leagues signed them?

There was one other consideration that undoubtedly had some bearing on the matter. A number of the major league teams rented out their facilities to the Negro teams, among them, for example, the New York Yankees, who received some $100,000 a year from renting out Yankee Stadium and their stadia at Newark, Kansas City and Norfolk.

Another area of the problem was also covered in MacPhail's report—that of contract violation if the major leagues were to deal directly with the black ballplayer who had been playing for one of the Negro teams.

After much discussion with the rest of the committee and other owners, MacPhail's plan involved bringing the Negro leagues into organized baseball.

Then, through an orderly process, a plan would be developed whereby only a certain number of Negro players each year would be drafted by the major league clubs in a manner similar to the drafts of today. The last place clubs from the previous year in each league would have the first choices, the second to last clubs the second choices, etc.

Also, a set price would be established, depending on the quality of that player, as the amount awarded as compensation to the owner of the Negro team for the loss of his player.

Branch Rickey wanted no part of these longer range plans. He wanted more immediate action and decided to go it alone. He had carefully selected the man he chose to break the color line.

Jackie Robinson was a great athlete and a college graduate. Rickey took the time and effort to satisfy himself that Robinson not only had the ability to play major league ball but also the courage to turn the other cheek against all the abuse that would be hurled his way on the base paths, at bat, on the road, at hotels and restaurants.

Rickey also relished his role as the crusader. He claimed that he alone was willing to bring a Negro into organized baseball.

In a speech he made to a predominantly black audience at Wilberforce State University, a black college located at Wilberforce, Ohio, on February 16, 1948, he claimed that a report had been circulated to each major league owner and in it Rickey was condemned for his efforts in bringing Robinson into organized baseball.

He also claimed that each copy of this report had been collected after each owner had read it. Unknown to Rickey a reporter was in the audience and his speech was reported in the press the next day.

A number of the owners responded immediately. Bob Carpenter of the Phillies called the allegations by Rickey that the other magnates were trying to prevent him from breaking baseball's color line as "ridiculous." Phil Wrigley called Rickey's statement an unqualified lie. Clark Griffith of the Washington Senators said he had never heard of the report.

Rickey eventually backed down to a degree, saying that it was actually a part of a larger report concerning other matters facing major league baseball and that it was possible that some owners had overlooked that portion of the document that dealt with integration. He did admit that the removal of copies of the report might have been for reasons of secrecy and security rather than anti-black sentiment.

The actual existence of this portion of the document seems never to have been entirely substantiated.

Whatever his claim to the title of crusader, the fact remains that Rickey felt no obligation to compensate the Negro team or teams whose players he decided to sign. Robinson was the first.

Rickey dealt directly with him, completely bypassing the owners of the Kansas City Monarchs. Tom Baird, one of the white owners, was livid and threatened to appeal to the commissioner. If he received no satisfaction from that quarter he was determined, then, to take his case to the courts.

Baird and his fellow owners were in a delicate position. Their objections might be seen as opposition to integration when exactly the opposite was true. Finally, Baird's partner, J.L. Wilkinson, convinced Baird to withdraw his protest and Rickey's gamble that the owners of the Negro teams would not dare oppose his actions paid off. It was a move completely consistent with his well-earned reputation as "El Cheapo."

The other owners of major league teams strongly disagreed with Rickey's cavalier attitude of ignoring the interests of the owners of the Negro teams regarding compensation. Many, if not most, of the owners of the major league clubs felt that Rickey was just jumping the gun to try to get the best black players for himself.

Conversely, when Bill Veeck brought Larry Doby to his Cleveland Indians ball club, thus being the first club owner in the American League to sign a black ballplayer, he paid Mrs. Effa Manley, owner of the Newark Eagles, $10,000 for Doby's contract and an additional $10,000 when he made the club.

17

An Eight-Game
World Series—
Seven on the Field and
One at the Biltmore

The World Series opened at Yankee Stadium on September 30 before a record-breaking crowd of 73,365 and was broadcast to millions of fans throughout the country and over the Armed Forces Network. Television was still in its infancy with a limited number of sets available, but radio carried the play-by-play instantly to every corner of the country. The action was graphically reported by Red Barber, still the voice of the Dodgers, and Mel Allen, representing the Yankees.

The first two games were to be played at the Stadium, the next three at Ebbets Field and, if necessary, the sixth and seventh games back at the home of the Yankees. "The House That Ruth Built" had never been more colorful, reminiscent of the day earlier in the year when the Bambino had been honored. He, along with Commissioner Chandler (who, with MacPhail, were photographed hugging each other), Ty Cobb, Cy Young (then 80 years old), Tris Speaker and many of the more recent stars of the game were in attendance.

Prominent political figures were also there, including former President Herbert Hoover, Governor Thomas E. Dewey of New York, Secretary of State George C. Marshall, Mayor William O'Dwyer and MacPhail's old boss, former Undersecretary of War, Robert Patterson.

Burt Shotton, who was named as Rickey's interim manager during Durocher's suspension, had picked the ace of his staff, Ralph Branca, as his starting pitcher for Game One. Although Branca was only 21 years old, he had won one game for each of those tender years, and was a logical choice. Bucky Harris had countered with Frank Shea who, despite his occasional arm trouble, had compiled a record of 14 and 5 in his rookie season.

The Dodgers manufactured a run in the first inning when Jackie Robinson stole second base after coaxing a walk from the cautious Yankee pitcher. Dixie Walker brought him home with a line single and the Brooklyns led 1-0. Shea settled down but, with the Yankees mounting a rally in the fourth inning, Bucky had another rookie, Bobby Brown (now Dr. Bobby Brown who retired from the medical profession when he was named president of the American League to succeed Larry's son, Lee MacPhail), pinch hit for Spec and Brown walked with the bases loaded. Before the inning was over the Yankees led 5-1.

Joe Page came in to finish the game and, although he allowed two runs, closed the Dodgers down the rest of the way. That night Harris continued a ritual he had done so many times during the season when he raised his glass in his frequent and somewhat superstitious toast: "Here's to Joe Page."

Game Two was a debacle! It started off routinely enough with the Superchief, Allie Reynolds, dueling the little southpaw, Vic Lombardi. In the top of the fourth Dixie Walker homered to tie the score at 2-2. Then the dam broke loose against the hapless Dodgers.

The deep center field at the Stadium was designed to showcase the abilities of great center fielders like DiMaggio. Those ballplayers who could dash back with the crack of the bat and spear the ball at the last second could bring wild cheers from the crowd. Normally, Pete Reiser was this type of superstar. But not in Game Two.

Billy Johnson hit a deep, but otherwise routine fly ball to dead center and after circling around, Reiser fell down. By the time he had retrieved the ball and thrown it back in, Johnson was standing on third base with a triple.

This was followed by another routine fly by Phil Rizzuto

to Gene Hermanski in left field and it too fell to the ground for a double. With no outs, Bucky Harris had the next batter attempt a sacrifice to move Rizzuto over to third. Jackie Robinson could not come up with the bunt and all hands were safe. It was just not the Dodgers' day!

Before Brooklyn could retire to the sanctuary of their clubhouse the Yankees had scored in every inning but the second and eighth, had run up 10 runs on 15 hits, and worn out four Dodger pitchers—Lombardi, Gregg, Behrman and Barney. Reynolds had gone all the way and racked up a total of 12 strikeouts.

The Bums were charged with only two errors but that was just because they had not touched several other balls that had to be called hits. It was a day to be forgotten in Flatbush. But they would take heart. The Series was now moving to the friendly confines of Ebbets Field.

It seemed that every game in this seven-game Series was different. Game Three was a wild one. Shotton started Joe Hatten and Harris countered with the much-traveled Bobo Newsom. The latter was certainly not unfamiliar with the home of the Dodgers, having pitched there for MacPhail back in '42.

In the first inning an event happened that seemed insignificant at the time but which later caused many people to second-guess some strategy employed by Harris in Game Four. Pete Reiser walked and was out trying to steal second. Another rookie, Sherm Lollar, was catching and threw Pete out with a perfect throw. In sliding into second Reiser turned his ankle and had to leave the game. At the time it seemed just a bad sprain, but later it developed that he had also broken a bone. Had Bucky realized the extent of the injury he most certainly would have made a different decision the next day.

After Hatten had held the Yankees without a run in the first two innings, the Dodgers went to work on Newsom in their half of the second. Before it was over Brooklyn had scored six runs, had knocked Bobo out of the box, and had continued by treating Vic Raschi rudely in his World Series baptism.

Even though the Yankees kept coming back with two runs each in the third, fourth and fifth innings, the final score was Brooklyn 9, New York 8. DiMaggio had blasted a two-run home run and Yogi Berra, batting for Lollar, had gotten the first pinch-hit home run in a World Series, but it was not enough.

The two great relief pitchers, Joe Page and Hugh Casey, had finished up in masterful style by shutting out their opponents—Page from the sixth on, and Casey taking over in the seventh to finish up.

Incidentally, Bobby Brown had doubled and scored in the sixth. The rookie was never to be retired as a pinch hitter during the entire Series.

Game Four was the one that will never be forgotten. Many people can remember exactly where they were and what they were doing while listening to this historic contest.

Bill Bevens had had a rocky and inconsistent year for the Yankees, winning 7 games while losing 13. He was strong and, with enough rest, was hard to beat. This was his first start and he felt strong as an ox. He was also wild enough that he kept the batters from getting too settled in the batter's box and taking a toehold.

A rookie, Harry Taylor, with an impressive 10-5 record, started for the Dodgers. The Yankees looked as if they were going to break the game wide open in the first inning, loading the bases with no outs. Then DiMaggio walked, forcing in the first run. Still nobody out. Hal Gregg replaced Taylor and the sun shone on the Flatbush Faithful. George McQuinn popped up and was retired on the infield fly rule, and Billy Johnson followed by hitting into a double play—Reese to Stanky to Robinson—the Dodgers escaped the big inning. It could have been much worse.

Bevens walked two in the Dodger half of the first inning and kept dodging the bullet through the first eight frames. During this period he walked eight but, miraculously, did not allow a hit during those first eight innings.

In the top of the fourth, Billy Johnson led off with a tremendous triple and Johnny Lindell followed with a run-scoring double. It looked like a promising inning, but Gregg wiggled out without any further damage. Then, in the bottom of the fifth the Dodgers scored without a hit. Bevens continued his wild streak and walked the first two batters. A sacrifice moved the two base runners up and an infield out scored the man from third. It was 2-1 going into the top of the ninth.

Again, the Yankees almost blew the game wide open. Gregg had been taken out for a pinch hitter and Hank Behrman had come in to pitch the eighth inning. He also started the ninth but, when the Yankees loaded the bases on two singles and a fielder's choice, Shotton brought in his ace reliever, Hugh Casey, to face Tommy Henrich.

The last time the two of them had faced each other was in the World Series of 1941 when Mickey Owen had dropped that third strike for what should have been the third out. Henrich had beaten the throw to first and that started the deluge that buried the Dodgers.

Whether the thoughts of that previous encounter went through the minds of the two facing each other or not, things have a way of evening out. There was one out and when Tommy tapped the ball back weakly to Casey, the burly pitcher started a home-to-first double play and the side was retired. In the entire seven-game Series, Casey was to pitch in all but the second game blowout.

Then came the Dodger ninth and that incredible finish!

Bruce Edwards, the Dodger catcher, was the first man up and hit a towering fly ball that finally came down in Johnny Lindell's glove in front of the left-field wall. One out. Two more and Bevens would achieve something that no one before him had ever accomplished—a no-hitter in the World Series.

Carl Furillo worked Bevens for a walk, the ninth free pass issued by the right-hander. The next batter was the third-baseman, John (Spider) Jorgensen, who had had a good year during the season, compiling a .274 average as a rookie. He was trying to hit to right to get Furillo over to third but in so doing, popped up to George McQuinn in foul territory. Two out. Just one more and the game would be history.

Furillo was not all that fast and Shotton had to make a move that would increase their chances of getting a man to second. So, he put in Al Gionfriddo to run for Carl. Little Al was fast on the bases and an excellent outfielder defensively—not much of a hitter but a good replacement in the late innings to protect a lead. Now, however, the only thought was to get some speed on the bases.

Hugh Casey was due up next and everyone in the ball park knew he was through for the day. But who would Burt send

up to hit for him? There was only one left-handed batter left
in the dugout and that was the man who had limped off the
field with what later proved to be a broken foot the day
before—Pete Reiser. Shotton called on him and, disguising
the injury as much as possible, Pete moved to the plate accompanied by the raucous, hoarse cheering of the ever-faith-
ful screaming Flatbush fans.

With the count two and one on the batter, little Al made
his move and just beat Berra's throw to Rizzuto at second.
Reiser had not swung at the pitch which was called ball three.
Now first base was open. Harris had a real decision to make.
Should he walk Reiser and play for a force play? After all, that
would go against all baseball tradition—putting the winning
run on base. Or should he let the injured but gutsy outfielder
hit away? Bucky didn't hesitate. He signalled for Bevens to
throw an intentional wide one. Reiser limped to first base and
was replaced by a pinch runner, Eddie Miksis.

Peewee Reese has really chuckled about the decision. He
has said that if Bucky had had any idea of the real extent of
Reiser's injury he never would have walked him, knowing
that there would be a pinch runner anyway and that the
chances of Pete even hitting the ball in his condition would
have been slim—let alone getting down to first base to avoid
being the third out. At any rate, that's what happened. A
manager gets only one shot at making the right decision, and
who knows what actually would have happened had Reiser
been allowed to hit?

Now there were men on first and second. Still two out. The
no-hitter still intact. All Bevens had to do was just get that
one more out and he had it—undying fame and the first no-
hit game in a World Series.

The next batter was the steady, but light-hitting, Eddie
Stanky, the "Brat." But Shotton made another move. For only
the second time all year he called Eddie back from the on-
deck circle and sent Harry (Cookie) Lavagetto up to hit for
him.

Cookie missed the first pitch entirely. But, not the second.
The ball was hit high and far to right field. Henrich leapt like
a Masai warrior but no one could have reached it as it caromed
off the concrete wall above Tommy's head. With two outs

both runners were off with the crack of the bat. Gionfriddo scored easily to tie the game and Miksis kept coming. He slid home safely and the incredible ball game was over.

The Bums had pulled the chestnut out of the fire, had scored a total of three runs on only one hit all day, and Bill Bevens had missed his date with history. But it was a game never to be forgotten!

The fifth game was another cliff-hanger. With the Series tied at two both teams knew that they would be returning to Yankee Stadium for the sixth game and it just remained to be seen which team would go in there with the 3-2 edge.

Harris' pitching rotation had been much easier to decide than had that of Shotton. This was especially true for Bucky when, because of the luxury of having won the first two games, he was able to gamble with Newsom in Game Three. After starting Branca in the first game and losing, Burt's selection for starters and early relievers seemed sometimes to be the result of a coin flip. Hugh Casey was always ready for the last few innings.

Frank Shea had been the winning pitcher in the first game and had only pitched five innings in that one. So he was well-rested and strong to start Game Five. Ralph Branca had pitched in Game Three so Shotton felt he could not come back with him that quickly. After wrestling with the decision Burt picked Rex Barney to face the Yankees. Barney had not started a game since Independence Day, but had posted a 5-2 record for the season.

Shea was masterful, both on the mound and at the plate. He set the Dodgers down on four hits and got two of the Yankees' five hits himself. Frank batted in the first run for the Bronx Bombers in the fourth with a line single and through the first five innings against the Dodgers he allowed only two base runners, one on a walk and the other on a single, with nobody advancing as far as second.

In the meantime Barney was dodging the bullet. He bid fair to break Bevens' World Series record of 10 walks set the day before, and undoubtedly would have had the Bums scored some runs so that Shotton would not have had to pinch-hit for him. Rex gave up nine bases on balls in the four and two-thirds innings he pitched.

He had faced DiMaggio three times before being taken out. The first two times he was successful, setting the Yankee Clipper down on strikes with the bases loaded in the first and making him hit into a double play the second time he faced him in the third. However, the third time was too much and, on the third pitch on a 2-0 count, Joe deposited the ball in the upper deck to give Shea a fifth inning lead of 2-0.

The Yankee rookie pitcher went all the way, winning his second game of the Series, this time 2-1. Shotton had to use four pitchers—Barney, Hatten, Behrman and, of course, Hugh Casey. The ninth inning was reminiscent of the day before with Cookie Lavagetto coming to bat with two out, the tying run on second and the Yankees leading 2-1. This time the script was a little different. Cookie went down swinging and the ball game was over.

Now, it was back to Yankee Stadium where the Dodgers had yet to win a game. Their back was to the wall.

Game Six. A new World Series record crowd of 74,065 came to see their Yankees close out the Series. Allie Reynolds, the Superchief, was, like Shea the day before, well-rested and raring to go. He had had an easy time of it in Game Two and was looking forward to the same type of afternoon in the same park in which he had had his previous romp.

However, there are few things more unpredictable than sporting events. That's what makes horse racing. The odds would have been great against the Yankees losing that day. MacPhail was very confident, with everything going for his Yankees. But some things are just not meant to be.

The Dodgers started right in against Reynolds as if they had not read the script. Eddie Stanky and Peewee Reese led off with line singles and Johnny Lindell suffered the same indignity the Dodger outfielders had gone through in Game Two when he let Jackie Robinson's routine fly ball in left field drop for the third single. Bases loaded. Nobody out. Before they were retired, the Dodgers picked up two runs. It could have been worse.

Vic Lombardi started for Brooklyn and retired the first six Yankees. From then on, for both sides, it was "Katie, bar the door." Records other than for attendance were set this day. A total of 38 players were used in the game, 21 by New York and 17 by Brooklyn. Bucky Harris used six pitchers, Burt Shotton four. The game took a record 3 hours and 19 minutes to play. Enough statistics.

The Dodgers got to Reynolds again for two runs in the top of the third and Allie retired for the day. But the Yankees were not going to sit back and quit four runs down. They tied it up with four in their half of the same inning against the little left-hander and his replacement, Ralph Branca.

New York went ahead again 5-4 with a single run in the fourth, but the lead lasted only until the top of the sixth. Joe Page was now pitching for the Yankees and with a one-run lead he figured to shut Brooklyn down the rest of the way. But this was not meant to be. They teed off on the great fireman and his successor, Bobo Newsom, and, before the Dodgers went to the field they had a three-run lead, 8-5. This was an unaccustomed luxury for Burt Shotton. He was now able to make defensive moves to protect that lead.

Even though it had been Lavagetto's double against Bill Bevens in the fourth game that had brought in the tying and winning runs and had prevented the Yankee pitcher's no-hitter and victory, Burt Shotton had credited Al Gionfriddo and his steal of second base as the key to the game. Burt had used the little outfielder often during the season as a defensive replacement, usually for Pete Reiser. In this sixth game, Gene Hermanski had started in left and, when Eddie Miksis had pinch-hit for him he had also replaced him in the sun field for an inning. Now, with his three-run lead, Shotton sent Gionfriddo to left. It proved to be a stroke of genius!

In the last of the sixth little Al made one of the greatest fielding plays in World Series history. A further change in the lineup had Joe Hatten taking over the Dodger pitching at the same time. He proved to be no mystery to the Yankees but did manage to get two outs while he had walked Stirnweiss and allowed a single to Yogi Berra. This brought the potential tying run to the plate in the person of the Yankee Clipper, Joe DiMaggio.

Over 70,000 fans rose as one as they watched Joe send a screaming shot 415 feet toward the bull pen in left-center field. The three runs would tie the score at eight. But Gionfriddo was off with the crack of the bat and caught up with the ball at the last split-second as it was going over the fence into the bull pen. The usually publicly unflappable DiMaggio almost broke his toe kicking second base as he saw the ball sink into Gionfriddo's glove. The inning was over.

The Yanks did pick up a run in the last of the ninth but Hugh Casey got the save, his fifth appearance in six games, and the Dodgers prevailed, 8-6. MacPhail did not take kindly to the defeat and, when he found out that the reason Lindell had not finished the game was that he had had a broken rib before the game started, he climbed all over the outfielder. Johnny had gotten two hits before he had taken himself out. Well, anyway, tomorrow was another day.

Another day? Now, the whole season and the entire World Series came down to one final game. Each manager would use everybody on his team if necessary. They could rest all winter.

As so often happens, most of the dramatics had been used up getting to this seventh game. The game itself was rather routine. Bucky Harris had planned on starting Bill Bevens but switched over to Frank Shea who had already won two games.

However, the Dodgers got to Spec for two runs in the second and Bucky then brought in the man who had come so close to World Series no-hit fame. Bevens did an adequate job and when he was taken out for a pinch-hitter in the last of the fourth, the Yankees had gone ahead 3-2 before the start of the fifth.

Now, Bucky Harris had a big decision to make. Whom should he bring in to go the rest of the way? The Dodgers had been able to come back several times in the Series already. He had both Allie Reynolds and Joe Page warming up in the bull pen. In fact, he had almost everybody to pick from if the situation demanded it.

John Shulte was the bull pen catcher and, as such, was the man to advise who "had it" and who did not. Harris' coach, Frank Crosetti, was on the phone in the dugout relaying this information to Bucky who was at the other end of the dugout. Just around the corner, hanging around the runway next to Harris' end of the dugout, was Larry MacPhail.

Word came back from Shulte on both men. Crosetti yelled it on down to Harris:

"Shulte says Page hasn't got it, but the Indian (Allie Reynolds) is knocking the mitt out of his hands. Who do you want?"

At this point Bucky spotted MacPhail who had also heard the comments Crosetti had yelled across the dugout.

"Larry, you've got as much to lose on this deal as I do. Page or Reynolds?"

Page had been bombed for four runs the day before. There didn't seem to be much choice.

Larry growled:

"Bucky, you've been calling them all season and for six games so far in the World Series. There's no reason to change now. You pick the man."

Harris turned back to Crosetti who had been waiting for instructions. All the players on the bench had heard the entire exchange between Shulte and Crosetti and even the much more subdued conversation between Harris and MacPhail. There were many disbelievers in the dugout when Bucky yelled back to his coach one syllable:

"Page."

Larry, in reminiscing about the decision, observed:

"That took guts, but Bucky never flinched. I looked over at the Dodger bench when Joe came in and old Burt Shotton couldn't believe it. They certainly didn't expect Bucky to come back with the same guy they murdered the day before."

All the great fireman did was to shut the Dodgers down for five innings on one hit, that a harmless single by Miksis in the ninth inning that was erased in a double play. The routine and businesslike ending was in stark contrast to the wild and unpredictable ones that had preceded it.

Baseball is a funny game. The day before, Page had gotten his ears pinned back. Today, except for two pitches, he had thrown nothing but fast balls that looked like aspirin tablets, had faced the minimum of 15 batters and walked off the mound to thunderous applause. How do you figure it?

The Yankee clubhouse was bedlam! All the emotion that had built up during the Series spilled over in the outpouring of happy congratulations and flowing champagne. It was a typical scene in a winner's clubhouse. The doors were open to the press and others at the same time the players came in from the field.

Then, in the midst of the jubilation, the ever-emotional MacPhail stole the spotlight from Bucky, his players and his coaches—an uncontrolled performance whose timeliness he greatly regretted many times in the future.

With tears streaming down his puffy cheeks he screamed:

"That's it! It's all over! I'm through. No more pressure! I'm retiring from baseball and resigning as president of the Yankees."

At the time few people believed him. Most thought that he was just overreacting to the emotion of the moment. But, as he kept repeating the statement many times throughout the evening, they started to take him at his word.

Actually, maybe his decision was not as unpredictable as it seemed. Many times and events in his life gave testament to the fact that it was the creating, the building of things that was the driving force that impelled him. Once the goal was attained the fun was gone. It was the getting there that counted. This was the denouement. He was president of the World Champions! What was there left to achieve in baseball?

As he walked out of the clubhouse back through the grandstands a chance meeting occurred that gave evidence to the finality of the Larry MacPhail–Branch Rickey relationship that had had so many emotional ups and downs over their years in baseball.

Rickey had just left the Dodger clubhouse where the emotions of a different nature had also been overflowing. His shoulders were hunched in the despair of defeat when he ran into MacPhail. The stands still held the stragglers, some of whom were still savoring the victory and others who were just trying to avoid the crowds.

The bitterness of defeat and the deterioration of their relationship came through on the part of Rickey in the short conversation. MacPhail put his arm around the older man in a conciliatory gesture. Rickey took the hand that was extended to him and forced the words so low-pitched that MacPhail could barely hear them: "I am taking your hand only because so many people are watching. But don't you ever speak to me again!"

The victory party was at the Biltmore. And what a party it was!

Every detail had been meticulously planned. The food and drink were lavish in both quality and quantity. Anyone even remotely connected with the Yankees, major league baseball, the World Series, politics or almost any other area of public interest was invited.

The emotion that Larry had expended in the clubhouse after the game was strictly a warmup for what followed at the victory celebration. The rambunctious redhead was now the roaring redhead and ready to take on all comers. What followed was later dubbed "The Battle of the Biltmore."

John McDonald, the traveling secretary who had been with him so long in Cincinnati and Brooklyn, had by now retired from the Dodgers and had co-authored an article in the *Saturday Evening Post* shortly thereafter that dealt mainly with his relationship and experiences with MacPhail during that time. Larry had violently resented the piece and had even referred to McDonald as a Judas! Seeing him at the bar, Larry first berated him unmercifully and then knocked him down with a right to the eye.

Now he was completely out of control! He saw George Weiss, whom he had earlier publicly given credit for having built the Yankees to their present position of dominance, and fired him on the spot.

Later in the evening and small hours of the morning there were further discussions, arguments and resolutions between and among the three owners of the Yankees that resulted in Topping and Webb buying out MacPhail for $2,000,000. It was an emotional and turbulent ending to three highly successful years during which Larry was able to rebuild a great dynasty.

He was to reflect and question many times thereafter, when he licked cancer twice and a heart attack another time, whether he would have been able to overcome these physical problems had he continued under the pressure of the major league baseball scene in the manner in which it was his nature to operate.

18

Down on the Farm

Larry had always wanted to own and live on a farm—to relax and get away from the pressures that always seemed to build up in any activity he undertook. Baseball had taken a toll on his personal life.

In late December of 1937 and the first two weeks of January 1938, Larry was negotiating with the Brooklyn Trust Bank about whether and under what conditions he would take over the running of the Dodgers. By this time, his daughter, Marian, was living in New York and he asked her to go out and take a good look at Ebbets Field and its facilities. She reported back to him that her overall impression was that it was really only one or two steps above those at old Neil Park in Columbus, which they had abandoned in favor of building the new and magnificent Columbus Red Bird Stadium. Of course, this not unexpected report was the type of challenge MacPhail loved, and it merely whetted his appetite.

When Larry got the arrangements he wanted for running the Dodgers, he and Inez moved to New York and took up residence at 1 Beekman Place. They also persuaded their daughter to move in with them, at least temporarily.

Marian was their firstborn and four and a half years older than Lee. In her childhood, their family relationship had been a very close and warm one. During the period of Larry's involvement with the Columbus baseball team and the building of Red Bird Stadium, Inez became almost a baseball widow. Still, in Columbus each of the members of the MacPhail family was happy and popular, the children were growing up in a typically active and normal environment and Inez was busily engaged in all that that entailed. Larry's time-consuming in-volvement in the demands of baseball was not only under-standable but also tolerable in their marriage.

However, the life of a superactive baseball executive in the big leagues, and especially in Brooklyn and New York, put a much greater strain on the family ties. Then, when Larry and Inez moved from the city to Larchmont, New York, this put even greater distance, both emotionally and geographically, between them.

In Columbus, Inez had many friends and much social ac-tivity that occupied her time and energy. This was almost totally cut off when they moved to New York, both in the city and in Larchmont. There were many things of a cultural nature to do in the big city, but it was really a lonely place in which to do them without the friendships Inez had known in Columbus.

As the days and months went by and the union of the Brooklyn Dodgers and Larry MacPhail became more and more integrated, his marriage union suffered commensurately. Run-ning the Dodgers simply consumed his time and energy. This, coupled with the proximity of a most attractive young lady who was constantly at his elbow during his working hours, spelled doom for his marriage. It is not a story unique in the business world—or the baseball world.

Incidentally, Larry's own experience may have been part of the reason he was originally against his son, Lee, going into the baseball business. Leland Stanford MacPhail, Jr., later president of the American League for a number of years and recently president of the Major League Baseball Player Rela-tions Committee tells of his father's opposition to his enter-ing the sport:

"When I was growing up, baseball was part of our family life the whole time. I just assumed that I would work in baseball and I had gone to Swarthmore College, which he had helped me find. The reason he had recommended Swarthmore to me is that he was working for Branch Rickey at that time and Mr. Rickey had sent his daughter, Alice, to Swarthmore. And, because of that, I had gotten to know Mr. Rickey a little bit and he had offered me a job running one of the Cardinals' minor league teams when I got out of school.

"I had just assumed that I would go to work for my father in the Dodger organization. In those days recruiters from various companies were coming around to the colleges to interview prospective candidates for jobs in their companies. I hadn't gone to any of those meetings since I knew that I was all set with my father. The assistant dean called me up one time and asked me why I wasn't going to any of those meetings. I told him that I was going to work in baseball, so there was no need for me to have those interviews.

"So, you can imagine I was more than a little shocked when I went home for spring vacation and my father said:

" 'What are you going to do when you get out of college?'

"It was then when he gave me the argument that I shouldn't go into baseball—that I should go into business school or law school. He gave as his reasons for not going into baseball that it was too small and the opportunities were too limited for someone to get ahead.

"He said, 'I'll make a deal with you. If you'll try something else first and, if at the end of the year you still want to go into baseball, I'll give you a job running one of our minor league teams.'

"I said, 'Well, that's fine, except that I have passed up all those job interviews in college, and I wouldn't know where to go to look for one now.'

" 'Don't worry about that,' he answered. 'I have something in mind for you. I'll fix it up for you. Fay Murray, who owns the Nashville club, is in the livestock business and I know he is looking for young people to go into the business.'

"I told my father that I was a city boy and that no one knows less about livestock than I do.

"His response to that was, 'Oh, it doesn't matter whether it's livestock or what it is—whether it's nuts and bolts in the steel business. It doesn't matter what the product is.'

"So, I got the job and they sent me down to a stockyard in Florence, South Carolina (he had said that you'll be working at a desk, anyway). I got there and walked between those aisles in the stockyard, between the cattle and the hogs, and

got as far as the office in the back of the yard. I could smell
it when I got about two miles away. The office was about 12
feet square and there were two desks—one for the manager
of the yard and the other for his secretary. I knew right then
and there that it wasn't going to be any desk job.

"It was a very interesting experience and I stayed about
a year and a half. At the end of this time my father realized
that I was really interested in baseball and his resistance, for
whatever reason, was over. He gave me a job running the
Reading, Pennsylvania team."

Getting back to 1941, Larry filed for divorce that year but
in those days it took almost five years for the decree to become final. Jean says:

"We bought the farm in 1941. Or, rather, he did since we
weren't married until 1945. So, you can see it was quite a long
romance.

"We started looking in New Englnd and upstate New York
for a farm we liked. I wanted one in Vermont, but not Larry.

" 'No way am I going to live in Vermont, having been
brought up in Michigan,' he insisted.

"So, we continued to look in New York and then broad-
ened our search to include Virginia and the Eastern Shore.
I don't think we looked in Pennsylvannia, but we finally
ended up in Harford County, Maryland, near the small town
of Bel Air, northeast of Baltimore.

"We had seen all these beautiful places which, in 1941, you
could buy for a reasonable amount of money. The Eastern
Shore was really not convenient because it was not on the
Pennsylvania or B & O and we couldn't get back and forth
from New York very easily. Well, after we had seen all these
lovely locations, including many in Harford County, we went
back to our good friend, Broadax Cameron, an attorney in Bel
Air.

"We finally went to this farm—the most horrible thing I
had ever seen—and stood out on this hill where the house
was, the main house. There were the two of them, Broadax
and Larry, looking all around them and raving about the possibilities it had!

"I stood there and said, 'Larry, if you buy this farm I'm never going to marry you!' Of course, he didn't pay much attention to that—and, so, he bought it.

"Paul Menton was sports editor of the *Baltimore Sun* at that time, and Larry asked him to send out a photographer to take a picture of the place and run a page on it in the roto section.

"So, the photographer went out there, looked it over and went back to Baltimore empty-handed. He told Paul:

" 'That's no farm he bought. He must have been drunk or crazy.'

"Paul said, 'I didn't ask what you thought. Go back and take the pictures.'

"He did and they ran the picture in the *Sun* over the caption 'Larry MacPhail bought this farm.' "

The before and after pictures bear out Jean's assessment. There wasn't even a blade of grass. She didn't want anything elaborate, just something nice, and this property wasn't it. But she freely admits that Larry saw possibilities that were later borne out and Glenangus Farms, the romantically Scottish name Larry gave the place, became a showplace of the county.

Although they (or, rather, Larry) had bought the farm in '41, they weren't able to do much with it until '42. With the war on then they were just able to get a tenant house built so that a manager could live there. With Larry's running the Dodgers and trying to repeat their pennant-winning success of the previous year, not much else was accomplished on the farm that year. Then, of course, MacPhail went back in the service in the fall.

With Larry in Washington, Jean left the Dodgers and spent 1943 running the farm with the help of a man named Boone who had been one of Larry's lieutenants when they were both overseas during the first World War. He was a teacher in New Jersey and would come down on weekends to help run the place. Occasionally, Larry could get away from the Pentagon and come up on weekends as well. Jean remembers, "We also had a couple of high school boys and six French sailors who were sort of at liberty while their ship was being repaired in

Baltimore. The repair work took a long time, so they were available all summer long. I can't remember where I dug them up, but we put them up at the inn in Bel Air and they would have lunch with us at the farm.

"Actually, they must have been there into the fall. In the room that became the library we had a large table, several big benches and a huge pot-bellied stove. When we sat with our backs to the stove we almost burned up, so we all had to sit on the other side of the table. Boone, the two high school boys and I couldn't speak a word of French and the sailors not a word of English. So, we really had quite a time.

"A man by the name of Waddell was the manager at the time, and not a very good one. Somehow we had located 13 or 14 German prisoners-of-war in the nearby town of Edgewood and would transport them over to our farm under guard.

"I can remember one time Larry came up from Washington on a surprise visit and, not seeing Waddell or the POWs, asked me where they were. I told them that they were over on a nearby farm we had rented, getting in the hay, and he drove over to see them. When we got there he saw no activity at all. Under each pile of hay were two or three German POWs sleeping. Waddell and the guard were asleep in the truck. Well, you know, all hell broke loose. Wow, did that change fast!"

There really wasn't much more accomplished on the farm during this period. Larry's thoughts and actions, like those of so many other people, were devoted almost exclusively to the war effort. At the end of '43 Larry asked Jean to join him at the Pentagon and work as his secretary so their visits to the farm were rare.

Larry's divorce from Inez became final in early May in 1945 and on the 16th of that month he and Jean were married at the Belvedere Hotel in Baltimore. Many members of the Maryland press corps were in attendance. After the ceremony and the wedding breakfast the entire party went out to Pimlico to the horse races.

Commissioner Chandler had issued an ultimatum to the effect that no one connected with major league baseball would be allowed to go to the racetrack. Of course, MacPhail was not about to be dictated to as to where he could or could not spend his leisure hours and he relished the publicity that followed in all the papers the next day. Nothing was heard about this defiant activity from the commissioner's office.

With the war about over and Larry now running the Yankees his activity revolved mainly around bringing the pennant and World Series championship back to the Yankees.

In the meantime he also found time to devote to making his vision of a showplace farm a reality. In typical fashion he studied all facets of animal husbandry, farm management, total landscaping and other elements that would contribute to attaining this goal. He had read somewhere that the federal government would provide, free of charge, quantities of multiflora roses if the recipient would keep detailed records on their growth and proliferation and report back periodically to the Department of Agriculture. Gradually the neat white fences that separated the fields and lots at Glenangus Farms were covered with these beautiful blossoms, also called Japanese roses. When a visitor to the farm would comment on the beauty of the roses, Larry was wont to point out with a friendly poke to the ribs, "and you don't have to paint the fences."

As might be surmised from the name he gave to the farm, Larry's first endeavor in the livestock business was to start building a prize herd of Black Angus cattle. It was not long before he had one of the top herds in the country and set several records at cattle sales. He imported a number of top-quality heifers directly from Scotland to be serviced by his prize bulls.

Then, while still continuing his strong interest in improving the quality of his cattle herd, he directed his attention to the business of breeding thoroughbred horses.

He purchased the first three brood mares from his friend, Alfred G. Vanderbilt, for $34,000. Each of the three was in foal, with two producing colts and the other a filly. By the summer of 1948 he had these six horses at Glenangus plus two more yearling colts and two fillies of the same age that he had purchased from Adolphe Pons, who ran the Country Life Breeding Farm in Bel Air.

Larry always considered patience a virtue, but not a very

important one. He just couldn't wait for his yearlings and foals to grow up. So he ordered Jimmy McGee, who trained for him, to keep his eyes open for a young juvenile. The last week in June, at Jimmy's suggestion, Larry bought a two-year old bay colt named Jacopone for $15,000 from Walter Jeffords even though the horse had finished sixth, seven lengths behind the winner, in his first start on June 22 at Delaware Park.

The colt was by a stud named Jacopo-Fleur by Pennant. It might have been the fact that a horse named Pennant was in his bloodlines that had attracted Larry to him in the first place. Before the year was over, Jacopone had justified McGee's judgment by becoming the Squire of Glenangus' first winner carrying the maize and blue colors he had adopted from the University of Michigan.

Larry's wide range of interests was expressed in the various names he gave to his young horses. The Jockey Club accepted "B Minor" as the name of one of the foals, but rejected the name "Battery B," taken from his World War I outfit, for another because it had been used too recently at that time. It also turned down the name "Ladies Day" for one of the fillies for the same reason. One of the yearlings had been called "Leonidoff" in honor of the prominent producer and ballet master of the day and another was known as "Country Date." The rumor that one of the colts was to be named "Branch Rickey" was ill-founded.

In August, Larry, Jean and Jimmy left Glenangus and went to the races and sales at Saratoga. Most people had figured that he would not be a buyer, but he and McGee had given careful study to the sales catalogs that had been distributed a month and a half earlier and before the sale was over MacPhail had spent almost $40,000, paying top prices for the best-bred fillies and passing up the desirable colts. He was interested not only in racing them the next year, but also in building up his broodmare ranks for the future.

Larry had already learned much about the thoroughbred breeding business. He figured that if he stuck to quality in his mares he could always buy the services of the top stallions as long as he could show their owners that they would be mated to well-bred and good-producing matrons.

The roaring redhead never did anything halfway. If he was

going into the horse breeding business he wanted to know all there was to learn about the industry. Other than his occasional trips to the track around New York during his baseball days in there, his familiarity with the bangtails was basically restricted to his trips to the betting windows.

He knew that the sharpshooters in the business would be laying in the weeds for him to peel off some of the $2,000,000 he left baseball with and would be rubbing their hands in anticipated glee at the thought of plucking some of that green stuff from this greenhorn. Some of those in the baseball fraternity might have advised their brethren in horseracing that MacPhail might not be the easy touch they thought him to be.

With typical MacPhail intensity, he interviewed owners and trainers, read dozen of books on the subject of thoroughbreds and their breeding, became acquainted with bloodlines and generally studied the many and varied phases of the business.

In the early part of 1949 he was in full swing. At an auction at Belmont he was the most active spender when he bought three fillies out of the dispersal sale of Walter J. Chrysler's stable. After carefully studying the bloodlines of these three ladies, he peeled off $27,300 from his bankroll to bring them over to Glenangus. For Our Hostess, a three-year old daughter of the imported Bull Dog-Epitine, Larry paid $13,600, and $7,000 for Pretty One, another filly from Bull Dog. The third horse, Invariant, was sired by one of the most successful sires of the time, the imported Blenheim II.

At Pimlico, just before the Preakness, he grabbed off an honor highly prized in the horsey set of Maryland, when one of his home-bred colts came out the yearling champion of the Pimlico show.

Not only was he starting to learn much about this new business, but he was also able to apply some of the lessons he had learned from his trading of players during his baseball days.

Larry sent 10 yearlings to the summer sales at Saratoga in 1950 and when the intelligentsia of racing studied the catalog they were amazed to discover that the 10 yearlings were sired by 10 of the leading horses doing stud duty, sires that few outsiders had ever been able to secure for their mares.

The judging of horseflesh is an imprecise science at best and it is difficult to determine what is in the mind of a prospective buyer. One of the yearlings was a chestnut filly by Grand Slam-Green Shed who was bought by a horseman of many years experience, named Del Holeman, for $2,900. The new owner then brought his purchase to Kentucky where she was broken and trained and fed for two months.

It should be pointed out that, at that time, there was a considerable difference between the sales at Saratoga and those at Lexington, Kentucky a couple of months later. Thoughts of the glitter at the Saratoga spa conjure up a picture of lovely ladies parading about and perspiring in their minks and sables. Such was not the case at Lexington where, although some of the same wealthy persons who wanted a stakes horse at almost any price were present, a much higher percentage of the buyers were trainers and very knowledgeable about the animals with which they were getting involved.

At any rate, Holeman, having spent considerable time and money on the Grand Slam filly, then put her up for sale at Lexington. She had been given a public trial on the Sunday prior to the sale and had run reasonably well. She came up in the first morning's sale and brought $1,800. And, who do you suppose bought her? Leland Stanford MacPhail!

So, now he had the filly back, was spared the expense of training and feeding her in the interim, plus $1,100. And, as if that were not enough, a man who had been at MacPhail's side and had watched him bid her in at $1,800, later came around and offered to buy the filly for $2,500. Larry could not pass it up and accepted the offer, ending up without a horse, but with an extra $700.

MacPhail probably expressed it best when, comparing the two prominent locations of the horse sale areas, he said at Lexington:

> Down here a yearling without much pedigree, but an extremely good individual, will bring a really good price, when the same yearling at Saratoga would go for nothing. Those buyers at Saratoga—they're label drinkers.
>
> You know, of course, how a man who can drink nothing but Johnnie Walker Black will be quite happy with Old Sluefoot if he sees it come out of a Johnnie Walker bottle,

and in fact I have made some experiments like that on a few friends.

Well, at Saratoga a majority of the buyers will insist on something by Blenheim or Mahmoud or Bull Lea, even if it has crooked hocks or a light forehand. That's possibly because at Saratoga the owners have a big hand in the buying and they want a fashionable pedigree, sometimes neglecting to note that there isn't much horse attached to it. Furthermore, if a horse looks as if he would be hard to train—well, it's the trainer, not the owner, who has to fret with it. At Lexington, where there are many more trainers involved, these trainers have enough grief without asking for more trouble.

Another event occurred in 1949 that ranked as the most important transaction, both financially and sentimentally, that the Colonel (the name Larry liked to be called now) was to make during his time in the horse business—the purchase of a yearling named General Staff for $25,000 from the Crispin Oglebay's dispersal sales.

General Staff was the royally-bred son of the aforementioned Mahmoud, winner of the Epsom Derby and the leading American sire of 1946, whose other offspring were to win seven stakes races in 1950. His dam was a horse named Uvira II who had won the Irish Oaks.

General Staff won three races toward the close of the 1950 racing season and finished third in the Pimlico Futurity, not a mean accomplishment for an owner so new to the sport of kings. In retrospect, both Larry and Jimmy McGee wished they had rested their prize horse at that time. He had had some trouble with his ankles, but they didn't realize that total rest would have been the cure that would have allowed General Staff to not only compete in, but also have an excellent chance of winning, the Kentucky Derby.

It boggles the mind to think that Larry would have been the first man to parlay a world's championship in baseball with the greatest prize in horseracing!

However, hindsight is very easy. The fact is that they decided to bring the horse down to Florida and race him in early '51. Larry admitted, "We got too greedy and couldn't wait."

On January 24, General Staff ran his first race of the new

year at Hialeah, and absolutely scattered a mediocre field, winning by five lengths. Racing writers were highly enthusiastic about how well the "General" ran, and Larry was delighted to read their praises. Trainer McGee, who was not a Johnnie-come-lately to the sport, was quoted as saying:

"He acts and runs like the best horse I've ever trained, and he's just beginning to get good. I don't know how good yet. He was a problem as a two year old, in spite of doing all right. Now, he's a race horse, sound, steady, and hard-hitting."

Bill Corum, successor to the legendary Matt Winn as president of Churchill Downs and thereby becoming the new "Mr. Derby," was a Hialeah visitor when General Staff won this race and was greatly impressed by the looks and performance of MacPhail's horse. He wrote:

> There's a colt that is just beginning to bloom. This race yesterday, which he won loping, after running between horses to take the lead around the last bend, was General Staff's first as a three-year-old and of the winter season. He hadn't been out since he ran third behind Big Stretch in the Pimlico Futurity, after getting some bad breaks and a none-too-well judged ride from Jockey Ira Hanford.
>
> Ira let him run about a sixteenth of a mile in yesterday's seven-furlong sprint. To be sure, he wasn't beating any Derby horses in this one. But, it was hard to watch him and not see him as a bright prospect for the Flamingo and the Rose Run as of now.
>
> After all, following two educational races at two, he now has gone to the post seven times without being out of the money at distances from six furlongs to a mile and a sixteenth. He twice finished second, beaten a half length and a head, then won three straight, followed by his third in the Pimlico Futurity and yesterday's galloping score.
>
> Look out, little red Kentucky Rosebuds, there may be a red-headed man coming into your lives. Those who know MacPhail won't say "no" too loud. There are four-leaf clovers in the man's spinach. He's been lucky in everything he has ever tried. Why not horseracing?

Joe H. Palmer, who wrote *American Race Horses*, an annual publication of the Sagamore Press, heard Corum's comments and also displayed enthusiasm when he chirped in with thoughts of his own:

"He's a beautifully-bred horse, half-brother to two stakes winners, so you could expect him to have class. As a Derby horse he's a long-shot, as every horse is until he comes up to the race itself, but I like the way he ran, and I'd give Larry MacPhail a chance to be the first man to double the World Series and the Kentucky Derby."

There was only one trouble with all these encomiums. Not only were the writers impressed, there was another man, Mr. Charles McLennan, the racing secretary and handicapper at Hialeah, who was equally impressed. And, this was a man who had it within his power to load a horse down with unwanted weight.

Those from the baseball community who were taking early pre-spring training vacations under the warming rays of the Florida sun had cases of deja vu when they heard the mooselike roars that echoed throughout the Peninsula State from the lungs of L.S. (Loud Stentorian) MacPhail when Mr. McLennan determined to burden General Staff with 122 pounds for the Bahamas Handicap on February 3.

Larry was roughly quoted as screaming:

"What are you trying to do, break my animal's back? If you put that kind of weight on my horse, I might as well ride him myself! Where is the justice? Where is your sense of fair play? Where are my constitutional rights?"

It was even suggested that MacPhail compared this injustice to the officials of baseball insisting that Peewee Reese or Scooter Rizzuto be asked to carry the batboy around the bases on their shoulders. Although the Society for the Prevention of Cruelty to Animals might have awarded Larry a medal for his efforts, it was to no avail.

Larry withdrew General Staff. Four days later, in typical unpredictable MacPhail style, he entered General Staff in another race at the same weight. He won by four lengths. He was next entered in the famous Flamingo Stakes and ran a peculiar race, sprinting into a lead, suddenly pulling up and finishing eighth.

Although he was scratched from the Kentucky Derby, he

did run an exciting race in the early spring at Laurel, the Cherry Blossoms Stakes. The handicapper had assigned 124 pounds to the "General," who remained the favorite despite carrying six more pounds than his nearest rival. Two of the horses with 113 pounds on their backs were Repertoire and Alerted. It was a thriller all the way and as they rounded the turn for home they looked like three chargers side by side at the head of a chariot, matching each other stride for stride.

Larry was out of his seat, arms flailing, teetering precariously over the rail, yelling himself hoarse, "Come on, General! Bring it home!"

It was a photo finish, but Larry knew his horse had lost. Trainer Jim McGee was the first to greet him:

"He did exactly as we'd planned," he consoled the Colonel. Grimly, Larry conceded:

"He'll be all right," he mumbled. Just then the jockey came up and Larry put his arm around the young man's shoulder, "You ran a fine race, boy. You did just what I wanted you to." Turning slowly to his wife, he said unsmilingly, "Let's go home, Jean."

MacPhail really regretted racing General Staff in those winter stakes races. In looking back he reflected:

"I'm convinced that if we had rested him after the Futurity he would have won the Kentucky Derby in '51. When he broke down before the Derby, we had to fire him and he didn't race again until he was four. Then, he won eight races and wound up winning $157,800 all told, a lot of money in those days."

19

Challenges, Opportunities and Celebrations

A momentous event that greatly affected the 60-year-old Squire of Glenangus occurred during this period. In Baltimore, on October 26, 1950, there was born to Jean and Larry Mac-Phail, a daughter, named Jean Katherine MacMurtrie Mac-Phail after her mother and paternal grandmother. Minutes after the birth Larry went to the same Belvedere Hotel at which they had had their wedding reception to celebrate the new arrival.

In the bar he ran across their old friend, Millard Tydings, then a United States senator from Maryland. In a jubilant mood Larry clapped him on the back and said:

"Millard, let me buy you a drink. I am celebrating."

Tydings readily accepted and inquired:

"Larry, to what do I owe this happy largesse?"

"Well, old friend," MacPhail replied, "congratulate me. Jean just became the mother of a bouncing baby girl!"

"I'll be damned, Larry," Tydings answered, "whom do you suspect?"

Also, during this time, MacPhail advanced in his new field so rapidly (for anyone except MacPhail) that his fellow horsemen elected him president of the National Association of Thoroughbred Breeders. However, this pace was really not fast enough for him and, on January 27, 1952, Larry closed a deal for the purchase of Bowie Racetrack in Maryland.

There had been four tracks in the Free State—Pimlico, Laurel, Havre de Grace and Bowie. Apparently there had been an effort by the interests behind Pimlico and Laurel to close out Havre de Grace first (which they were able to do) and then gobble up Bowie, thereby eliminating the competition for the racing dates and splitting Bowie's 25 dates between themselves.

Although Larry headed the syndicate that bought the track, there was little doubt in anyone's mind who would be running the show. As in every endeavor he entered he had the wonderful talent of delegating authority—to himself. But it always seemed to pay off for his fellow investors.

Bowie had been kicked around like a stepchild by the Maryland Racing Commission, getting the worst racing dates while Pimlico and Laurel were dividing the plums. Larry let it be known that he was not about to be satisfied with 25 dates when each of the other tracks was favored with 36 or 37. He was a fast learner and, in typical fashion, immersed himself in his new activity immediately.

The actual sale of Bowie was announced at the Belvedere Hotel on Sunday, January 27 by Charles F. Simonelli, a New York motion picture executive:

> Acting for the syndicate headed by L.S. (Larry) MacPhail and Donald Lillis, nationally prominent financier and partner in Bear, Stearns and Company, investment bankers, I have contracted to purchase 7,382 shares, or approximately 60 percent, a controlling interest, in Bowie Racetrack, subject to approval by the court, the conditions of sale, and if the racing commission allots satisfactory dates for 1952. Legal details must also be worked out satisfactorily. The new ownership should take over on February 20, the closing date under our agreement.
>
> Mr. MacPhail made a study of the Bowie plant and its operations during the past year. He has some very definite ideas as to the improvements necessary to make Bowie one of the outstanding tracks in the East. . . . Further statements regarding policies which will govern the operations at Bowie or improvements contemplated will come from Mr. MacPhail.

Larry was vacationing with Jean and Jeanie in Naples, Florida, but his mind was whirring with plans for Bowie. As he had in baseball in Columbus, Cincinnati, Brooklyn and at Yankee Stadium, the first thing he would do was to renovate the facilities at hand and do all possible to make the physical plant an enjoyable place to visit. It was, therefore, vintage MacPhail for him to send ahead the following message:

> Bowie is located midway between the world's capital and America's sixth-largest city. It can become one of the country's outstanding tracks. Bowie will be modernized in the interest of its patrons as fast as possible under existing government regulations. Secondly, we will have the best interests of horsemen and breeders definitely in mind, with increased facilities, better purses, and better horses. We are certain we will not have to worry about the support we can expect from the racing public of Baltimore, Washington and the Eastern seaboard.

The Bowie track had been in receivership since February, 1951, as a result of dissention among its officers and stockholders. Now, with new and dynamic ownership, it was thought that a racing program geared to the level of Pimlico and Laurel would enable Maryland racing to compete more favorably with racing in New Jersey. For the last few years Maryland had not been able to compete on equal terms with the three-track New Jersey circuit.

Earlier, MacPhail had also been quoted as saying:

"Racing is badly in need of a sound public relations program. It has some big problems to face, among them the fact that racketeers and gangsters and small-time hoodlums have muscled into it, much to its detriment."

The closing on the Bowie purchase was completed as scheduled on February 20 and Larry was raring to go. He did not want to conduct racing at Bowie until at least the main part of the renovation was completed so the spring meeting was held at the Laurel track. He scheduled the reopening of Bowie for November 17, 1952, so there was much to be done.

The syndicate paid $1,997,160 for 60 shares of the Bowie stock. Larry was given carte blanche and total control. He in-

sisted on being able to do as he pleased and spend as he pleased
and most of the plans were his own.

MacPhail started out with the idea of spending $700,000
on improvements the first year, but by mid-October expenditures had already passed $1,500,000. This meant, of course,
that before the track would be opened for the first race, the
syndicate would have over $4,000,000 sunk in the venture.

Shortly after the closing, some members showed signs of
hedging on their assignment of total control to Larry and
wanted to put some reins on his authority to hire and fire,
and to commit unrestricted funds to the renovation. They
quickly fell back in line, however, when the rambunctious
redhead stormed out of a meeting with the threat: "I quit!"

This was the last challenge to his authority and he immediately started studying blueprints and outlining the changes
he was to bring about. No one thought he could accomplish
such an ambitious program as he had in mind by the November opening date, but, within a matter of days, bulldozers were
at work on the track, center field and parking lots, while
carpenters, plumbers, painters and their laborers, went at the
grandstand, clubhouse and other buildings with the fervor in-
spired by the new boss.

Larry had some surprises in mind to welcome the turf fans
on opening day: a resurfaced racetrack including a new seven-
furlong and mile-and-a-quarter chute, twin artificial lakes
decorating the infield, a modern sloped concourse to provide
a perfect view for standees, increased facilities of all kinds
and a new saddling paddock behind the stands. And, in Larry's
own words: "That's only the beginning."

A poetic accolade appeared in the *Turf Flash* of March 8
written by a racing writer named Raleigh S. Burroughs:

With Larry at the Bowie helm,
Improvements soon will grace the place—
Conveniences that overwhelm,
And better Thoroughbreds to race.

He'll stretch the present parking lot
To care for fifty thousand hacks,
And cushion benches, like as not,
To ease our sacroiliacs.

The clubhouse, some predict, will be
A bettor's dream of paradise;
The quarters for the bourgeoisie
Will be like home, but twice as nice.

But, there's a flaw in Bowie's plant
That challenges the able Mac
If he can fix it, then I'll grant
He's served the patrons of the track.

The Bowie players face the sun
To watch the gallop for the prize,
And, when they view the backstretch run,
The setting sun gets in their eyes.

So, Larry, you're without a doubt
The best improver anywhere,
If you can turn the sun about
And shield our optics from the glare.

Despite his far-reaching plans, there is no record that Mac-Phail was able to accomplish this solar turnabout. But, to the amazement of almost everyone except the redheaded dynamo himself, Bowie opened right on time. And, the program he planned was typically commensurate with the plant improvements. He had promised great stakes races and the promise was fulfilled.

Although the amounts of money pale in today's rarefied prize atmosphere, they were very attractive in 1952. For Opening Day, Larry scheduled the $20,000 Barbara Frietchie Handicap of a mile and a sixteenth, for fillies and mares of the older division. It attracted some of the smartest of the sex developed in the previous several years.

However, Lady Luck let Larry down for one of the few times of the many occasions when those two faced each other. The opening turned out to be a colossal flop! Only two races were run and that night there was even a question as to whether the track would actually reopen again.

MacPhail's detractors, and this was not an inconsiderable group, chortled in glee. They read with relish the reports in the newspapers that night and the next day.

First off, the fog was so dense that at noon, three-quarters of an hour before the start of the first race, the track was invisible from the grandstand. Larry postponed the start for an hour.

Then, the jockeys refused to ride because they said the entirely new racing track was unsafe. Jimmy Lynch, the local vice-president of the riders' guild, said that the strip had not been given time to settle and that the rain two days earlier had evidently washed out the bottom of the surface.

"You gallop along and all of a sudden your horse's foot sinks down 12 to 18 inches," Lynch said.

There was talk that the 18-day meeting might be transferred to Pimlico whose session had just been completed two days earlier, but MacPhail was adamant and refused even to consider it, of course.

In trying to save the day, two of the stewards made a speech to the jockeys and 10 of them volunteered to run in the first race. There was no mishap and 12 agreed to get up in the saddle for the second run. But, as the runner-up, Annamae L, crossed the finish line, the filly stumbled and she and her jockey, Abelardo De Lara, fell to the ground. Fortunately, neither horse nor rider was hurt, but that was the final straw.

With tears running down his ample cheeks, Larry gave in and announced the cancellation of the other six races, including the feature Barbara Frietchie Handicap, to a crowd of over 12,000. When asked about his plans for the next day, the seldom discouraged or pessimistic MacPhail answered, "I honestly don't know."

The next morning Larry cancelled both Tuesday's and Wednesday's cards, and by Wednesday night the track seemed to be rounding into shape. Horses had worked out that afternoon. Exercise boys, using about two-thirds of the track, reported that the strip "seemed to be in good shape."

The track superintendent, Martin Meyers, said he was sure the entire oval would be ready for the resumption of racing on Friday. MacPhail was so sure of himself on this score that he even agreed to move the balance of the meeting to another track, probably Pimlico, if Bowie were not in prime condition by that time.

Larry's confidence was justified and the second reopening came off as planned with the balance of the schedule being resumed at that point. The meeting came to a close on December 6.

In addition, two $50,000 races were carded, one being the Maryland Gold Cup for two-year-olds on November 22, and the other the President's Plate Handicap for three-year-olds and older horses at a mile and a quarter on closing day. He was trying to appeal to the owners of a wide range of horses.

The schedule of fall dates had the added advantage of having no competition from any track between Washington and New York, so Larry could attract patronage from both cities and such crowded waypoints as Baltimore and Philadelphia.

The year 1952 was pivotal in several ways. His thoughts and energy were mainly directed toward his responsibilities as president of Bowie, but his personal fortune was tied up more and more at Glenangus where the money he had put into the thoroughbred-breeding game was now running close to $1,000,000—half of the amount he received from his share of the New York Yankees.

General Staff had won the Narragansett Special and was still racing, but was destined for stud duty along with the aging Grand Slam down on the farm. MacPhail's primary interest at this time was the breeding of thoroughbreds for the market.

He now owned about 30 of the most fashionably bred brood mares, who are annually mated to the foremost stallions of both Kentucky and Maryland, and he was gradually moving toward leadership among the country's commercial breeders.

The first Glenangus sales consignment went to Saratoga in 1950, when 10 yearlings brought $77,700, and the next season the average was practically the same when 15 of the MacPhail youngsters realized $116,200. In August of '52, Larry took 27 colts and fillies to the Saratoga Spa auction ring and came home with $195,200—an average price of $7,230.

But this year brought a more calamitous thing—the first of three great challenges to the life of this fiery fighter—his first bout with cancer.

It is difficult to single out one quality in the character or personality of Larry MacPhail that stands out more than others, but certainly one of the most prominent would be his thoroughness and attention to detail. Whenever he approached a new project or problem he would first learn everything there was to know about the subject. In his mind, it was only then that he would be able to take intelligent and decisive action.

Shortly before the late-November opening of Bowie, Larry, a chain-smoker, came up with a not infrequent case of laryngitis. When this had occurred in the past, he would give up smoking for a few days, try to restrain his bellowing, and the hoarseness would go away. But, not this time. After two weeks passed by without any relief, he consulted a specialist in Baltimore. The doctor took a sample of tissue from his throat and submitted it to three pathologists.

The report came back, in due time, that one of the three thought the cells indicated malignancy, but that the other two said there was no sign of cancer. For a few hours this gave Larry some encouragement, but his lifetime of thoroughness brought him back to the fact that the report was not unanimous.

His daughter, Marian, was married to one of the finest doctors in New York City, Dr. Walsh McDermott. Larry contacted him and told him what had transpired. His son-in-law told him to send the slides up to him immediately.

On New Year's Eve, Larry and Jean were drinking a toast to each other and welcoming in 1953 when the phone rang. Larry thought it was one of the neighbors extending greetings and answered cheerily. However, it was long-distance from New York, and Walsh was on the other end of the line. The tone of his voice told all there was to know. He said, "Larry, hang on to your chair, because what I have to tell you is not good news."

Then MacPhail heard the news that three of the top cancer specialists in New York agreed that he had a malignant condition in his larynx. "Get up here without delay," he was commanded.

Larry poured himself a double scotch, slumped down in his chair, and grimly contemplated his future.

The next day he went to New York where another examination of his throat confirmed the diagnosis. After discussing his condition further, Walsh took his father-in-law first to Boston and then to a Dr. Kirk in Philadelphia. Everyone else had said that an operation was absolutely necessary and that Larry would then be mute for the rest of his life. However, Dr. Kirk said there could be one alternative. The other choice would be a rigorous course of radium x-ray treatments.

Rather than surrendering to despair, Larry returned to Glenangus to decide objectively on which of the courses to choose. First, he wanted to find out how it would be to be voiceless. He didn't utter one word for three days, communicating with Jean and others by writing what he wanted to say on paper, much as Damon Runyon had done during the last two years of his life.

Since his childhood and the compulsory piano lessons so typical of those days, Larry had enjoyed music and had a not inconsiderable talent at the keyboard. He had even played the organ in church as a youth.

When he bought the farm, one of his first purchases was a theater-size organ which he often played during the quiet evenings at Glenangus. Once he told Stephen Early, formerly press secretary to President Franklin D. Roosevelt and later a prominent Maryland racing official:

"You've got to have something to do after the sun sets in the country and the animals go to sleep. There's nothing like an organ—it gives you a sense of power."

The taste of this man of many parts ran to Bach and Brahms and during these days the most prominent sounds heard in the house were classical notes rising above the massive organ.

What would life be like with an existence based on one-sided conversation? Jeanie was now two and the apple of her father's eye. How would their relationship be affected by the restrictions imposed if he elected to have the surgery? Finally, after 72 hours of self-imposed silence, this most voluble of men rasped, "I can't stand it!"

The decision having been made, Larry and Jean moved to the Westbury Hotel in New York to start the x-ray treatments. For 75 grueling days he received the radium. In off-hours he would go to nearby Carnegie Hall to take organ lessons, which proved to be wonderful therapy. He and Jean would go out to dinner in the evening to help pass the time.

At the end of the course of treatments, Larry and Jean threw some bags into one of their cars and headed south without any definite plans. After wandering about the Carolinas they decided to motor to Miami, fly to Nassau in the Bahamas, wrestle gently with some bonefish, and generally just soak up the sun. This was the final touch to his recuperation and when they returned to New York for a checkup with Dr. McDermott, all were amazed to find that he had apparently licked the dread disease at least for now.

The quality of his thoroughbred stock was ever improving and with it his reputation as one of the best horse-breeders in the country. Nor did his fame as a raiser of top black angus cattle suffer because of it. He continued to hold highly successful cattle dispersal sales at Glenangus, attracting buyers from all over the East and Midwest.

But, as his success with horses continued to grow, Larry aimed more and more for the big money and prestige of the yearling sales every year at Saratoga. This was a week-long dispersal sale that built to a climax on Friday night. The excitement, quality of breeding and sale prices would escalate as the week wore on.

For the earlier years, the last night of the sales belonged to A.B. Hancock Sr. After he had retired from the business his place was taken by Mr. Henry H. Knight, and, for many years, Friday night became known as "Knight's Night," dedicated to the sale of a big draft of yearlings from Knight's Almahurst Farm. This session usually produced many of the auction's top prices, as well as some of its most successful future runners.

Knight retired from large scale breeding after the sales in 1955 and his absence threatened to leave a formidable gap in the Saratoga lineup. However, stepping in to fill this void was probably the only man who could do so, the Master of Glenangus himself, L.S. (Let's Sellemall) MacPhail.

Larry had been one of the heaviest purchasers at the Knight dispersal sales the previous years, and his own sales during this period kept building up toward his taking over the Friday night vendue in '56. He could point with pride to the fact that two of the two-year-olds he had sold at the '55 sale, Fair View and Thin Ice, had run to victory at Saratoga during the earlier part of the '56 meeting carrying the Greentree Stable's silks. Greentree's co-owners were John Hay Whitney and Mrs. Charles Shipman Payson.

But, now it was "MacPhail Night"—and what a night it was!

Larry arrived on the scene early, resplendent in white bib and black tie. He seemed to feel the quiet confidence of a man who knew the evening would be a real winner. He sat down unobtrusively some 10 rows from the front and just awaited developments.

The crowd was slow in arriving and filling the white chairs that had been labeled with some of the most famous names in racing—Mrs. Elizabeth Graham, Fred W. Hooper Jr., Mrs. Anson Bigelow and the above-mentioned co-owner of Green-tree Stables, Mrs. Charles Shipman Payson.

A casual patron of the sales got to chatting with Larry and inquired as to his expectations for the evening. He told the gentleman that this was the largest consignment he had brought to Saratoga and that he was offering a total of 41 yearlings.

"I'll need an average of $12,000 to make any money," he said, "and I think I'll do it. I may be prejudiced, but these yearlings are the result of the best breeding and bloodlines. The knowledgeable buyers who attend these sales are aware of that."

Greentree opened the sale by going to $42,000 to get a powerful-looking brown son of Nimbus from Ariostar, by Solario, three well-known names in recent racing lore. This colt, a classic type, had a definite resemblance to another famous horse of the time, Tom Fool, which presumably attracted Mrs. Payson.

Thereafter, there were more bidders as the late-arrivals filled the clean white chairs and the bidding became more competitive. Mrs. Bigelow made her presence known when she went to $30,000 for a handsome son of Mahmoud, half-brother of Larry's favorite General Staff.

MacPhail was in his element and enjoying every minute of it. The total sale topped "Knight's Night" of the previous year by an average of $5,395 per horse, for one of the most sensational sales in Saratoga history.

Larry's 41 yearlings brought in a total of $667,700 for an average of $16,285, considerably above the $12,000 he had said he needed to come out ahead. The last animal the auctioneer brought the gavel down on was a brown son of Heliopolis from Roman Miss for the top price of the evening of $57,000. It was a night to remember!

Lest the impression be created that the fires in the old boy were being banked and that the roaring redhead had succumbed to the sedentary life of a country gentleman, one has only to recall his trip to the Preakness earlier in the year.

The four-lane highway to Pimlico had been altered to handle the traffic for the event. Instead of the usual two lanes each way, the state police had designated three lanes to handle the incoming traffic prior to the race, with the fourth lane for the few cars that would be going in the opposite direction.

Since Larry felt that patience was an unimportant virtue and certainly secondary to his desire to get himself and his friends to the track, he pulled his big Chrysler out of the line of slow-moving bumper-to-bumper traffic into the only lane left for departing vehicles. By doing so, he attracted a minimum of six cops on motorcycles and in squad cars but he ignored their sirens until it came time for him to turn into the track.

An officer of the law, speechless, approached the driver's side of the limousine. Larry lowered the window, stuck out his leathery visage and said only:

"MacPhail."

"Yes, SUH, Colonel MacPhail," stammered the cop, "....Jest you follow me!" And, it was right to the gate.

Larry MacPhail was a very complicated person. His life seemed to bounce back and forth between tranquility and turmoil. And these moods and emotions could change in a flash, from one to the other.

It also seemed that the "getting there" was far more important than the "being there."

In the very short period of his activity in horse and cattle breeding, he had already achieved heights—he had set another record with the top sales at Saratoga of two-thirds of a million dollars. He pondered the future:

"I have too much work looking after 150 horses. I think I'll dispose of the brood mares and spend more time racing. I'll have 40 more head at the Saratoga yearling sales next summer and that will end it. Getting out a catalogue for that event is a major job in itself. There isn't an agency around that's qualified to handle a brochure of that type."

Quite possibly this decision was influenced by a return to the New York hospital in May of 1957 for another battle with cancer, this time in the intestines.

By this time, Dan Parker, of the *New York Mirror*, and Larry had become very close friends, as had Dan's wife and Jean. Dan visited his old friend at the hospital and, looking out over the sun-bathed rooftops of Manhattan from his 13th floor room, Larry sighed:

"The worst of being in here is that it takes me away from the farm down in Maryland at a time when it is at its most beautiful. There are four mockingbirds' nests near the house and they provide free concerts for us.

"This thing kicked up on me last December, and I was in here for a week, but they couldn't find anything wrong. They suggested that I wait until it flared up again and then return for more x-rays. The day of the Robinson-Fullmer fight it came back and I chartered a plane to bring me up here quickly from Bel Air. This time, they found the area where the blockage was located. It could be caused by anything from a kink to a tumor of some kind. I don't relish operations any more than the next fellow, but I want to find out what's causing this periodic disturbance, so I gave them the go-sign. So, what's with baseball?"

Now, as usual, Larry was off and running on one of his favorite subjects:

"Day baseball is through," he continued. "The minors are dead. The trend now is for people interested in linking the sport with television and radio to buy clubs. John Galbreath of Pittsburgh told me recently that I got out at the right time, because no one is making any money now. Branch Rickey has spent $3,000,000 of John's money at Pittsburgh trying to rebuild.

"I remember when Jim Norris and Art Wirtz were talking

about getting control of the Yankees and of Madison Square Garden. They made an offer for the ball club, but I wouldn't vote for any deal that would give them control of the club."

Larry's comments seem prophetic in light of both the astronomical salaries being paid to ballplayers today and the recent purchase of the Chicago Cubs from the Wrigley family by the Tribune Company of Chicago. The Tribune Company owns not only the *Chicago Tribune* newspaper, but also the television superstation, WGN. Preceding this development was the purchase of the Atlanta Braves by Ted Turner and his nationwide superstation, WTBS.

Returning to Parker's conversation with MacPhail, the two old friends who had had many great times sparring with each other, reminisced together and then Dan left the hospital room.

The next day, Larry had the operation. It was revealed that he had the beginning of a cancerous growth. The section was removed and, once again, he had beaten the rap by taking timely and decisive action.

True to his word, "MacPhail Night" at Saratoga on August 16, 1957 was his swan song at the Saratoga Spa. He sold his 40 yearlings, picked up his money and walked off. It was the end of another phase in the life of this astonishing man, another smashing climax achieved in a remarkably short period of time.

20

A Cure for Complacency

The year 1957 also brought to the fore the many problems facing baseball—dwindling attendance, the competitive attraction of other spectator sports such as professional football and basketball, and other competing diversions for America's entertainment dollars, especially participation sports such as softball, boating, golf, and tennis.

People who recognized and were willing to face these problems knew that it was a time for change and improvement, not in the game itself, but in a need to attract a more national audience.

Life was a potent force in the magazine world at that time and, as spring training approached, they sought out the opinion of a man who they knew would not only be good copy but would also offer some revolutionary approaches for curing the ailments that afflicted baseball—Larry MacPhail.

In their February 24, 1958 issue, *Life* featured an article MacPhail wrote entitled "A Pulmotor for Baseball" in which he delineated the ills of the game and backed them up with facts and statistics to try to shake out the complacency of the owners.

He had been out of baseball since his Yankees had won the World Series of 1947 against Branch Rickey's Brooklyn Dodgers so he had the perspective of one with plenty of experience in the management and ownership of major league baseball without the bias of present day financial involvement.

He felt that in 1958 baseball was no longer the "national pastime." In the previous decade pro football and pro basketball had grown tremendously but the attendance at the ball parks in 1957 was half of what it had been in 1948. Nearly a third of the major league clubs had deserted their original cities in the East and Midwest for the big potential rewards in the expanding markets of the West and Southwest. Related to this shift was the effect these moves had on the minor leagues. More than half the minor leagues had folded and the ones that were left were barely hanging on financially. Attendance at professional baseball games had dropped from a peak of 62,000,000 in 1949 to a low of slightly over 32,000,000 in 1957.

Although the biggest part of this decline was in the minor leagues, an analysis of many of the major league cities over this period was equally disturbing. The attendance at Yankee Stadium had dropped from 2,373,000 ten years earlier to 1,476,000 in 1957 even though during that period they had won eight pennants and six World Series. The number of fans who had gone through the turnstiles at Cleveland during those same years was down 72 percent. Washington was still in the American League at that time and had dropped 43 percent in attendance, Detroit 27 percent and Boston 24 percent. The Philadelphia and St. Louis clubs had already moved for financial reasons and the story in the older National League was pretty much the same.

Larry did not pretend to have all the answers but felt he could point out some of the reasons for the decline, which he did at a dinner party in New York. He said that all but three of the 16 Major League parks were antiquated. Warren Giles, then president of the National League, took strong exception to the statement and his rebuttal in the press made interesting reading.

In an interview the next day, Giles called MacPhail a "sensationalist without recent experience, someone whose only contribution to baseball consisted of painting the seats at Cincinnati, Brooklyn and New York red or yellow instead of green."

Larry wrote that "Mr. Giles is an estimable gentleman—amiable, easygoing and optimistic. That is one reason why he is President of the National League. But somebody ought to tell him about the facts of life. Most of Mr. Giles's ball parks are as obsolete as the streetcars that carried the fans out to the games in the good old days when mustaches were worn by National League players."

Let us put the date of this article in perspective. Walter O'Malley had requested and received permission from the rest of the owners of National League teams to move the Brooklyn Dodgers to Los Angeles. Although he had tried to pressure Mayor Wagner of New York City to have the city participate in the construction of a new stadium for the Dodgers, it became apparent that he really had no intention of remaining in New York. He fully realized the tremendous potential of the rapidly expanding Los Angeles market. He also was fully aware of the complications involved in his being the only National League team on the West Coast, so he prevailed on Horace Stoneham, owner of the Dodgers' historic rivals, the New York Giants, to move west with him. It was incredible that two out of the three major league teams in the largest city in the United States were deserting it and that the National League had agreed to turn over New York City as the exclusive province of the American League and the New York Yankees.

Prophetically, Larry made an amazingly accurate observation on the Dodgers' move. He said, "I predict right now that if Mr. O'Malley sticks to his plan of not televising home games (which is what he did), the Los Angeles Dodgers will draw three million people this year and set the all-time record for major league attendance. When and if they get a modern stadium with adequate parking instead of the Coliseum, they can probably draw four million."

The most visionary part of the entire article in *Life* was Larry's proposal to establish two big leagues, each to contain two divisions of six teams each. Both he and *Life* sometimes refer to four major leagues but, in actuality, he develops the idea of an East and West Division in each of the two major leagues. Each six-team division was formed on a geographical basis and it is absolutely amazing how accurate these predictions were. He wrote:

> There is just one way, in my opinion, in which baseball can regain its former position as the national sport. First, the men who run it must get together and act together.

They must recognize the fact that the world has moved ahead, that the habits and interests of the average American have changed. They must admit that the present system of major and minor league territorial rights which was set up in 1903 is now hopelessly outmoded. Baseball is sick. It can't get well by taking a couple of sugar-coated pills and maintaining any status quo. Baseball must take a deep breath and revise its whole operation.

With the minor leagues dead for all intents and purposes, major league baseball must be expanded to include all sections of the country. The South and Southwest are not now represented in either major league. The Pacific Coast is not represented in the American League. The entire eastern seaboard has only one National League club. Canada, with two great metropolitan areas, has no major league baseball at all. What can be done about it?

The obvious solution is the creation of four instead of two major leagues. I proposed this when subpoenaed and questioned by a congressional committee in 1951. I feel certain that today the commissioner of baseball (Ford Frick) is in complete agreement with this proposal. Careful analysis proves that this is the step that should and must be taken.

There are more than enough large cities with adequate qualifications to fill out four major leagues. Here are some important things to consider:

1) There is no reason why, in this age of airplane travel, major league baseball should be limited to the continental U.S., especially when Montreal, Toronto, Havana and Mexico City are four of the best baseball towns.

2) There are eight cities in North America without major league teams but with larger area populations than three cities—Kansas City, Cincinnati and Milwaukee—that already have major league clubs.

3) Milwaukee, which has set a National League attendance record since getting major league ball, was, as a minor league town, consistently outdrawn by Montreal, Denver, Toronto and Seattle, which are still minor league cities.

4) There are at least 30 cities in North America whose metropolitan areas are large enough (populations of almost a million, or more) to support a major league club. At least 11 of them could support two major league teams if they had modern ball parks.

In any expansion of the major leagues the first logical step would be to authorize one additional club in New York, Los Angeles, Detroit and either San Francisco or Philadelphia. All of these have metropolitan populations of more than four million except San Francisco, which has almost three million. With the grant of additional one-club franchises in the Montreal, Toronto, Mexico City and Minneapolis-St. Paul areas, each league could be divided into two six-club leagues. The four leagues would shape up something like this:

NATIONAL LEAGUE (East)	Metropolitan Area Population	AMERICAN LEAGUE (East)	Metropolitan Area Population
*New York	14,400,000	New York	14,400,000
Philadelphia	4,000,000	Detroit	3,600,000
*Detroit	3,600,000	Boston	2,400,000
Pittsburgh	2,300,000	Washington	2,000,000
*Montreal	1,600,000	Cleveland	1,700,000
*Toronto	1,400,000	Baltimore	1,500,000
NATIONAL LEAGUE (West)		**AMERICAN LEAGUE (West)**	
Chicago	6,200,000	Chicago	6,200,000
Los Angeles	5,900,000	*Los Angeles	5,900,000
San Francisco	2,700,000	*Mexico City	3,800,000
St. Louis	2,000,000	*San Francisco	2,700,000
Milwaukee	1,100,000	*Minn/St. Paul	1,300,000
Cincinnati	1,100,000	Kansas City	1,000,000

*New Franchises

In his article, Larry then goes beyond the concept of four six-team divisions or leagues and adds two more to each division to make a total of 32 clubs in major league baseball. Among other cities he suggests are Dallas-Ft.Worth, Houston, Atlanta and Seattle, all of which, of course, have teams today. Two other cities that he mentions—Denver and New Orleans—are still likely candidates in the next expansion phase.

Larry argued that giving major league baseball to the entire country would bring about a complete renaissance and once again make it the "national pastime." It would revitalize the old areas and create tremendous new interest in the new areas. New stadiums would be constructed with municipal help that would create new civic pride in the local team. Other older parks would be rehabilitated to make them much more attractive places to bring the entire family.

254 • The Roaring Redhead

He concluded with a warning: "When baseball makes up its mind to do a job it does a pretty good one. But it better get on with this one. If it doesn't, it may never again get the chance."

Not all of MacPhail's suggestions were followed in their entirety, but look at baseball today in light of the above. Over 28 years have passed since he wrote this article and almost everything he predicted has transpired. Year after year the attendance records of major league baseball are broken. This is the greatest testament to the validity of his contributions and his inspiration for the future of the game. A quote from his last paragraph says it all:

"If the club owners give major league ball to the whole country, and if they get about the business of preserving its heritage as a team sport instead of another entry in the entertainment field, my grandchildren will be able to celebrate the 100th anniversary of the World Series in the year 2003. I don't know whether the opening game will be played in Yankee Stadium or on the moon, but I'm sure that baseball will have been re-established as the national sport and pastime."

21

The Roaring Redhead Till the End

Over the years golf had been a game Larry had not only played well, but one that had been most enjoyable for the companionship it afforded. Back in Columbus he had been a member of a regular foursome that played every weekend he could make it. But when he moved on to the big leagues he found fewer opportunities to enjoy golf.

However, when he bought the farm in 1941 he started adding to the acreage as more land became available until he had acquired almost a thousand acres. One day, as he looked out over the flower beds, the shrubs and the impeccably groomed lawn, he envisioned a championship golf course on the floor of the lush, green valley, right at the bottom of the hill.

So, he threw himself into his new project with the same fervour, zest and thoroughness he had shown so many times before at the ball parks and the race track. Larry hired one golf architect, got into an argument with him over some suggestion and promptly fired him.

After more difficulties with the next architect, the beautiful 18-hole championship course was completed at a cost of $300,000. He then sold it to a group of local residents around Bel Air at a price that covered his costs. He held the 20-year mortgage on the property now named the Maryland Golf and Country Club.

Larry MacPhail, without a project to occupy his boundless energy, was like a geyser about to erupt. He seemed to delight in the controversies he would create as much as he enjoyed the success of his many accomplishments.

Shortly after the completion of the golf course he got it into his head that the last nine holes needed more time for the grass to mature and informed the membership that he would prevent them from using those holes. It was strictly an arbitrary decision on MacPhail's part, but he threatened he would get an injunction to keep the golfers off. He finally relented.

Another time he gave permission to the golf pro, Paul Haviland, to let the golfers use his nearby horse training track for practice shots. Several days later he was looking out his huge living room window when he saw some golfers down in the area. He stormed out of the house and raced down to the area bellowing his approach and warned them that they were trespassing on his property. They told him that they had permission from the pro, but this cut no ice with Larry and he told them to get moving or he would call the police.

Some of his actions were completely inexplicable and often indefensible and humiliating in retrospect.

One day he refused to let some residents of a nearby area use an access road that was on the end of his property. He even put up a steel chain across the road to prevent cars from using the road and stood guard over the entrance with rifle in hand.

Another time, while walking over his property, he noticed several men working on some wires atop a pole along the road. Subconsciously he had been looking for something worthy of his inimitable moose-like roar and this seemed to fill the bill. He screamed some endearing epithets at the men, which action accomplished its desired results. The crew climbed down, gathered up their tools, got into their truck and left Larry with a self-satisfied smirk on his face.

That evening, when he turned on the light switches, he found he was in total darkness, the food was starting to spoil in the refrigerator and the air conditioners were silent. That is when he tried to reach someone at the Gas and Electric Company to see what could be done to rectify the situation. The men he had chased off his property were with that utility and had been trying to restore electricity to Glenangus.

The last years of his life were tragic ones for Larry Mac-Phail. The ravages of age and the debilitating effect of the long overuse of alcohol were beginning to take their toll. However, his entrepreneurial drives ran unabated.

With these forces in conflict his business judgment was affected and a number of financial schemes went sour. He put money in a venture to invent a machine that would remove paint from airport runways. Another can't-miss deal involved a process to develop a non-eroding and night-visible paint for highways. He concocted various schemes that had to do with the Grand Cayman Islands, all of which were financial disasters.

Glenangus Farms required considerable upkeep and there was no money coming in from any source. Too proud to ask for help from his children, he denied the existence of any problem.

He feuded with his son-in-law, Jim Duncan, Jeanie's husband, when Jim tried to help control his expenditures. He refused to stay in Bel Air where he was in good hands and would leave Jean and take various trips to Grand Cayman and other places, leaving without any funds. There were several embarrassing and difficult incidents that, fortunately, did not involve any serious injury to Larry or other people involved, but were very sad and humiliating.

At last his family was able to convince him that he needed constant medical care but, instead of entering some private institution, he insisted on going to a Veterans' Hospital in Miami. It was almost as if he were trying to bridge the span back to his days with the 114th Field Artillery in France in World War I.

During his stay there, toward the end when his mind was slipping, his two biggest delights were the ice cream that was served to the patients every afternoon and the huge American flag that waved in the breeze just outside his hospital room window. And, in those final days, he was not always an easy patient. He was obstreperous at times—the "roaring redhead" till the end.

Larry had cheated death several times—enemy bullets in World War I, a heart attack and two bouts with cancer—but, finally his heart gave out and he died on October 1, 1975.

Services were held in Cass City, a little city in the "thumb" of Michigan, and that is where he is buried—the same town where he had been born 85 years earlier.

After his death, his beloved Glenangus Farms was sold at auction.

22

The Hall of Fame—
Finally, But Posthumously

As time went on and MacPhail was not elected to the Hall of Fame in Cooperstown, New York, he became more and more determined that, if elected, he would not accept the nomination.

His close friend, John F. Steadman, sports editor of the *Baltimore News American*, recalled asking him how he would react if he were elected:

"I don't want to go in. The Hall of Fame is for players— not executives, managers, contributors to the game, but only to the players . . . period."

Steadman persisted. "But, what if you were selected?"

"Well, I won't go. I'm telling you, I won't go. For God's sake, how many times do I have to tell you? I won't let them put me in the Hall of Fame."

About a year later, Steadman brought up the subject again and reminded him that he had said that "if they had put him in a strait-jacket, he would kick and holler and not let them enshrine him in the Hall."

That does conjure up a vision of the roaring redhead pulling another first and emulating Calvin Coolidge in refusing his proposed renomination to the presidency. Only in Larry's case it would have been done with much more fanfare and commotion. Nobody had ever refused the baseball honor.

But, this time, in a calmer mood, he reflected on the subject and said:

"Look, about the Hall of Fame, I'll do whatever you tell me to do. If you want me to go in and they select me, then I'll go. If you don't want me to go, then I won't."

There seems to be little doubt that, for many years, Warren Giles not only voted against Larry's nomination, but actively campaigned against it with his fellow members of the 12-man Veterans' Committee.

Giles resented MacPhail and his flamboyant approach to many of the hallowed traditions of baseball. He let few opportunities to criticize Larry pass by, claiming that the only thing he did for baseball was to paint the parks he was connected with in garish colors.

Unquestionably, his greatest resentment was caused by the amount of credit Larry received for putting together the National League pennant winning teams in Cincinnati in 1939 and 1940. MacPhail had been gone for two years and was succeeded as head of the Reds by Warren Giles. Even so, most people familiar with the situation gave Larry credit for assembling the heart of the team through trades, signings or the farm system.

Frankie Frisch, the Fordham Flash, and himself a member of the Hall, had also been a member of the Veterans' Committee in 1972. Frank H. Eck, of the Associated Press and another close friend of Larry's, appealed to Frisch to do all he could to get Larry nominated and elected in that year. Frisch had always been for it and this time he tried especially hard, feeling that it was most important to get Larry in while he was still alive.

One hour after the committee of 12 met, Frisch called Eck and told him:

"I couldn't swing it. Warren Giles said Larry MacPhail wasn't in baseball long enough."

Eck felt that there had been no oversight by the Veterans' Committee. It had been a deliberate act on the part of Giles and was "pure and simple stubbornness and a dislike for the best promoter baseball had ever known."

In February of the following year, Frisch had been injured in an automobile accident near Elkton, Maryland, and Larry went to visit him in the hospital. While they were talking, the subject of the Hall of Fame came up, Frisch indicating that he thought it was awful that Larry was not a member. He said he was really going to raise hell with the committee this time.

MacPhail continued to insist that membership should be restricted to players only. At any rate, Frankie was unable to help any further. The injuries proved fatal and he never left the hospital.

Larry's insistence on "players only" certainly ran counter to the prevailing view. There was another category of those already admitted to membership under the general heading of "meritorious service." The list included, among others, Judge Kenesaw Mountain Landis, Will Harridge, Ford Frick, Branch Rickey, Connie Mack, George Weiss, Ed Barrow and many others of MacPhail's contemporaries.

Although the winter of 1972 brought MacPhail's annual rejection for entry in the Baseball Hall of Fame, an honor from a totally unexpected source reached him on his 82nd birthday.

He was formally notified that he had won the award for being the breeder of the country's top broodmare and the dam of that year's Kentucky Derby winner, Riva Ridge. It certainly was a fitting consolation prize and a welcome birthday present.

Three years after his death in 1975, he was finally elected to the Hall of Fame.

In that year, 1978, there was a major change in the composition and size of the Veterans' Committee. It was expanded from 12 to 18 members, with two of the new members being Buzzie Bavasi of the California Angels and Joe Reichler of the commissioner's office.

It would have been hard to have picked two men more in Larry's corner than these two. They were ardent campaigners for his election.

When asked about when he first met Larry, Bavasi waxed sentimental and started reminiscing:

"Well, he gave me my first job. I guess it was late March in 1939. I was just graduating from college and one of my best friends was Ford Frick's son. Ford was like a father to me.

"As a graduation present I was given a new car and a year off to do anything I wanted to. Well, the only thing I wanted to do was to go to Clearwater and spend two months watching the Dodgers in spring training.

"So, I went down there to see all the clubs the Dodgers would be playing and Ford came down and got a little annoyed with me. He told me I had to go to work.

"So, he made me go back to New York with him. He took me to Larry's office and told him that here was the fellow he had been talking about.

"Larry took me into his office and said:

" 'Do you know anything about baseball?' I replied:

" 'Mr. MacPhail, I know the game, itself, but I don't know anything about the operation of a baseball team.' He said:

" 'Good. You've got a job. I have too many people around here that think they know how to run a ball club.'

"That's how I got the job—by being ignorant."

Joe Reichler, in the commissioner's office, is one of the foremost historians of baseball. He has written 19 books, the most famous of which is his definitive tome entitled *The Baseball Encyclopedia* which is "the complete and official record of major league baseball."

He was a close friend of Larry's and, in the encyclopedia he stated bluntly, "MacPhail belongs in the Hall of Fame despite everything he did to discourage election."

In 1978, The Veterans' Committee met at the Americana Hotel the morning after the 55th annual meeting of the New York Baseball Writers' Association. Over the years this sequence had become the custom and often there was much disagreement between the two groups.

Sixteen of the 18 members of the comittee were present. Bill Terry had just resigned from the committee and his replacement had not yet been named, and Bill DeWitt was snowbound in Cleveland.

With a two-thirds rule in effect, a candidate had to receive 12 votes for election.

Buzzie and Joe campaigned hard and apparently it was still not an easy job. Reportedly, the jury was deadlocked. It was a tie between MacPhail and Tom Yawkey, who had died the year before, in 1977. By the new rules, only one non-player could be chosen each year by the Veterans' Committee.

Larry finally won in a runoff.

Two others were elected to the Hall for induction at the same time as Larry. Addie Joss, the great Cleveland pitcher of the first decade of the 20th century, was the player named by the committee, and Eddie Mathews had previously been elected by the Baseball Writers' Association of America.

It was also most fitting that, on the same platform, the first Ford C. Frick Award would be presented to Red Barber and Mel Allen for broadcasting excellence. Barber's professional life was so intertwined with MacPhail's and, between them, Barber and Allen reported baseball for nearly 60 years.

Red had campaigned for years for Larry's election to the Hall. In his column of congratulations in the *Tallahassee Democrat* just after MacPhail's election, he recalled an incident that had been told to him by Tom Meany, the sportswriter.

It occurred during a crucial series between the Dodgers and Cardinals as they were battling for first place near the end of the 1941 season. Meany and MacPhail were listening to the night game at the press room bar as the game began:

"The Cardinals got the first man on with a walk. The next batter singled to right and the runner tried for third. He slid, just as the ball got to the third baseman.

"The umpire waved 'out.' I said. 'He's out!' Then, the ball got loose and the umpire changed his sign to 'safe.' I said, 'No—he's safe.'

"Hymie Green, the bartender, said: 'Listen to that Barber— he can't tell out from safe.'

"MacPhail said: 'You tend bar and let Barber broadcast.'

"Green said: 'You can't talk to me that way.'

"MacPhail said: 'I never will again. Get your check—you're through.'

"In my book, MacPhail was a hell of a man."

The actual induction ceremonies occurred at the Hall of Fame in Cooperstown on August 7, 1978. Sons Lee and Bill accepted the plaque and most of the family were in attendance, including his widow, Jean Bauer, his two daughters, Marian McDermott and Jean Duncan, and six grandchildren.

A year after the induction, at the Baseball Writers' meeting in New York, Ken Smith, then head of the Hall of Fame, wrote a nostalgic piece for their Scorebook, which included much

of Lee's acceptance speech and some of the great parodies of
past years' shows:

> Greater New Yorkers in the crowd under the Coopers-
> town elms gloated like proud relatives when Larry Mac-
> Phail was embronzed last year with Eddie Mathews and
> the late Addie Joss. They had the obstreperous Dodgers'
> and Yankees' autocrat for eight years.
>
> After son Bill introduced Allen, Bruce, Lisa, Kathy and
> Leland MacPhail IV (Lee's children), son Lee, accepting his
> father's citation started on a tour of his life—" . . . you've
> heard of his promotional firsts, how he organized Old
> Timer's Day, organs in ball parks, stadium clubs, the yellow
> ball . . . " A senior in the crowd found himself humming
> Arthur Mann's song from the 1938 Writers' show.

> When your club begins to fall
> Introduce a yellow ball
> I've got a pocketful of schemes.
> If the crowds you draw won't do,
> Paint the stands a turquoise blue,
> I pay 10 grand to Mungo
> Just to hit an occasional fungo . . .

> Dream over, son Lee was going on " . . . you've heard
> about his bringing night baseball to the major leagues . . ."
> Mr. Senior fell into another trance, remembering the night
> that the writers smeared their hands with phosphorus, and
> in darkness, waved in unison as superb writer-director, Jim
> Kahn, led them singing:

> It's a big holiday over there
> 'Cause the Dodgers are lit up and on the air.
> It's a live-wire gent
> That we proudly present
> Mr. Thomas A. Edison MacPhail.

> Back to reality on the Cooperstown platform, Lee was
> saying ". . . my favorite story about Dad was how he bought
> the Yankees . . . " We fade back to the Waldorf and Louis
> Effrat in his smash hit theme song . . .

> Do you recall the days of yore
> When MacPhail was in power
> We quenched our thirst while Larry cursed
> And downed a whiskey sour.

A man assigned to Ebbets Field,
To write the game each day,
Just did his work like any jerk,
In an alcoholic way.

An elevator rushed us up
To Larry's little bar.
And there we never lacked for fun,
Or fisticuffs, by Gar!

But, times are ever changing,
Those days we used to know.
Will Branch black out that picture,
Or will the liquor flow.

Will the lights go on again
In Larry's saloon.
Will the fights come on again
Come April and June.

Will big shots still come here
Danny Kaye, Toots Shor or Georgie Raft.
Will Branch serve Rupperts beer
Or Seven-Up on draft?

Will they set 'em up again,
When twilight begins.
Or will all the baseball scribes
Go over to Flynn's?

It seems a shame to waste the gin,
And serve us Rickey Finn.
Will the lights go on again
In Larry's saloon?

The spell over . . . Lee was going on . . . "he battled all his contemporaries but bore no grudges, he'd forget those overnight. I don't feel he had any real enemies in baseball. He was a business man, but he was proudest of being successful making baseball deals . . .

"He was aggressive, garrulous, unpredictable, flamboyant, breaker of traditions. He was loud, and after a couple of martinis, insulting and pugnacious on occasion. But, he was a brilliant promotional genius and visioner . . . everyone laughed when he wrote there will be 24 major league teams . . .

"Larry MacPhail had great personal charm; he loved people he worked with—Bucky Harris, Charley Dressen, Red

Barber, Burleigh Grimes here on the platform, Buzzie Bavasi and many others. His sense of the dramatic prevented his continuing beyond the climax of the World Championship.

"In many cases he was a religious man, and if somehow he could know or see what goes on here today, he would be very, very proud and very, very happy."

Bowie Kuhn finished with "Did you notice that the sun came out while Lee was talking?"

The text for his plaque was written by Joe Reichler:

LELAND STANFORD MacPHAIL

"LARRY"

DYNAMIC, INNOVATIVE EXECUTIVE MADE HIS MARK AS PROGRESSIVE HEAD OF THREE CLUBS—CINCINNATI REDS, BROOKLYN DODGERS AND NEW YORK YANKEES—FROM 1933 TO 1947. WON CHAMPIONSHIPS IN BOTH LEAGUES—WITH DODGERS IN 1941 AND YANKEES IN 1947. PIONEERED NIGHT BALL IN CINCINNATI IN 1935. ALSO INSTALLED LIGHTS IN EBBETS FIELD AND YANKEE STADIUM. ORIGINATED PLANE TRAVEL BY PLAYING PERSONNEL AND IDEA OF STADIUM CLUB. HELPED SET UP EMPLOYEE AND PLAYER PENSION PLANS.